B2B Exchanges 2.0

Not all e-markets are "dot-bombs"

W. William A. Woods
co-author of
*B2B Exchanges: The Killer Application in the
Business-to-Business Internet Revolution*

www.b2bexchanges.com

Any questions or comments regarding this document should be forwarded to
W. William A. Woods at wwaw@csi.com.

Published by ISI *Publications*
ISBN: 962 7762 77 6
Copyright © 2002 W. William A. Woods
All rights reserved
Published in Bermuda

This book is available at special quantity discounts for use as premiums or for
sales promotions, in corporate training programs, or for academic institutions.

For more information, please contact Sarah Barham, CEO of ISI Publications,
at sarahb@isipublications.com, tel: (1 441) 292 5666 fax: (1 441) 292 5665
or visit ISI's web site: www.isipublications.com. Also available through
www.booksonbiz.com.

To Sarah, Zoe, and Ella, with all my love

Contents

Part I:

Analyzing the B2B Exchange Market Space

Analyzing the B2B Exchange Market Space

Introduction

In 1999, I co-authored a book entitled *B2B Exchanges: The Killer Application in the Business-to-Business Internet Revolution*. I have written this sequel as an update on recent developments in e-business.

Although we are still at an early stage in the development of e-business there are numerous examples of how e-marketplaces — what I call B2B exchanges — are revolutionizing the way that companies do business and communicate with one another.

In this book I try to document the history of B2B exchanges, analyzing what has and what has not been working and taking a look ahead. I use a fictitious company, Metal Co. Inc., in several places throughout the book to illustrate certain points. But mainly I use real world examples of B2B exchanges to show how they have affected, or will affect, traditional industries.

W. William A. Woods
July 2002

Acknowledgments

For their role in the preparation of this book I would like to especially thank Sarah Barham and Carol Bonnett, my editors at ISI Publications in Bermuda, and Ian Hallsworth for his production work in Hong Kong.

I would also like to thank Arthur Sculley, Nick Earle at StreamServe, Gale Daikoku at Gartner, Chris Prior-Willeard at PricewaterhouseCoopers, Ruben Lee at Oxford Finance Group, Paul Ellis at CreditTrade, Rod Tasker at Identrus, and Dan Jankowski at Covisint for reviewing my draft manuscript and providing many insightful comments.

All judgments and opinions in this book are, unless otherwise stated, my own, and not necessarily those of people who provided advice to me, or the institutions for which they work. Despite their invaluable assistance, any errors or omissions in the book remain fully my responsibility.

Chapter 1

The Rise and Fall of B2B Exchanges

"I believe that it is way too soon to write-off B2B exchanges as failures and that they are now mounting a concerted comeback."

In 1999, when B2B mania was just picking up speed, some analysts predicted that more than 100,000 B2B exchanges would be operational by 2001. At that time there were probably around 300 B2B exchanges. Indeed, there was a tremendous explosion of B2B exchanges in 2000 and by the end of that year GartnerG2, part of Gartner, Inc. the leading B2B analyst, was actively tracking nearly 2,000 B2B exchanges worldwide.[1]

Since then, most start-up B2B exchanges have merged, simply run out of money, closed down completely or been converted into software vendors. In fact, there have never been more than 2,500 B2B exchanges established worldwide to date and, of those, only approximately 1,000 are still operating, and only around 250 are likely to survive as true exchanges.

With the collapse of the Internet-led investment boom of the 1990s, and the subsequent huge declines in the market value of B2B-related stocks, many pundits now claim that B2B exchanges have been a total bust.

"If today's companies are to survive, they are going to have to reinvent themselves and integrate the Internet into everything they do."

That is the opening statement in the book I co-authored with Arthur Sculley called *B2B Exchanges: The Killer Application in the Business-to-Business Internet Revolution*. This was the first book written on B2B exchanges and was published at the end of 1999. Despite the large number of dot-bombs, dot-gones and other sad stories in the B2B space, that message is just as pertinent today.

This, my second book on B2B exchanges, analyzes what went wrong, what went right, and what B2B exchanges need to do to succeed. I also explain why B2B exchanges are *still* a killer application in the e-business revolution.

I believe that it is way too soon to write-off B2B exchanges as failures and that they are now mounting a concerted comeback.

But first…. let's look at the history of B2B exchanges over the last three years.

The Rise…

B2B exchanges promised to empower buyers and enable them to source, negotiate the price, and arrange delivery of, the supplies and direct materials that they needed, much faster and much cheaper than ever before. They also offered to enable suppliers to find new markets, reduce inventory levels, lower their input and selling costs, design products faster, and deliver goods and services more efficiently.

During the second half of 1999, the media swung its attention to the B2B revolution and an increasing number of securities analysts started to focus on B2B exchanges. As the B2C star began to fade, analysts realized that the fastest future growth would be in B2B. Those investors, particularly institutional investors, who had missed out on the "dot-com" phenomenon, decided that they were not going to be left out this time.

The highly successful IPO by the Internet Capital Group, Inc. (NASDAQ: ICGE) (www.internetcapital.com) in August 1999 made Wall Street focus on B2B e-business in the same way that the Amazon.com and Yahoo IPOs had ignited interest in B2C. The company had an opening day gain of 103.7% when its stock closed at $24.44 a share, up from its offering price of $12. ICG's business model was to invest in B2B start-ups, help them grow and then take them public. At its peak, ICG had a stake in several B2B exchanges including: Onvia.com (office supplies); PaperExchange (paper); Autovia (car parts); FuelSpot (fuel); eMerge Interactive (cattle); and Verticalnet (59 e-marketplaces). ICG also invested in CreditTrade in the summer of 2000, one of the most successful B2B exchanges in the financial services sector and an exchange I study in some detail later in this book.

ICG's share price reached $200 in January 2000, giving it a market capitalization in excess of $56 billion. Other prominent companies in the B2B sector such as Commerce One, Ariba, and i2 Technologies also reached fantastic valuations around that time.

Todd Hewlin, at the Internet Capital Group, wrote the following, in 2000:

"Ultimately, digital marketplaces promise to fundamentally transform industries and our global economy. They are already reducing both process and product costs. They are delivering higher revenues at reduced cost of sales. They are integrating supply chain transactions in unprecedented ways. And they are enabling businesses to outsource many non-core business activities to increase flexibility and reduce management complexity. In fact, once all of these outcomes of the B2B transformation are taken into account, many industries expect 15%–30% reductions in end-to-end costs of their supply chain. Over the coming years, this profound impact on industry economics may well reflect the greatest incremental change in corporate productivity ever."

During 1999 and 2000, about 2,000 independent, dot-com exchanges were set up by entrepreneurs and/or enterprising executives who saw the potential for a B2B exchange in their industry. Not to be left out of the B2B revolution, a number of large "bricks and mortar" companies decided to form their own B2B exchanges. The promise of costs savings and increased efficiency drove even the largest competing manufacturers to work together to launch B2B exchanges. For example, in 2000, GM, Ford, and DaimlerChrysler got together to create an auto exchange called Covisint. They have now been joined by PSA Peugeot-Citroen, Renault of France, and its affiliate Nissan Motors of Japan.

These types of exchanges are called "industry consortia" because they are formed by a consortium of existing buyers or sellers in a particular market space. By the start of 2002, there were over 50 such industry consortia (approximately 5% of the total number of surviving exchanges).

Other leading consortia plays include:

- CPGmarket.com
- Cordiem
- E2open
- Exostar
- GlobalNetXchange
- IntercontinentalExchange

Analyzing the B2B Exchange Market Space

- Omnexus
- Pantellos
- Quadrem
- The WorldWide Retail Exchange, and
- Transora.

During 2000, business magazines and the mainstream media ran endless stories about the promise of B2B exchanges. In their thirst for information about this new B2B phenomenon, thousands of people flocked to seminars organized by new media groups like NetMarketMakers, which was acquired by Jupiter Media Metrix in April 2000. NetMarketMakers regularly attracted up to 6,000 delegates to its popular "GroundZero" series of B2B conferences on the East and West coasts of the US.

And the Fall...

Today, ICG's stock trades around $0.40 and its market capitalization is below $100 million.

The grand demise started in the spring of 2000. Share prices in the B2B sector fell heavily after March 2000, along with the rest of the NASDAQ-listed technology stocks.

Since then, many B2B exchanges have failed to launch as announced or merged with others. Many have simply run out of money, closed down, or been converted into software vendors. And the B2B exchange carnage has not been limited to dot-com companies. Several prominent industry consortia have also failed to launch, collapsed or refocused including: BondBook, MetalSite (recently acquired and re-launched by MSA), MetalSpectrum, Petrocosm, Packtion, RetailersMarketXchange, and C-StoreMatrix.

As we shall see, the B2B e-business revolution has, and is, taking longer to complete than any one initially imagined.

Let's take a look at one prominent example — Ventro.

Case study: Ventro (born as Chemdex and now called NexPrise, Inc.)

With the benefit of hindsight, the absolute peak in B2B market mania turned out to be the end of February 2000, when a high-profile B2B exchange in the chemicals sector, called Chemdex, announced that it was changing its name to Ventro Corporation (NASDAQ:VNTR) and planned to launch multiple e-marketplaces. The share price immediately leapt by 100% and the company was obliged to make a further press release to emphasize that there had been no actual financial transactions associated with the change of name.

Ventro's stock traded as high as $243.50 per share at the end of February 2000. By mid-March 2001, just one year later, Ventro stock was trading below $1 — a decline of about 99.5% from its high.

In May 2001, several law firms announced that they had filed class action suits on behalf of all individuals and institutional investors who had purchased the common stock of Ventro during 2000.

The complainants charge that Ventro and certain of its officers and directors violated the federal securities laws by providing materially false and misleading information about Ventro's financial condition and future growth potential, and as a result of these false and misleading statements Ventro's stock traded at artificially inflated prices during February–December 2000. Specifically, the claim states that in early 2001 it was revealed that Ventro's CEO and the other defendants had realized by December 1999 that Ventro's business model of independent e-marketplaces didn't make sense. In addition, it is alleged that by mid-February 2000 it was evident to the management of Ventro that Ventro did not possess the technology to successfully compete as an e-marketplace. The plaintiffs claim that management knew this would severely impair Ventro's future revenue growth. However, the management wanted to raise additional money through debt offerings before the bottom fell out of Ventro's stock price. Thus, the claim states that the management continued to make positive but false statements about Ventro's business and future revenues.

On 6 December 2000, Ventro announced a restructuring in which it closed down two out of three of its main B2B exchanges, including its original e-marketplace called Chemdex.

The class action claims that the management's misconduct has wiped out over $4 billion in market capitalization after Ventro stock fell when the truth about Ventro, its operations and prospects, began to reach the market.

On 5 September 2001, NASDAQ threatened to delist Ventro as its stock was not in compliance with the $1 minimum bid price requirement for continued listing as stipulated in Marketplace Rule 4450(a)(5), by trading below a $1 for too long. However, NASDAQ subsequently suspended the operation of that rule for the market as a whole following the tragic events of 11 September 2001, giving Ventro a reprieve.

Analyzing the B2B Exchange Market Space

On 15 January 2002, Ventro announced that it had changed its name again, this time to NexPrise, Inc. The NASDAQ market symbol was changed from "VNTR" to "NXPS". The stock continues to trade at around $0.30.

From B2B Exchange to Software Vendor

Many attempts to form B2B exchanges ran out of money before they achieved critical mass. Others switched their focus from providing a central marketplace to providing software — especially integration software. The failure to generate transaction volume through their systems drove many B2B exchanges to refocus their efforts on providing software applications to companies on a service bureau basis — the "application service provider" (ASP) model. In Chapter 5, I describe the corporate history of AviationX, which started out to be a B2B exchange for the aviation industry and ended up trying to be an ASP for that industry.

A similar change of focus has occurred among some consortia exchanges too. For example, Novopoint, which started out as a public exchange for food now calls itself a "vertical service provider". The RetailersMarketXchange, which stated at its launch that it "plans to offer the first Internet trade exchange designed as a full-service marketplace for all convenience-store and small-business retailers and their suppliers", now describes itself as providing "the software and services infrastructure to power communication and commerce for the fuel and convenience retail channel".

Among the best-known names in the B2B sector are Ariba Inc., Commerce One Inc., and i2 Technologies Inc. These companies aimed to provide the "picks and shovels" that would enable other companies to mine the B2B gold. In the process, they would license the marketplace software and charge a license fee based on the value of the transactions run through the applications. For example, Wall Street postulated that, if the automotive manufacturing industry in the US makes annual procurements of over $300 billion, then the company that supplied the software that moved all that procurement on-line might be able to charge a 10% fee — generating gross revenue of $30 billion per annum!

Based on this conceit, the share price of Ariba (NASDAQ: ARBA) went as high as $169 and the company had a market capitalization in excess of $40 billion with gross revenues of less than $280 million and a net loss of $792 million for the financial year ended 30 September 2000. Today, the stock is trading below $4. Commerce One experienced a similar collapse in its share price (which cost me personally).

Of course, in reality no large manufacturer would be prepared to transfer its current procurement onto an electronic exchange that charged such high transaction fees. It made more sense for the major manufacturers to build their own exchange and try to capture all of the potential cost savings. Hence, the development of the industry consortia exchanges.

Case study: Verticalnet

Verticalnet, Inc. (NASDAQ: VERT) started as a B2B exchange for the electronics industry. It then expanded its ambitions in 1999, to be an operator of industry-specific websites designed as on-line B2B communities for 59 industry-specific marketplaces. In October 2000, it switched focus to be a "B2B e-commerce enabler" and then changed direction again to be an "enterprise software provider" in September 2001. When Verticalnet acquired Atlas Commerce in December 2001, it finally switched to become a "developer of extended enterprise management applications". Atlas Commerce was a privately-held software company, specialising in providing private exchange software and strategic sourcing applications. Verticalnet now focuses on connecting suppliers to various buyers in enterprises by supplying the software required to build private network exchanges — so called "collaborative supply chain solutions". The company claims that its new, combined strategic sourcing applications, with multi-party collaboration features, can help drive efficiencies and strengthen relationships throughout the supply chain.

In 1999, Arthur Sculley and I had predicted that horizontal exchanges like Verticalnet's 59 e-marketplaces would not survive. In February 2002, Verticalnet announced that it would sell off its suite of 59 e-marketplaces to focus on selling its complex software solutions to large enterprises.

Case study: e-STEEL

On 13 November 2001, e-STEEL Corporation announced that it had changed its name to NewView Technologies Inc. (www.newview.com) to more accurately reflect its expanded product offerings and strategic direction. The firm had just completed the migration of its technology platform and business plan to a licensed software model. Its inter-enterprise software supports a broad portfolio of network business processes essential to managing complex direct material supply chains.

The change in name reflects the evolution of the company from a dot-com B2B exchange for the steel industry to an inter-enterprise business process software innovator for multiple industries. Michael S. Levin, NewView Technologies' Chairman and CEO, claims that the company's software solutions lower material acquisition, possession, and distribution costs and provide customers with a rapid return on investment. However, NewView continues to operate the e-STEEL exchange, a leading B2B exchange for the global steel industry.

The day the music died

During 2001, NetMarketMakers stopped updating its website at www.nmm.com after rapidly declining attendance at its B2B seminars left it short of cash. Today, good information on B2B exchanges is harder to find, although Tim Clark (formerly the leading analyst at NetMarketMakers) now publishes an excellent newsletter called *B2Bwatch*.

Current B2B information is also available from Line 56 (www.line56.com). The strange name comes from the Shakespeare's infamous quote "To be or not to be", which happens to be the 56th line of Act Three, Scene One in *Hamlet*.

What Went Wrong?

In the late 90s we got our first glimpse of what was possible in B2B. Unfortunately, everyone became over-optimistic in terms of how quickly it could happen. Analysts sold on the concept of "Internet time" just assumed that it would happen "overnight," in two or three years. B2B became so over hyped that it could never deliver on its true promise in that time frame.

Wall Street's brief love affair with B2B failed, therefore, because it was over-optimistic.

But B2B has also disappointed many business executives on Main Street. The major reasons for the disappointment caused by B2B exchanges so far, are:

- the failure of many B2B exchange business models due to an inability to build sufficient liquidity;
- the failure to build-out many exchanges beyond a simple Internet trading platform, and thereby failing to capitalize on "early mover" advantage;
- the belief that the B2B revolution could occur "overnight" without regard for the time required to achieve integration of disparate IT systems;
- a miscalculation of the relative importance of "neutrality" versus market domination; and
- the confusion of market turnover for revenue and profitability.

Let us analyze each of these issues in more depth.

Failure to build sufficient liquidity

The most prominent service an exchange provides is a centralized market space, and the more likely a buyer or seller is to make a satisfactory transaction on an exchange, the more likely they are to sign up and use that exchange over its rivals.

"Liquidity is king" for exchanges, so it is essential to build liquidity as quickly as possible.

Many B2B exchange start-ups failed to generate sufficient liquidity to survive. Unfortunately, it often takes longer than expected to get established industries to change their old procurement practices. Moving procurement on-line represents a major cultural change for many companies. Many B2B exchanges and B2B analysts underestimated the time it would take to convince procurement managers to move their business on to the Internet.

I discuss ways for B2B exchanges to build a critical mass of liquidity in Chapter 4.

Liquidity is easier to build when the products are highly standardized, as in financial services, where on-line trading of liquid, commoditized products such as US Treasury securities and corporate bonds is now commonplace on exchanges like eSpeed, BrokerTec, and TradeWeb. For example, in the fourth quarter of 2001 alone, eSpeed recorded total electronic volume in excess of $7 trillion. In March 2002, TradeWeb announced that its cumulative trading volume has surpassed the $10 trillion mark since trading began in 1998. TradeWeb's current product offerings include US Treasuries, US agency debt, euro-denominated sovereign debt, agency mortgage-backed securities, and commercial paper.

In many cases, the struggle for a critical mass of liquidity was compounded by the proliferation of start-ups in the same market space. This is well illustrated in the list of prominent successes and prominent failures at the end of this chapter.

In the financial services environment during 2000 and 2001 there was an explosion of B2B trading platforms for products ranging from US Treasuries, through corporate bonds and repos to foreign exchange. During that period, over 100 on-line trading systems were launched — many chasing the same buyers and sellers. Inevitably, there have been many failures. BondBook, a prominent US-based trading platform for high grade and high yield corporate bonds, closed down in October 2001. Corporate bonds are still relatively illiquid and far less commoditized than US Treasuries. BondBook was backed by a "who's who" of Wall Street, including Goldman Sachs, Credit Suisse First Boston, Deutsche Bank, Merrill Lynch, Morgan Stanley, Salomon Smith Barney, and UBS Warburg — but still failed. The system, which allowed counterparties to interact anonymously with each other, faced the issue of trying to completely change the traditional way of trading corporate bonds by phone — and went bust before it achieved critical mass. It is a major challenge to get existing voice brokers in bank dealing rooms to migrate their trading to an on-line system. Many sales people feel their job is threatened by a move to on-line trading and they stick with voice broking to preserve their position.

Many B2B exchanges faced exactly the same cultural resistance to change in their chosen market space and ran out of money before generating sufficient trading volumes and revenue.

Failure to build-out the exchange and capitalize on "early mover" advantage

Understandably, most B2B exchanges focused at the start on providing an on-line trading platform. However, many B2B exchanges never even made it past the first phase of providing an information portal and an on-line catalog (e-catalog) for an industry sector. Some second generation exchanges, especially industry consortia, managed to get as far as providing auction functionality, automated request-for-proposal and request-for-quote systems, and — in a few cases — continuous trading.

But few start-up B2B exchanges focused on the logistics of fulfilment, clearing and settlement, and payment processing. These un-sexy areas are what the securities industry calls "back-office functions."

As we shall see, successful third-generation B2B exchanges are able to extend their value proposition for users to include fully-integrated clearing and settlement functionality, derivatives trading and, ultimately, web-based services.

Providing settlement and other back-office functionality is not an "either-or" choice for public B2B exchanges. To be successful, exchanges must provide it all.

The securities markets provide plenty of examples of how successful exchanges must provide more than just a trading floor — physical or virtual. The NYSE, for example, which has been around for more than 200 years, is not just a trading floor. The NYSE owns part of the US clearing and settlement organization called DTCC. It also owns two-thirds of the Securities Industry

Automation Corporation (SIAC). SIAC is not just a major technology provider to the NYSE — it also provides the back-office systems used by the brokers who use that exchange.

In Europe, the Deutsche Börse has its own clearing and settlement organization. It is also in the process of buying 100% of a Pan-European clearinghouse called Clearstream.

Successful securities exchanges also offer back-office software packages for brokers that are tightly integrated with the exchange's trading engine. This helps members of the exchange grow their businesses while simultaneously locking the members into using that exchange.

These examples show that an exchange with longevity must offer a whole suite of services, not just a trading floor. In fact, many of the efficiencies of Internet trading can only be realized when the exchange also acts as a processing hub for all the back-office functions.

In the B2B world, exchanges discovered that on-line trading only works quickly for a subset of products that are fairly standardized or that are commodity items (eg, materials, repairs, and operations (MRO), indirect supplies such as light bulbs, stationery, etc.). On the other hand, the back-office functions are required in respect of all products, including direct supplies — no matter how they are traded. A B2B exchange can only become a hub for a whole industry if it provides back-office functions for all the products traded by that industry. In other words, the central e-marketplace can only survive if it is a part of a wider set of services offered by the exchange.

For example, MSA MetalSite (recently re-launched by MSA) and NewView Technologies (formally e-STEEL) are both continuing to provide a public e-marketplace for metals. However, the provision of the e-marketplace is now just one service in a community of services — just part of their plans to create a full service B2B exchange.

In Chapter 11, I explain why smart exchanges provide clearing and settlement services.

Analyzing the B2B Exchange Market Space

Underestimating the time required to integrate disparate IT systems

No one now doubts that the Internet offers an unrivalled vehicle for information exchange. But to realize the full benefits of the Internet in business, it is critical that a seamless flow of information is achieved, not only within a company but also between that company's customers, its suppliers, and all the parties associated with a transaction. For this to be achieved, all those parties must be included in the information flow, which requires the sharing of information and the sharing of the underlying networks conveying that information.

B2B exchanges host functionality and information that in many cases is also needed within a user's internal applications and needs to be integrated into the user's secure systems.

In a network-based e-business environment B2B exchanges cannot be islands on the Internet.

Unfortunately, many B2B exchanges were just that — islands that were isolated from the infrastructure of the companies that use them.

Achieving the necessary level of integration was one of the greatest challenges facing start-up B2B exchanges. And it is the complexity of the technology issues raised by integration that has prevented many B2B exchanges from delivering on their promise and achieving their full potential so far. In many cases, B2B exchanges have failed because they simply ran out of cash before they could achieve their true value proposition of fully integrating with the users' internal systems.

In Chapters 9 and 10, I discuss how and why the necessary level of integration is now occurring.

Neutrality: is it like virginity?

A perception of "neutrality" is critical to the success of a B2B exchange. However, neutrality is not a binary state — like virginity. Many B2B exchanges fell into the trap of believing that you are either totally neutral or you are not neutral at all.

In reality, you just need to be neutral enough to attract a wide enough membership base to achieve critical mass.

A successful exchange must get the largest number of buyers and sellers, and ensure that the largest buyers and the largest sellers use its central e-marketplace. If an exchange has to give up a piece of "neutrality" to achieve that, so be it.

It is true that B2B exchanges are judged on how well they serve all their members and how fair and equal they are. The winner is normally the exchange that demonstrates that it is operated in a neutral way so that all buyers and sellers feel comfortable in joining that market. But a consortium that includes some of the big players in that industry can still own the exchange.

Many independent dot-coms clung to neutrality and failed to co-opt the big players, who then launched their own industry-led exchanges. Industry-led consortia have the major advantage that they are well funded by their bricks and mortar parents. An additional advantage for consortia plays is that they bring tremendous natural liquidity to the exchange — in the form of combined buying or selling power. For example, Covisint can, in theory, expect to capture the combined parts procurement volume of all its owners — which amounts to more than $300 billion per annum.

On the other hand, such consortia faced the issue of how to establish sufficient operating neutrality for the exchange to succeed. One of the most hotly debated issues in B2B became whether consortia plays could retain sufficient neutrality to attract other buyers and sellers outside of the founding group. For example, a consortium of buying automakers established Covisint. The major car parts suppliers, such as Delphi, were naturally reluctant to join an exchange, the sole purpose of which seemed to be to combine the buying power of all Delphi's largest customers so that they could collectively drive Delphi's prices down.

Case study: MetalSite

MetalSite, an early leader as the first B2B exchange in steel, ceased operations on 15 June 2001, when it could no longer secure sufficient operating capital. The original founders and equity investors in MetalSite included Weirton, LTV, Steel Dynamics Inc., Bethlehem (now in Chapter 11 bankruptcy), and Ryerson Tull. In the 12 months to June 2001, MetalSite claimed that it handled over 2 million tons of product and conducted over 100,000 auctions.

In August 2001, Management Science Associates (MSA) announced that it had bought the assets of MetalSite Inc., and would relaunch MetalSite and ScrapSite (for scrap metal). Dr. Alfred Kuehn, founder and chairman of MSA, claims that "the lesson of MetalSite is that a viable exchange cannot be owned by an active participant. The barrier to MetalSite's and ScrapSite's growth in usage by non-equity firms during their final year is overcome by this purchase.

Industry concern about profits accruing to competitors from use of these exchanges can now be put to rest." (See Chapter 5 for my views on this.)

NewView Technologies, MetalSite's main competitor and an independently funded exchange, had constantly criticised MetalSite because of MetalSite's industry consortium ownership model.

The outcome has been that many industry-led exchanges used up much of 2001 in developing a hybrid corporate governance structure under which they have become sufficiently independent to operate in a totally neutral way. For example, Covisint now has independent management and most of the major car parts suppliers, including Delphi, have joined the exchange.

See Chapter 5 for a more detailed discussion of the pros and cons of industry consortia.

It's not what you take, it's what you make

Every commercial enterprise that wants to survive — from the smallest grocery store to the largest auto manufacturer — knows, that "it's not what you take, it's what you make" that counts.

Unfortunately, during the Internet boom a rather dubious habit became common for some B2B exchanges: booking the entire value of trades as revenues, rather than merely the profits earned on those trades (something which is not permitted for banks or stock exchanges).

For example, EnronOnline reported revenues of over $100 billion in 2000 and over $130 billion in the first three quarters of 2001. In reality, it only made $8 billion in 2000. It had fully exploited the device of reporting trading volume as revenue.

Imagine if a securities exchange, like the NYSE, started using its total trading value as its gross revenue. In 2000, the annual trading volume on the New York Stock Exchange, Inc. (NYSE) reached a record of 262 billion shares, with a total value of $11.1 trillion. However, the audited accounts state that the gross revenue of the NYSE and its wholly-owned subsidiaries in 2000 was $815.3 million. Not the entire value of all trades, but still the highest revenue in the history of the NYSE. Take the Bermuda Stock Exchange, of which I used to be the CEO. It has a "print market" where annual trades worth over $270 billion are reported. But the BSX cannot, alas, report that figure as its gross revenue.

Some of the Survivors

Marketspace	Company Names
Automotive	Covisint
Aviation/ Aerospace	Exostar, Cordiem, Aeroxchange, Airparts, Partsbase
Metals, minerals and mining	e-Steel (now part of NewView Technologies), MSA MetalSite and MSA ScrapSite, Quadrem
Chemicals	ChemConnect (merged with Envera and CheMatch), Elemica, Omnexus
Plastics	ChemConnect, Omnexus, Satyamplastics
Electronics	E2open, Converge, TraderFirst
Retail, consumer packaged goods	CPGMarket, GlobalNetXchange, WorldWideRetailExchange, Transora
Financial services	CreditTrade, eSpeed, BrokerTec, TradeWeb, MarketAxess, Currenex, FX Connect, FXall
Insurance	Catex, Inreon, RI3K, Riskclick, eReinsure
Intangible assets	The Patent and License Exchange (pl-x)
Energy, oil, gas, electricity	Intercontinentalexchange (ICE), HoustonStreet, Trade-ranger, Pantellos, ChemConnect
Freight	NTE
Shipping	Balticexchange, Levelseas, ShipyardXchange, Inttra
Paper	PaperSpace
Food, fruits, fish, cattle, etc	Agribuys, eMerge Interactive (cattle), PEFA

Analyzing the B2B Exchange Market Space

General trading   BayanTrade, DaewooTrade, Eficentrum, FreeMarkets, Goodex, ProcuraDigital

B2B news, research and analysis   B2Bwatch (www.factpointgroup.com), Line56.com, Communityb2b.com, eaijournal.com, emarketect, eMarketer, Gartner, Goldman Sachs, www.b2bexchanges.com

Source: Author, eMarketer.com

RIP

The following B2B exchanges have either failed to launch as announced, closed down, or completely revised their business plans to the point where they are no longer acting as exchanges.

Marketspace	Company Names
Automotive	Autovia, Autotradercenter
Aviation/ Aerospace	AviationX, Avolo, Skyfish, Aerospan, TradeAir
Metals, minerals and mining	MetalSpectrum, Aluminum.com, Copper.com
Chemicals	E-chemicals, Promedix, Chemdex
Plastics	PlasticsNet
Retail, consumer packaged goods	Novopoint, RetailersMarketXchange, FoodUSA, C-StoreMatrix, Packtion, ICSFoodone
Financial services	Atriax, BondBook, Visible Markets, BondClick (merged with BondVision), BondConnect, BondUSA, CFOweb, Limitrader. BondLink has been acquired by MarketAxess.
Insurance	Dotrisk, Global Risk Exchange, WISe
Intangible assets	Techex

Energy, oil, gas, electricity	Altra Energy Technologies (liquid gas trading acquired by ChemConnect), EnronOnline, Petrocosm, Silicon Valley Oil
Freight	FreightWise
Hospital supplies	Neoforma
Shipping	Shipdesk
Paper	PaperExchange, PaperX
Office supplies	Onvia
B2B news	NetMarketMakers

Source: Author

End Note:

1. *Debunking the Myth: E-marketplaces are not dead!*, Gale Daikoku, GartnerG2 Report, October 2001.

Analyzing the B2B Exchange Market Space

Chapter 2

A Reality Check: Why B2B has Not Been a Total Bust

"Despite all the failures and adverse publicity, B2B exchange volumes just keep on growing."

I believe that B2B exchanges are here to stay.

Although B2B exchanges have failed to meet the unrealistic growth expectations of Wall Street, they are not about to disappear. Many of the B2B exchanges that have survived through the last three years are now likely to flourish, although there will continue to be consolidation generally, some more will fail and growth rates will be slower.

Gale Daikoku, the leading B2B analyst at GartnerG2 (part of Gartner), predicts that by 2005, public and private B2B exchanges will be a dominant B2B trade mechanism for thousands of companies.[1]

Let us take a look at some of the positive indicators with respect to B2B exchanges.

B2B Exchange Volumes Keep On Growing

Despite all the failures and adverse publicity, B2B exchange volumes just keep on growing.

At the end of 1999, Arthur Sculley and I predicted that the total value of e-business passing through B2B exchanges would reach $600 billion by 2004 in the US alone. Our prediction was based on the assumption that about 40% of

Analyzing the B2B Exchange Market Space

all e-business would pass through B2B exchanges. At that time, the industry consensus forecast for overall B2B e-business was around $1.5 trillion by 2004.

In 2001, total e-business passing through B2B exchanges in the US, including private network exchanges, exceeded $250 billion. This represented at least a 75% increase over 2000, which Gartner estimates was around $140 billion, and suggests that our estimate of $600 billion by 2004 is very conservative.

For example, during 2001 in US auto manufacturing alone, customers contracted for more than $100 billion in raw materials, parts, and components for current and future vehicle programs using Covisint's electronic quote management (e-RFQ) product and more than US$51 billion through Covisint's on-line auction product. Approximately 85% of the auction volume represented direct materials purchases for building cars and trucks. The Global Web Trading Association (GTWA) has reported that trading through its 32 member B2B exchanges grew by several thousand percent in 2001 and exceeded $6 billion.

These estimates exclude financial services, where B2B exchanges such as eSpeed and TradeWeb are already trading volumes in the low $ trillions.

Worldwide B2B e-Business Keeps On Growing

B2B e-business is already much larger than on-line B2C commerce. A US Census Bureau report released in March 2002 shows that B2B transactions constituted 94% of e-business in 2000, with on-line sales to consumers making up the other 6%.

eMarketer published its latest *E-commerce Trade and B2B Exchanges Report* in March 2002 (www.emarketer.com).[2] eMarketer projects that worldwide B2B e-business activity will grow by almost 74% in 2002 to $823.4 billion by the end of the year, up from $474.3 billion in on-line transactions in 2001. And that it will reach $2,367 billion by the end of 2004. Other research firms forecast even larger numbers. For instance, Gartner, the leading firm of B2B analysts, now estimates that total B2B e-business will exceed $8.5 trillion by 2005.[3]

eMarketer uses a four-step process of aggregating, filtering, organizing and analyzing data from the leading research sources worldwide and then adding concise and insightful analysis of the facts and figures, along with its own estimates and projections, to create this valuable market report.

eMarketer's forecasts are more conservative than other research firms in large part due to its tighter definition of e-business, which includes only Internet-based transactions. While some researchers include traditional EDI within their forecasts, eMarketer includes only web-EDI. eMarketer also excludes the transaction of business services via the Internet, while some industry analysts include business services in their forecasts.

And eMarketer's report[2] shows that this growth is worldwide, not just in the US. For example, although Europe is still not a truly common market, eMarketer continues to forecast that B2B e-business will reach an estimated $797.3 billion in Europe in 2004. Germany is forecast to account for the largest portion of on-line trade, at $230.7 billion in 2004, followed by the United Kingdom at $214 billion. Examples of on-line exchanges that are based in Europe include a number of shipping sites, namely: the Balticexchange, Inttra, Levelseas, and ShipyardXchange; several insurance exchanges: including Inreon, eReinsure, Riskclick and RI3K; one of the leading consumer packaged goods sites: CPGMarket.com; and several trading hubs: including Goodex, and PEFA.com.

eMarketer also states that e-business is thriving in Asia, both through government-supported technology initiatives and the demand for Asian-based suppliers to join the networks set up by overseas trading partners. eMarketer projects that B2B e-business will grow to exceed $300 billion in the Asia-Pacific region in 2004, and will shortly thereafter experience accelerated growth.

BayanTrade is one example of a successful B2B exchange that eMarketer identifies as operating in the Asia-Pacific region. Based in the Philippines and founded by a consortium of six large enterprises, BayanTrade has conducted more than $74 million in transactions, the majority of which were on-line auctions. Other examples of active B2B exchanges in the Asia-Pacific region include electronic components exchange TraderFirst.com, and several trading hubs, including Satyamplastics.com, and Daewootrade.com.

Finally, eMarketer estimates that B2B e-business in the Latin American region will grow from $2.85 billion in 2000 to more than $58.3 billion by 2004. eMarketer predicts that a rapid acceleration of e-business growth will occur in this region sometime after 2005, once the telecommunications firms have developed a more reliable Internet infrastructure. Eficentrum is a leading trading hub in the Latin American region.

Analyzing the B2B Exchange Market Space

An Intense Period of Consolidation

Over the last 24 months, there has been a period of intense competition between entrepreneurial B2B exchanges and industry consortia plays in various vertical markets. The "winner takes most" effect has driven mergers and consolidations and one dominant exchange — with the greatest liquidity — has started to emerge in many verticals.

For example, in the chemicals industry ChemConnect acquired Envera in June 2001 and has now merged with CheMatch.

ChemConnect, the leading B2B exchange in the chemicals and plastics verticals (a combined market of $1.7 trillion), bought its rival CheMatch in a stock swap in February 2002. CheMatch, which trades chemicals, polymers, feed stocks, and fuel products on-line, is now fully integrated with ChemConnect. The two companies have been growing steadily since their creation more than two years ago. In 2001, ChemConnect reported $3 billion in transactions, while CheMatch posted $1 billion. ChemConnect is now reporting that it will be profitable by the end of 2002.

Although ChemConnect was emerging as the market leader, there was intense competition between the two exchanges. The merger has been welcomed by the industry and the combined revenues of the company, as well as the cost-savings associated with the merger, look like they will guarantee the merged exchange's success as the dominant player in the chemicals and plastics industries. In March 2002, ChemConnect expanded further by acquiring a natural gas liquids marketplace from Altra Energy Technologies. Natural gas liquids are used in the production of some plastics. It is possible that ChemConnect will now seek to merge with, or establish, an interoperability agreement with Elemica — which would give it total market domination in both chemicals and plastics.

In the metals industry, MSA MetalSite has recently acquired the Global Steel Exchange. Another form of merger is illustrated by the way Partminer is now working with E2open. The electronics exchange, E2open — founded by industry heavy-hitters like IBM, Hitachi, Lucent, Matsushita, Nortel, and Toshiba — entered into a revenue-sharing partnership with PartMiner, which was best known for its database of electronic component information. PartMiner's contribution to E2open was this database of over 12 million items and other transaction technology. Industry sources are suggesting that E2open will now merger with Converge.

Similarly, Cordiem and the Aerospace Hardware Exchange (AHX) have entered into a strategic technology and marketing agreement for hardware commodity transactions. The agreement allows Cordiem to connect its customers to AHX's two million line items of hardware commodities and its transaction and information management platform. AHX and Cordiem will market Cordiem's procurement and collaboration technology to AHX's global membership base, co-marketing both companies' services to a combined customer base.

As we have seen, over 100 on-line trading platforms developed in the financial services environment during 2000 and 2001 However, the Bond Market Association (www.bondmarkets.com) published a survey in December 2001 which showed that, in respect of fixed-income systems in the US, from a list of 68 systems at the end of 2000, 21 (about one-third) had merged with other partners or gone bust by the end of 2001. The survey reported that there are still 49 fixed-income systems in the US. The report attributes consolidation in the number of US trading systems to overcapacity, contraction in the Internet economy, and unsuccessful business models. Including derivative trading platforms (such as CreditTrade) the survey report identified a total of 79 electronic trading platforms operating in the US and Europe for all fixed-income products.

On the casualty list are BondBook, BondConnect, BondUSA, CFOweb, Limitrader and Visible Markets. BondLink was acquired by MarketAxess and BondClick merged with BondVision.

The clear leaders in the fixed-income area are now eSpeed, Brokertec, Market Axess, and TradeWeb. In foreign exchange trading the leaders are FXall (which was voted best overall multi-bank portal for research, for trading, and for straight through processing in the *Euromoney* Forex Poll released in May 2002), Currenex, and FX Connect.

I can confidently predict that there will be further consolidation in the financial services area and that only one trading platform will eventually dominate in each product vertical such as fixed-income trading and foreign exchange in each of the US and Europe.

The same process of massive consolidation is currently underway in most other industries.

Analyzing the B2B Exchange Market Space

B2B Productivity Improvements

One of the greatest claims of the new economy is that IT can deliver truly extraordinary productivity improvements. B2B exchanges were expected to contribute by reducing costs and increasing efficiency.

IT has undoubtedly increased productivity in the developed world. In the US, during the IT investment boom of the late 1990s, many new economy believers claimed that sustainable annual productivity growth in the US was as high as 3%–4%. Between the years 1995 to 2000, US companies nearly doubled the pace of their IT investment. However, it turned out that IT investment at that rate was unsustainable and data revisions show that, during the same years, labor productivity grew at an annual rate of 2.5%. That is still nearly twice the 1972–1995 rate of 1.4%. The revised data for Q4 2001 now shows that US labor productivity in the non-farm business sector grew at 5.2% in that quarter and a staggering 8.4% annualized rate in the first quarter of 2002. Even though that rate is not sustainable, even the conservative view today is that trend productivity growth in the US is now above 2% p.a.

The McKinsey Global Institute (www.mckinsey.com) has released a study on US productivity growth 1995–2000[4], which suggests that the productivity improvements in the US are sustainable.

What is interesting is that the McKinsey study concluded that the productivity improvements we have seen already relate less to new IT and more to product, service and process innovations, competition, and to a lesser extent cyclical demand factors. However, they identified six specific sectors in which the Internet had clearly boosted productivity. One of these is the securities industry.

The McKinsey Report states: "*The securities industry was the only one of the six jumping sectors in which the Internet materially boosted productivity. By the end of 1999, roughly 40% of retail securities trades were done on-line, up from virtually zero in 1995, and the same number of front-line employees could broker ten times as many trades. At the same time, firms further automated the back end of the trading process. Competition ensured the rapid diffusion of successful applications of technology as on-line discount brokers, such as E-Trade and Charles Schwab, forced traditional brokers to develop their own low-cost, on-line trading capabilities. Specific regulatory changes increased competition and had a significant impact on productivity in two sectors. In the securities industry, the SEC's Order Handling and 16th Rules sharply reduced commissions and trading spreads. These reductions allowed institutional investors to take advantage of increasingly small price anomalies, thus boosting trading volumes and allowing the industry to leverage fixed labor."*

This shows that IT can deliver truly extraordinary productivity improvements by expanding labor capacity by an order of magnitude. As McKinsey discovered, on-line retail securities trading requires approximately one-tenth of the customer interfacing labor employed in traditional channels.

McKinsey concludes that the reason why the securities industry has benefited so much from IT is that the product itself is well-suited to IT because it is essentially intangible information that can be digitized.

B2B exchanges are similarly in the business of digitizing intangible information (purchasing decisions, orders, delivery information, inventory levels, etc.) and will deliver significant improvements in productivity for exchange users once the user's internal applications have been integrated and are able to talk to other users' systems.

The productivity benefits of full integration come from increased purchasing efficiency and reduced operational costs. By integrating the enterprise's internal systems with its trading partners, structured data from electronic transactions can automatically be fed into the relevant financial, logistics, and manufacturing management modules. This data can include, by way of example, product, customer and payment details, order volumes and delivery dates. This allows businesses to reduce their order cycle times by automating the purchase process and the accounting and payment process.

In addition, procurement processes, such as obtaining a request for proposal or requests for quotations, can also be made more efficient. B2B exchanges provide auction functionality that is significantly reducing purchasing costs for large companies. B2B exchanges are now focused on automating the "back-end" processes of clearing and settlement. As with the securities industry, increasing efficiency driven by straight through processing will drive further productivity improvements in other industries.

IT productivity improvements have, so far, been largely derived from the benefits of the greater information exchange made possible by the World Wide Web and by e-mail. This suggests that even greater productivity improvements are possible once we start to see true program-to-program integration and the integration of business processes through web-based services, much of which will be achieved through B2B exchanges.

Analyzing the B2B Exchange Market Space

XML — The e-Business Integration Panacea?

Two years ago, I believed that the Internet and eXtensible Markup Language (XML) would replace EDI and make e-business as easy as opening a browser window.

One of the main benefits of the Internet that I emphasized was inclusion. Small- and medium-sized companies, who could not afford the major services work of EDI or application integration, would be able to participate in the network economy by simply opening Netscape or Microsoft Explorer. However, while the Internet does provide a low cost communication channel, in practice the document standards that need to be supported are complex and daunting.

XML offered to solve all of these complex problems and has been highly touted as the e-business communication and integration panacea. XML, being a text-based language, does travel over the same Internet communications channels as traditional web browser traffic. But XML does not provide one standard for building and exchanging documents, it only provides a blueprint. So far, the efforts of developers to use XML have fragmented some of the data definitions and tagging, and XML, while promising a lot, is still very much in its infancy.

There is a common saying "The wonderful thing about standards is that there are so many to choose from." And XML could fall into this trap. Where 20 companies use XML to build a purchase order for their business then 20 different XML based purchase orders will emerge, reflecting the individual needs of the respective businesses. Fortunately, industry participants are beginning to come together to set more formal standards.

Today I can confidently re-state that XML is here to stay. XML adoption will be rapid in some industries, like hi-technology and financial services, and slower in others, but XML will become a component of document exchange in all successful B2B exchanges. However, rumors about the imminent demise of EDI have been greatly exaggerated.

Despite its shortcomings, EDI will remain a business communication vehicle many companies will need to support. The important point is that companies have significant investments in EDI and will need independent software vendors to support that investment. With the benefit of hindsight, it was naive to believe that organizations or value chain partners were going to rip out EDI systems. These systems represent multi-million dollar investments in time, resources, and effort, but more importantly, they work. For many organizations that have already made the investment in EDI and a value-added network infrastructure, EDI still represents the lowest cost, secure transaction processing infrastructure.

Although EDI will remain, program-to-program integration over the Internet is now truly possible and will drive us towards the "promised land" of business process integration.

Achieving this integration is one of the biggest challenges facing B2B exchanges. Over the next two years, third-generation B2B exchanges will struggle with systems integration and e-business communication as their users replace existing business processes with networked alternatives.

However, open access to, and the ubiquity of, the Internet will eventually address this issue and provide the optimal framework for integrating B2B exchanges with internal enterprise systems. In Chapter 9, I provide a detailed discussion of the integration issues being faced by B2B exchanges.

B2B Exchanges are assuming the Role of "Babel Fish" Communication Hubs

B2B exchanges are emerging as the critical communication hubs, through which suppliers, customers and trading partners can connect their systems and realize further productivity improvements.

The hub-and-spoke concept enables the numerous communications protocols to be "translated", so that different systems can talk to each other and avoids the need for companies to establish a large number of bilateral links to all other partners. When that integration is missing or weak it creates problems. Functionality overlaps, information has to be retyped or recaptured, separate databases are no longer synchronized, and document version control is lost.

Based on a B2B exchange's ability to integrate disparate systems, I have christened B2B exchanges as "Babel fish" communication hubs.

The late Douglas Adams invented Babel fish in his hilarious science-fiction novel *The Hitchhikers Guide to the Galaxy*. It is a small fish that you insert in your ear, its nutrition processes convert sound waves into brain waves, and it automatically acts as a translator for everything it hears — neatly crossing the language divide between any species you should happen to meet while travelling across the galaxy.

Analyzing the B2B Exchange Market Space

The complexity involved in implementing program-to-program integration standards creates an enormous opportunity for B2B exchanges to act as the translators — the "Babel fish" — that can communicate and map information between all the different parties, as illustrated in Figure 2A.

Each industry will have one B2B exchange that acts as a utility that allows every enterprise to have links with all the suppliers, customers, and logistics providers that they need to integrate with — on a "do-it-once" basis.

Private Network Exchanges are Flourishing

Over the last 12 months, smaller, private networks — that put a single e-business at the centre of the B2B network — have overshadowed large public B2B exchanges. Such private exchanges, as I call them, are web-based trading applications implemented by a single company with a select group of suppliers and customers.

Private exchanges offer increased collaboration with suppliers and a deeper view into the supply chain and are now fuelling new growth in B2B transactions.

With hindsight, it is possible to see that many companies were not ready to go straight to public B2B exchanges to begin their B2B efforts, because their own business environment was not sufficiently on-line. The result was that B2B exchanges only offered a novel procurement mechanism and could not deliver on the full potential of an on-line network, since that requires deep integration with the users' internal systems.

Companies are now progressing with the smaller set of B2B processes involved in linking up their existing suppliers and supply chain. As a result, many public exchanges are broadening their services by building and hosting private exchanges. For instance, CATEX, the insurance B2B exchange, has significantly broadened its base of services by assisting in the creation of several private insurance networks. Even big exchanges such as Covisint and E2open are building private exchanges for specific users.

See Chapter 6 for a detailed discussion of this new business model for B2B exchanges.

Behind the trend toward private trading networks is the desire for purchasing managers to have more control over their on-line relationships. Companies can use private exchanges to establish central control over purchasing through contracts with established suppliers.

Figure 2A: Babel Fish Communication Hubs

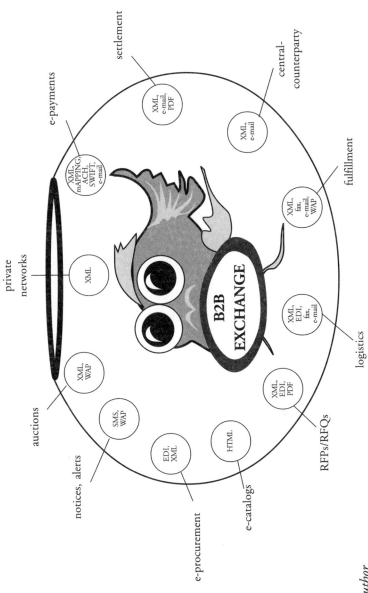

private networks

e-payments

settlement

central-counterparty

auctions

notices, alerts

e-procurement

e-catalogs

RFPs/RFQs

logistics

fulfillment

XML

XML, mAPPING, ACH, SWIFT, e-mail

XML, e-mail, PDF

XML, e-mail

XML, fax, e-mail, WAP

XML, WAP

SMS, WAP

EDI, XML

HTML

XML, EDI, PDF

XML, EDI, fax, e-mail

B2B EXCHANGE

Source: Author

Analyzing the B2B Exchange Market Space

One of the corner stones of the new economy was the concept that the Internet represented a "once in a lifetime" shift in power from suppliers to buyers. Nothing epitomized this more than the auction model, bringing multiple suppliers together on-line to compete for a buyer's business. Unfortunately, many B2B exchanges, which started by offering auctions, found that the buying members were using them solely to squeeze the prices of existing suppliers.

To create a sustainable business model, B2B exchanges have to find a value proposition that appeals to both buyers and sellers. Providing a platform for integrated supply chain management in the form of a private exchange is one way to provide real value to suppliers, as well as providing more efficient procurement platforms for buyers.

In doing so, B2B exchanges have to develop an e-business messaging and communications infrastructure that enables them to receive and deliver information and documents in a multitude of formats and channels (see Chapter 10).

Clearing and Settlement Issues Addressed

A critical component of any e-marketplace that seeks to expand its community of participants and facilitate automated and/or anonymous trading is an efficient clearing and settlement system.

Delivery of physical goods will always require the use of logistics companies like UPS and transportation services. Bulk trades of chemicals or car parts require a sophisticated fulfillment, tracking and payments process — which B2B exchanges are now addressing. This is the next frontier for developing B2B exchanges and no doubt will be a critical issue for the readers of this book, so I have devoted the whole of Chapter 11 to a fuller analysis of it.

The increasing awareness of the importance of the back-office functions is well illustrated by the insurance and re-insurance industries. Early movers in this space, such as CATEX and the Global Risk Exchange, focused on creating on-line trading platforms for insurers to buy and sell risk. In reality, on-line trading of risk has proved to be less attractive than the traditional method of placement through brokers, in all but the highly standardized capacities/ products. CATEX has seen over 1,400 trades, but it has taken five years to achieve even that modest number.

On the other hand, the industry has realized that tremendous value-add is available by streamlining the back-office logistics of the business. This covers everything from the finalization of the contract (after a company agrees to assume a risk), through contract amendments during the life of the contract and premium payment tracking, to claims handling and claims payment tracking. The newer B2B exchanges in this space, such as RI3K and Riskclick, are now heavily focused on providing workflow management and back-office processing functionality as the main driver of their business models (with on-line trading as just one component in a suite of value-added services).

The Introduction of Derivatives

Enron notwithstanding, I predict that derivatives are in the future of many B2B exchanges.

Many B2B exchanges have started by providing simple on-line trading mechanisms for physical products such as plastics, chemicals, and metals with spot buying and on-line price catalogs. Others are already focused on trading more sophisticated financial products such as forward contracts or securitized derivative instruments. For example, CreditTrade is trading credit derivatives, Enrononline.com (now called UBSWenergy) trades forward contracts on a whole range of assets including electricity, oil, and gas, and ChemConnect provides paper trades and exchange-traded futures in respect of Benzene products.

Having multiple competing buyers and sellers leads to inevitable market volatility. Because market volatility can involve adverse price moves, it substantially increases risk. B2B exchanges can be considerably enhanced if the core price discovery function for cash products is supplemented by the availability of financial derivatives that can be used to hedge exposures or arbitrage price differences in the underlying cash markets.

Many B2B exchanges will, therefore, seek to introduce financial products that allow their customers — the buyers and sellers — to manage these risks, hedge their exposure and speculate on future prices. This will enable them to expand their universe of participants to include players previously "unknown" to the original community of buyers and sellers of the physical products traded in the cash market. As the users of the successful B2B exchanges search for new tools to effectively improve risk management strategies, the exchanges must move quickly to introduce products, such as derivatives, to meet that demand and to increase transaction volume on the exchange.

Analyzing the B2B Exchange Market Space

But introducing derivatives increases the complexity of the exchange exponentially. Chapter 8 discusses the issues involved and explains how derivatives help to increase liquidity on an exchange.

B2B Exchanges are Better Funded Now

Many start-up B2B exchanges were under-capitalized based on the real timeframes required to build liquidity, integrate the users with the exchange, and build out the services offered by the exchange.

During the last three years, B2B exchanges were funded in three main ways:

- venture capital (VC) and seed capital (the three "Fs" — friends, family, and fools);
- an early IPO; or
- by industry consortia.

Venture capital and seed funding

In the face of a major pull back in technology stock valuations, a lot of VC funds scaled back or froze any further investment in private companies after April 2000. This acted like a fire blanket and deprived many B2B companies of oxygen at a critical time in their development. The pull back in VC funding was so widespread and so pervasive in 2000 and 2001 that both good and bad companies were affected.

Following the implosion of the dot-com boom, most investors have become less patient with money losing ventures and it is increasingly difficult for under-capitalized B2B exchanges to obtain additional working capital.

Premature IPOs and the "dot-bomb" phenomenon

During 1999 through mid–2000, we witnessed a period when many companies were convinced by the wizards of Wall Street that an early IPO would be a crucial ingredient in their formula for success. But as many of the companies that were floated sink without a trace, the lure of an early IPO has now been exposed as false magic.

At the end of 2001, over 250 companies listed on NASDAQ faced the prospect of being delisted because they were no longer in compliance with the $1 minimum bid price requirement for continued listing, as stipulated in Marketplace Rule 4450(a)(5).

A Reality Check: Has B2B Been a Total Bust?

Historically speaking, NASDAQ was set up to give young but higher growth companies a chance to access "cheap public money" before they could meet the prohibitive track record and/or profitability requirements of the Big Board — the NYSE. The reason why an IPO is considered "cheap money" is because the IPO valuation is considerably higher than in the seed and VC funding rounds. This enables a company to raise a larger amount of capital but only issue a small number of new shares. For example, many B2B-related IPOs in 1999 and 2000 offered only 10% of the enlarged issued share capital while raising amounts ranging from $50 million to $500 million, on the back of insignificant revenues and major losses.

Of course an early IPO appeals to the VCs and other early stage investors because it represents the "liquidity event" that is their holy grail.

The harsh lesson that many B2B companies have had to learn is that an IPO to the public and even a listing on NASDAQ are by no means a guarantee of success. Indeed in some cases, a premature IPO actually accelerates the company's demise.

The first problem with an early IPO is that the preparation process can take nine to twelve months of the senior management's time — including the preparation of a full disclosure registration document, an exhaustive due diligence process and a heavy pre-float PR blitz and road show. If the IPO is planned too early in the company's lifecycle it distracts the top management at precisely the time when they need to be completely focused on completing the product, establishing customers, building sustainable revenues, and driving the company to profitability — a crucial and tricky stage in its growth.

And after an early IPO, the company often does not have the luxury of sufficient time to achieve any of those things, if they have not been accomplished prior to the IPO.

Once the company has conducted an IPO and been listed, it is in the public domain — as well as being subject to rigorous statutory reporting and accounting requirements, it also finds itself much more sensitive to the vagaries of public and analyst opinion. The company's future becomes dependent on meeting the quarterly numbers that were forecast in the IPO. Managing investor relations becomes a necessity and a major continuing drain on management's resources.

If the company is not constantly moving forward at the speed predicted in the IPO, the share price will suffer. If the company has been floated before it is profitable, the IPO's proceeds are supposed to see it through to profitability. As we have seen all too often, when a newly floated company does not achieve profitability within the timeframe projected in the IPO, the "cheap public capital" starts to run out and the share price takes a dive. And then the chances of getting a second round of public funding are close to zero.

The truth is the leap across the chasm from private to public company can be too great for many early stage, pre-profit companies.

In the US the problem is compounded by the fact that the term "underwriting" is sorely abused. Leading Wall Street firms do not actually underwrite IPOs anymore. The so called "underwriting" commitment is nothing more than a "best efforts" commitment. This means that the lead underwriter builds a book of takers based on the red herring prospectus and an indicated price range. In order to actually price the issue and close the IPO, the lead underwriter requires the offering to be at least three or four times oversubscribed, to ensure there is sufficient aftermarket support to drive the IPO to a premium. For the issuing company, the IPO event is a binary one — it either happens and the stock soars to a premium over the issue price — or the issue never happens as the underwriter pulls it at the last minute.

For example, StreamServe, Inc. was literally hours away from pricing by the lead underwriter — Warburg Dillon Reed — in April 2000. Although the primary book was oversubscribed, the offering was pulled in the face of a rapidly weakening market.

IPOs should never be done that way. In most of Europe and Hong Kong the underwriter actually agrees to underwrite the offer on a firm basis and at a pre-agreed price. The underwriter then has "career at risk" incentive to sell the whole of the offering before the public offer period expires. In other words, the underwriter commits to fund the company and "take the hit" if he cannot sell it all. The major advantage of this mechanism for the issuing company is that the company gets firm committed funds right from the start and there is never a possibility that the IPO will not go ahead (except if a force majeure event occurs).

Fortunately, this story has a happy ending for StreamServe. Today, StreamServe is flourishing as a private company and is one of the largest software companies in Europe. In May 2002, *TIME* magazine listed StreamServe as one of the 50 hottest technology stocks in Europe.

A Reality Check: Has B2B Been a Total Bust?

Now that the madness of "dot-com fever" is over, B2B exchanges are remaining private until they can show sustainable profitability because their CEOs don't really fancy having to turn base metal into gold until they are really ready to.

Industry consortia

Industry consortia have the major advantage that they are usually well funded by their bricks and mortar parents. However, they must still retain the financial support of their founders long enough to survive the long growth phase (eg, MetalSite ran out of capital backing from its original founders before it achieved a sustainable position).

Whereas most independent, dot-com exchanges were launched with less than $50 million in capital, most industry consortia have several hundred million dollars in funding. For example, Pantellos had $100 million in organised funding.

Several industry consortia, such as Covisint and Cordiem, are rapidly heading towards profitability. I predict that we will see several industry consortia exchanges going public, by way of an IPO, during 2003 — once they have several profitable quarters under their belts.

B2B Exchanges Have the Opportunity to Move Offshore

A B2B exchange that supports cross border trading can effectively now choose where it wishes to be located. It can be set up and managed virtually anywhere, and the e-marketplace itself can be operated in a separate jurisdiction or in multiple jurisdictions.

This level of freedom is derived from the benefits of the knowledge economy and the specific nature of B2B exchanges.

In *Blown to Bits* (Harvard Business School Press), Philip Evans and Thomas S. Wurster pointed out that the Internet can blow away practically any business, and they write that the "glue that holds today's value chains and supply chains together" is melting. The Internet and web-based services are indeed creating the opportunity for companies to "unbundle the value chain" and place some high value functions in their location of choice.

For example, large multinational enterprises are now positioning their group procurement operations, their customer relationship management applications, their supply chain management solutions, and their intangible assets in offshore centers.

I argue in Chapter 12 that most B2B exchanges can be and should be incorporated offshore.

B2B exchanges are free from nearly all of the traditional constraints on physical location because they are:

- fully electronic members of the knowledge economy;
- restricted to business-to-business;
- virtual communities of members operating within a common, closed-contract system; and
- exclusive information sources.

This means that B2B exchanges, like companies, are able to locate some or all of their high value functions in offshore domiciles.

Third-generation B2B Exchanges are Already Emerging

By the end of this book, I hope that readers will be able to visualize the anatomy of a successful third-generation (3G) B2B exchange. 3G B2B exchanges will provide a wide range of services, all of which complement each other and attract users to join the exchange and, ultimately, to use the core trading service.

These exchanges are emerging and they will dominate their chosen market space. They will also be able to expand into new market spaces. The full range of services that these exchanges offer are listed in Figure 2B opposite.

Figure 2B: 3G B2B Exchanges

	B2B exchanges		
Functionality	1st Generation	2nd Generation	3rd Generation
1. Information portal — news, forms, etc.	√	√	√
2. On-line e-catalogs	√	√	√
3. Automated RFPs/RFQs	X	√	√
4. Auctions	X	√	√
5. Build and operate private networks for e-procurement by users	X	√	√
6. Fully-integrated clearing and settlement functionality	X	X	√
7. Supply chain management functionality	X	X	√
8. Continuous trading	X	X	√
9. Babel fish communication hub	X	X	√
10. Web-based value-added services	X	X	√
11. Derivatives trading	X	X	√

Source: Author

Analyzing the B2B Exchange Market Space

End Notes:

1. *Debunking the Myth: E-marketplaces are not dead!*, Gale Daikoku, GartnerG2 Report, October 2001.

2. *E-commerce Trade and B2B Exchanges Report*, Steve Butler eMarketer, March 2002.

3. *Global B2B Internet Commerce Forecast: Growth Pauses, but Expansion is on the Horizon*, Lauren Jones Shu, GartnerG2 Report, August 2001.

4. *US Productivity Growth, 1995-2000*, The McKinsey Global Institute, October 2001.

Chapter 3

Why B2B Exchanges are Still a "Killer Application"

"Many B2B Exchanges remain standing and are building true value for their owners, their users and the industries in which they operate."

The power of the Internet has resulted in the emergence of centralized marketplaces where businesses can buy and sell goods and services from each other. Just as centralized markets for the trading of stocks and bonds have become known as stock exchanges, I call these business-to-business markets B2B exchanges. Others call them net markets or e-markets.

Back in 1999, I asserted that "Based on their ability to bring buyers and sellers together on-line and thereby to create dynamic pricing, B2B Exchanges are the killer application in the business-to-business Internet revolution."

A "killer application" is a must-have application that drives people's usage of a particular computer technology and creates a mass market for it. In the early days of large, expensive IBM personal computers, the killer application that drove sales was the spreadsheet (originally Lotus 1-2-3). With the Internet, the killer application that has driven usage in both businesses and at home is the humble e-mail application.

Despite the common perception in the media that B2B exchanges have failed, e-business is inexorably penetrating deeper and deeper into business organizations, moving beyond customer-facing websites, and generating more far-reaching projects in back-office areas like logistics and supply chain management. In fact, companies are now focused on integrating the Internet into everything they do in order to survive.

Analyzing the B2B Exchange Market Space

Successful B2B exchanges are helping to provide the platforms for this new level of on-line collaboration across the supply chain and for improving trading efficiency. B2B exchanges provide significant opportunities to automate collaborative business processes with both customers and suppliers, thus generating internal efficiencies, and providing opportunities to reach new markets at much lower cost.

The B2B Internet stock market bubble may have burst but not everything has vanished. Many B2B exchanges remain standing and they are building true value for their owners, their users and the industries in which they operate.

B2B exchanges are being used in four ways:

1. As public, on-line marketplaces through which users secure improvements in the efficiency of the trading process, get greater price visibility, are able to set prices, and to find new suppliers;
2. As an important way to improve operational efficiency, supply chain management and product design through the development of private networks and collaborative communities (see Chapter 6);
3. As communication hubs through which suppliers, customers and logistics providers are able to interconnect their internal systems to realize productivity improvements and to access web-based services (see Chapter 9); and
4. As the platform for straight through processing of the "back-end" processes so as to improve logistics and fulfillment, enable product tracking, and secure efficient clearing and settlement and payment processing.

And more companies than ever are embarking on e-business projects to streamline their businesses in 2002/3. Businesses are now focused on using e-business to respond to the current harsher competitive environment by seeking to make operations more efficient and thereby cut costs — two of the key value propositions of B2B exchanges.

For the reasons set out in this chapter, B2B exchanges remain one of the killer applications that are driving the use of the Internet, and the rapid adoption of new Internet technologies such as eXtensible Markup Language (XML) by businesses worldwide.

Why B2B Exchanges are Still a Killer Application

Global Reach

The cost of accessing the Internet is falling daily and the cost of sending information by e-mail or over the Web is a fraction of standard telephone, fax, and mail costs. This means that sellers can reach out to buyers all over the world and the buyers can access sellers from all over the world. In the physical world, businesses and individual consumers will often pay a higher price or buy an inferior product simply because that is the only service available in their physical location. Now, B2B exchanges are able to bring fragmented buyers and sellers together on the "virtual" trading floor of the centralized market space.

B2B exchanges create a community of those buyers and sellers in a structured and organized fashion. After viewing the offers posted on the exchange, communications between potential buyers and sellers are specifically targeted to the interested parties. The on-line exchange thus generates great sales leads to pre-qualified buyers. Unlike e-mail on the Internet, communications through a central exchange can be organized, secured, authenticated, time-stamped, tracked, and verified.

The low cost of getting connected, irrespective of geographical distance, enables fragmented buyers and sellers to find each other through a B2B exchange without incurring real-world search and travel expenses or high commissions for using intermediaries. In addition, by aggregating multiple sellers in one place, an exchange creates a one stop shopping experience for the buyers.

Even when a supplier of parts puts up its own on-line store front to sell directly to the manufacturer, it will find that a B2B exchange is more attractive to many buyers. This is because a neutral, third-party exchange can post the store fronts of multiple suppliers in one place, facilitating the manufacturer's search for the best product at the best price.

The global reach of B2B exchanges is illustrated by the fact that leading consortium-backed exchanges such as Covisint, Exostar, and GlobalNetXchange have already established offices in Europe and Asia and are reporting significant transaction activity through their European operations. ChemConnect, the dominant chemicals and plastics exchange, has sales offices in Frankfurt, Rotterdam, Milan, Paris, and London.

Analyzing the B2B Exchange Market Space

Enabling E-procurement

A key goal of any procurement operation is to find the best deal, the right products, sufficient product availability, and acceptable prices. B2B exchanges have enabled companies to automate the procurement of goods and services from multiple suppliers.

Initially, this e-procurement was introduced to control the purchase of indirect supplies (eg, office supplies and goods for maintenance, repair, and operations (MRO) including: janitorial, electrical, bearings, tools, machinery, accessories, fire/safety equipment, etc.). Today, the same processes are being used to control the purchase of direct supplies, such as parts, components, and the raw materials used by manufacturers.

E-procurement allows a company to monitor its purchases more easily, and therefore reduce the amount of redundant or repetitive purchases. It is easier to manage the approval process when purchases are made on-line so the company can create tighter controls over spending authorizations. E-procurement also makes it easier to process the purchase transactions.

On-line procurement increases price transparency and facilitates new supplier discovery.

Finally, e-procurement enables a company to take advantage of dynamic pricing.

Dynamic Pricing

In the industrial world, most prices are set by a one-on-one negotiation or by the seller, who generally has the greater economic power, and can publish a hard-copy catalog with non-negotiable prices. An alternative method is to bring all of the potential buy and sell orders together and let those competing offers set the highest price or the price which maximizes the amount sold. This is the approach adopted by most stock exchanges with their central market matching systems for securities. It is also the price discovery mechanism adopted by eBay to run its on-line auctions for consumers.

Increasingly, dynamic price-setting mechanisms are being used by many B2B exchanges for business-to-business transactions, because the Internet's ability to interconnect companies very cheaply means that an Internet exchange can bring together bids and offers from all over the world. Initially, this may be as simple as on-line catalogs, which can have the price updated more regularly.

The next level is automated "request-for-proposal" mechanisms that enable buyers to get quotes from multiple suppliers. More sophisticated still is the use of real auctions to provide a dynamic forum in which competing bids are brought together.

Seller-driven auctions

In this approach, the seller drives the auction. The seller lists the item to sell and multiple buyers submit upward price bids for the designated item or service. This format tends to lead to an increase in the price bid as time extends and the close of the auction approaches. The system works well for sellers who can get the highest price for their goods while using the Internet to maximize their reach to a large number of potential buyers. This facilitates efficient market pricing and works especially well for unique or differentiated items which are relatively simple to describe and understand.

The system is less favorable to buyers, because there is no negotiation between the buyer and the seller — just a competition between all the buyers.

Seller-driven on-line auctions have proven to be a highly effective way of selling excess inventory. Businesses that use on-line auction sites to liquidate their leftovers report, on average, a 30% improvement in sales.

Buyer-driven auctions

What most distinguishes e-business from previous forms of business is the "once in a lifetime" shift of power from producers to customers. Customers are aware that they can demand the best quality, the best service, and the lowest prices; they also want everything customized and they want it immediately. They are far more demanding than in traditional commerce because they can now access suppliers from all over the world. In the world of B2B procurements, this process has seen the emergence of "buyer-driven" or reverse auctions.

In a reverse auction, the standard "eBay-style" auction format is inverted, with buyers specifying the items they want and multiple sellers competing for the buyer's business in an auction format. In this type of auction, the price tends to fall over time as the close of the auction approaches and the suppliers seek to undercut their competitors. This approach clearly favors the buyers, especially if there are multiple sellers able to offer items that come close to meeting the buyer's requirements. For a supplier that has had a long-standing relationship with the customer, the overwhelming fear is that a completely new competitor will come in and underbid them. The Internet enables that new competitor to be located anywhere in the world.

Analyzing the B2B Exchange Market Space

Reverse auctions can therefore be difficult for suppliers. For the salesman who has spent a career building a relationship with a critical customer, competing in a reverse auction can be his worst nightmare.

On the other hand, on-line reverse auctions have been proven to help companies significantly lower their procurement costs. FreeMarkets claims that buyers save more than 20% on average by using FreeMarkets' reverse auction applications. If there are five suppliers bidding on a contract, there are four suppliers who are happy to bid because they could win new business and only one supplier, the incumbent provider, who is being challenged.

For the main part though, reverse auctions are most appropriate for highly commoditized items such as indirect supplies (eg, for maintenance, repairs, and operations), where a deep supplier relationship is not critical and the quality and nature of the goods is highly standardized.

For direct procurement goods that tend to be more customized products (eg, a molded component required by a manufacturer) and for which quality is critical, a more complex approach is required.

Case study: FreeMarkets

FreeMarkets, Inc. (NASDAQ: FMKT) is a leading global provider of e-sourcing software and service solutions. FreeMarkets combines the power of web-based reverse auction technology with in-depth supply market information, market operations, and expert sourcing services. This enables the procurement of highly customized products through reverse auctions.

FreeMarkets has helped customers around the world source more than $30 billion in goods and services in over 195 different supply verticals and to identify savings of over $6.4 billion for those customers. Over 19,000 suppliers from more than 70 countries have actively bid through FreeMarkets since 1995.

FreeMarkets has developed a sophisticated system that allows the buyer to indicate a range of preferences over a series of parameters — rather than just price and volume. Although price is a factor, it is only one piece of the business equation, with quality, availability, time to volume, payment terms, and operations flexibility all playing a part.

In the manufacturing process, for example, quality, time of delivery, payment terms, and after sales service can be just as important and sometimes more important than the price. Similarly, a manufacturer may wish to link a particular purchase, or the amount of the product to be purchased, to another purchase

— for example where both products are needed but in different quantities in order to manufacture the end product. More sophisticated trading applications are now being developed that allow a buyer to build up a "profile" which indicates the buyer's preferences over these multiple attributes and links orders for different products into one "combination" order.

FreeMarkets works with its customers to pre-qualify a small group of suitable suppliers who meet the necessary supplier performance standards. The buying company indicates that the lowest price will not necessarily win the auction. The suppliers know this and can therefore continue to emphasize their core competencies. When buying a complex product the buying company may only select existing suppliers — eliminating the nightmare scenario for an incumbent supplier of losing a major account to a complete stranger.

After all the preparation, the procurement process comes down to a competitive on-line bidding process in which the buyer is able to establish the market price in say, one hour, rather than the complex, pre-Internet process that often took weeks to finalize the price.

FreeMarkets also works with its customers to perform continuous supplier performance analysis to evaluate not only prices, but also on-going attributes such as actual product availability, supplier responsiveness, service levels and delivery history, as well as customer-satisfaction ratings.

Revolutionizing Supply Chain Management
– Collaborative Communities

The process though which a manufacturer sources all the raw materials, components, and parts which go into producing its finished product is called a supply chain. Introducing e-procurement into the supply chain process is a much more complicated task than arranging occasional purchases from an on-line catalog. It is in the area of supply chain management where B2B exchanges are now delivering most value.

B2B exchanges are increasingly as focused on developing their supply chain management functionality as on building their central, public e-marketplaces.

A manufacturer can either build its own supplier-relationship management strategies or work through a B2B exchange as a central hub to tie all the parties together.

Analyzing the B2B Exchange Market Space

B2B exchanges, both private and public, have the capability to tie together the manufacturer with its suppliers (Tier 1) and its suppliers' suppliers (Tiers 2 and 3). This can lead to a collaborative process that generates greater efficiencies in the design of products and significant reductions in the time and cost of manufacturing.

The exchange therefore becomes a collaborative trading community. In this way, the benefits of the B2B exchange extend well beyond the function of bringing buyers and sellers together and result in major process improvements as well.

By enabling deep collaboration, supply-chain management functionality provides great benefits to suppliers which can help counter-balance the negative effects that suppliers perceive from reverse auctions run through a B2B exchange.

Some of these types of application are now called collaborative planning, forecasting and replenishment (CPFR). In order to be effective CPFR, and other e-business enabled supply-chain applications, must support:

- sourcing — to help locate suppliers, evaluate their offerings, and make comparisons;
- contract-management capabilities — to facilitate contract negotiation, maintain contract terms and pricing details, and ensure that the proper contractual terms are applied to each order;
- competitive bidding — to facilitate the generation of requests for quotes that include detailed line-item criteria, to share the RFQ with the suppliers and to manage the bidding process (see dynamic pricing above);
- collaboration with suppliers — to enable the manufacturer to share information about the state of the company to improve forecasting and demand planning and to promote efficiency by co-ordinating business processes; and
- collaboration from suppliers — to enable suppliers to respond to detailed RFQ specifications or to requirements received through integration with the manufacturer's enterprise resource planning (ERP) system. When a manufacturer's supply chain system can expose this type of data to its suppliers, the suppliers can respond with contract adjustments, new products or service packages and other cost saving proposals.

Supply chain management, therefore, requires deep integration between a company's purchasing process and the information residing in that company's inventory and logistics systems, with the information on the supplier's back-end systems. Connecting major ERP systems to other applications, such as supply-chain management and logistics systems, is one of the most complicated tasks facing e-business today.

As we shall see in Chapters 6 and 10, B2B exchanges are facilitating this process by setting the standards for whole industries, and by building private networks that link individual companies with their suppliers (based on those common standards) as well as by providing public marketplaces where buyers can identify potential new suppliers.

The main benefits to be achieved by implementing this level of collaboration through a B2B exchange are:

- reduced cost by building the functionality once for the exchange, so that each user does not have to deploy identical software in-house;
- establishment of common standards for the whole industry by the exchange;
- a common catalog standard as the basis for collaboration that eliminates common inconsistencies in trading partner and product identifiers; and
- reduced time to scale, since CPFR is now being offered as a standard service in some B2B exchanges (eg, the main retail and consumer packaged goods exchanges including GNX, CPGMarket, and Transora).

More Efficient Distribution Channels — B2O

Once a manufacturer goes on-line it can reach out and touch the end consumers of its products, without the need for retail distribution channels. Those distribution channels were developed to enable the manufacturer to achieve the maximum distribution of its products in a pre-Internet environment. The distribution channels also helped the manufacturer to manage inventory levels of completed products and to store that inventory, in return for a percentage of the sales price. Now a manufacturer can get orders from consumers directly over the Internet and then move to a "build-to-order" (B2O) program — just as Dell Computers has for PCs. A B2O business model can dramatically reduce manufacturing time, inventory levels, and distribution costs.

Dell's B2O program requires it to balance supply (what is available) with demand (what customers want). Dell has perfected the technique of adjusting for any shortage in a particular component by immediately informing customers of increased lead times on that product and offering other available options on promotion. This level of flexibility is only possible where the customers order on-line, and both Dell and Dell's suppliers can monitor component stock availability in real-time.

Analyzing the B2B Exchange Market Space

In addition, a B2O business model reduces the amount of inventory that sits unsold in the sales channels. This means that the benefits of new designs, reduced costs, and improved technology can be passed on to the end customers at a much faster rate.

General Motors offers its cars for sale on the Internet at www.gmbuypower.com, but also continues to sell its cars through its dealer network. However, in addition to selling its own cars, GM intends to become a car merchant and a buyer for the ultimate consumer, finding the right car for the buyer no matter who makes it.

GM is also a founder of Covisint, a giant, public B2B exchange. At the same time GM has divested itself of much of its manufacturing by spinning off into a separate company, called Delphi, the making of parts and accessories that together account for 60–70% of the cost of producing a car. Instead of owning — or at least controlling — the suppliers of parts and accessories, GM now buys them at auction on the Internet through Covisint from whatever source offers the best deal. GM still designs its cars, and it is now moving to assemble them using a B2O business model.

Catalysts for B2B Web Services

Web services are the latest tool for integration of software between businesses "across the firewall." Web services build upon an existing set of communications protocols that have been spectacularly successful — the Internet — and attempt to use it for true program-to-program integration.

Web services simply leverage the Internet infrastructure, formats, and protocols to let diverse applications interoperate in a simple, standard way.

A web service describes specific business functionality exposed by a company across its firewall, usually through an Internet connection, for the purpose of providing a way for another company or software program to use the service. Web services then extend the usage of the Internet to allow direct access to programs by other software applications, not just through a web browser. Web services comprise:

- providers, who publish the availability of their services;
- brokers, who register and categorize the services of the service providers; and
- users, who use brokers to find a provider's service.

In order for these three parties to communicate, a common language is required — XML.

Companies now face the choice of either establishing multiple bilateral links with each outside party that they need to integrate with, or establishing one link to a B2B exchange that sets the communications standards and enables users' applications to talk to each other (see Chapters 9 and 10).

B2B exchanges are communication hubs, through which suppliers, customers and trading partners can connect their systems — and are therefore acting as catalysts for the development of business web services.

The B2B exchange may not own all of the web-based services, but it acts as a portal, or what I call a "Babel fish" communications hub, which provides on-line access to those services and will thus accelerate the development of web services and continue to accelerate the use of the Internet by businesses.

Market Domination

B2B exchanges create an electronic, "virtual" marketplace that I call a market "space." Increasing returns will lead to a concentration of buyers and sellers in one B2B exchange market space for each product. One B2B exchange may operate several market spaces, but only one market space is likely to dominate for each product.

Eventually, all companies operating in a particular market space will have to join the B2B exchange that dominates in that space. The process of joining and connecting to that B2B exchange will continue to be one of the main drivers behind the use of the Internet and the adoption of XML by companies.

Examples of this process of market domination include ChemConnect in chemicals and plastics, Covisint in auto manufacturing, Cordiem in aviation, and Exostar in aerospace.

Analyzing the B2B Exchange Market Space

Part II:

Analyzing B2B Exchange Business Models

Analyzing B2B Exchange Business Models

Chapter 4

Building Liquidity on a B2B Exchange

"Exchanges can only generate liquidity if they are structured to maximize the satisfaction of the users and potential future users."

Achieving domination means having the greatest liquidity. A liquid market is a market where a large volume of trades can be quickly executed without a major impact on the price. The depth of the market's liquidity can be measured in terms of the number and size of trades that can be executed without a major impact on price. Liquid markets are more efficient markets.

The core service an exchange provides is a centralized marketplace, and the more likely a buyer or seller is to make a satisfactory transaction on an exchange, the more likely they are to sign up and use that exchange over its rivals.

As I state in Chapter 1, liquidity is king for exchanges, so it is essential to build liquidity as quickly as possible in order to survive and then to achieve domination.

The Nature of Liquidity

Liquidity is not necessarily about having the most members. Simply signing up lots of users does not guarantee that they will trade.

In order to create a trade you need a willing buyer and a willing seller. One or other side must be willing to make an offer (the "aggressive" order) and the other party must be willing to make an equal but opposite offer (the "passive" offer). To put it at its simplest, one party must be prepared to make a price and the other party must be willing to take that price.

The reason I call the first order an "aggressive" order is because that party is taking the risk of putting his price and other terms out into the market first. The risk he faces is that he has mispriced the good or service or that the market moves against him before he is able to subsequently revoke the offer. The other offer is a passive offer because it is accepting the terms tendered by the aggressive offeror.

The total number of members of an exchange is, therefore, not the most important factor — it is all about having users that are prepared to make aggressive orders and users who are prepared to accept those offers.

Liquidity can only be created quickly in the following two ways:

1. if the product is so innovative and compelling that traders just have to trade it immediately (very rare); or
2. if one or more creditworthy market-makers are prepared to quote two way prices on a continuous basis (ie, special forms of intermediary create the liquidity themselves).

In the absence of either of these, liquidity has to be built gradually over time — so called "natural" liquidity.

Unfortunately, few B2B exchanges have yet offered "must trade" new products. Rather they offer the ability to trade existing products on-line, with dynamic pricing to replace fixed price catalogs. In addition, it often takes longer than expected to get established industries to change their old procurement practices.

This means that B2B exchanges must either use market-makers or "prepare for the long haul" — in order to gradually build natural liquidity.

B2B exchanges are in good company — the world's largest securities markets have all had to build liquidity patiently over a long period of time. The NYSE took many years to build sufficient liquidity to move beyond a call-over market and progress to continuous trading. Building natural liquidity is all about building a complex set of parameters that collectively maximize trader satisfaction and add up to the right environment for transactions to get done. There is no one perfect form of market and the challenge of building natural liquidity has been faced by every marketplace ever opened — from the first agora to the NYSE.

Trader Satisfaction

Exchanges can only generate liquidity if they are structured to maximize the satisfaction of the users and potential future users. Trader satisfaction is driven by a combination of four main factors:

- the first is the number of other users who are willing to trade (or who the trader perceives are willing to trade);
- the second is the current value and volume of transactions — which conditions the trader's expectations of, and actual experience in, getting a trade executed;
- the third is the transaction costs associated with trading; and
- the fourth is the structure of the market.

Put another way, these four factors determine the attractiveness of the marketplace, as illustrated in Figure 4A.

Figure 4A: The Elements that Determine Trader Satisfaction and Drive Liquidity

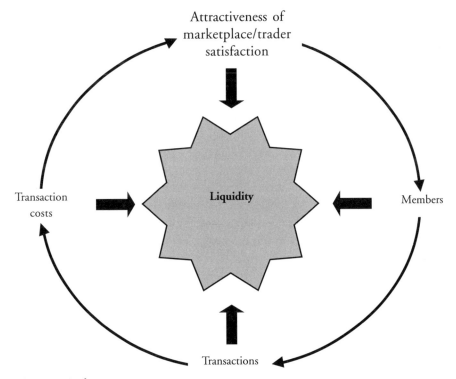

Source: Author

Analyzing B2B Exchange Business Models

B2B exchanges must be prepared to change periodically the variable attributes of their market — such as products traded, trading model, times of operation, rules for trading and costs of trading (transaction costs) — in order to find the right formula for their e-marketplace.

Number of users willing to trade

Liquidity is enhanced if you can build a critical mass of users willing to trade, as quickly as possible. This means that you must target volume traders in your vertical, whether buyers or sellers, and make sure that they sign up with you. In order to achieve sign-up, most exchanges have to waive the standard subscription fees in the early stages. Waiving fees at the start can put a lot of pressure on an exchange's finances.

However, transaction volume (which generates mind share) is worth more than profits in the early stages of the launch of a B2B exchange.

For example, Kevin English, the former CEO of Covisint, told me "Covisint has focused its early efforts on gaining traction with the large original equipment manufacturers and Tier 1 automotive supplier companies as a means of building a critical mass of customers who can influence broader adoption across the industry and, thus, build liquidity at a fast pace."

Actual volumes

Action speaks louder than words and actual trading volumes speak loudest of all. For example, in 2001 more than US$51 billion in automotive industry transaction volume was driven through Covisint, approximately 85% of which represented direct materials purchases for building cars and trucks.

Signing up key players who generate actual transaction volume creates a forward momentum that captures mind share, as press releases and the standard "industry grapevine" within each vertical pass on the word about the growth of an exchange. Conversely, low growth rates in the early stages can result in a serious loss of credibility. If an exchange creates a significant level of awareness at the launch and then does not deliver in terms of a credible level of transactions within a reasonably short time frame, then it will be harder to sign up more members. For example, CATEX has been operating as an insurance B2B exchange since 1997, but has only handled 1,400 trades in those five years. Consequently, some newer start-ups, such as Inreon and RI3K, are now generating more media attention and mind share in the insurance sector.

Building Liquidity on a B2B Exchange

This means that a successful exchange must organize a massive marketing and customer care program to win converts quickly. New users must be wooed, cajoled, and encouraged to sign up early and then smothered with good customer support in order to ensure that they trade on the exchange. This involves providing free training for each member's staff and constant contact with the member to make sure that user indifference does not prevent them from trading on your exchange in the early stages. For example, a dedicated client relationship management team at CreditTrade make on-site client visits to demonstrate website functionality.

Transaction costs

Transaction costs include overt costs, such as joining (membership) fees, trading fees and commissions payable. However, the total transaction costs of a particular market also include a number of hidden costs — such as settlement risk.

Clearing and settlement costs, plus settlement risks (eg, principal risk, market risk, and credit risk) are part of the overall cost of using a particular marketplace. B2B exchanges have used the Internet to dramatically reduce the front-office costs of trading (eg, searching for trade partners and negotiating the deal) but not, as yet, to reduce the back-office costs of clearing and settlement.

The Structure of the Market

The products traded

Liquidity is easier to build when the products are highly standardized. In financial services this has been evident with US Treasury securities and sovereign bonds that are traded on eSpeed, BrokerTec, TradeWeb, and Market Axess. In March 2002, TradeWeb announced that its cumulative trading volume had surpassed the $10 trillion mark since trading began in 1998. TradeWeb's current product offerings include US Treasuries, US agency debt, euro-denominated sovereign debt, agency mortgage-backed securities, and commercial paper. New products scheduled for introduction on the TradeWeb platform in 2002 include corporate bonds, agency discount notes, euro-denominated supranational issues, and euro commercial paper. eSpeed reported on-line volume in excess of $7 trillion in the fourth quarter of 2001 alone.

By way of contrast BondBook, which was backed by a roll call of Wall Street firms, only traded one product — corporate bonds. The system, which allowed counterparties to interact anonymously with each other, faced the issue of trying to change the traditional way of trading corporate bonds. It went bust in October 2001 before it achieved critical mass.

Analyzing B2B Exchange Business Models

In manufacturing industries, B2B exchanges that trade commodities or standardized products such as MRO supplies have been able to build liquidity faster than those exchanges that trade customized products — such as molded parts. For example, in the aviation industry, most of the transaction volume to date is for indirect procurement supplies, like light bulbs (which are pure commodity items) and for spare parts — rather than new parts (which are often modified for each separate airline).

The trading model

B2B exchange trading models can range from the simplest bulletin board websites to sophisticated continuous auction markets (which trade continuously during market hours, like the NYSE). In between are various forms of auction market and automated request-for-proposal/quote systems.

e-procurement functionality

Most B2B exchanges already offer e-procurement functionality that enables users to move their daily business e-procurement activities onto the exchange. On-line e-procurement leverages the power of the Internet to reduce procurement and search costs and increase operational efficiency. The key for a B2B exchange is to identify the specific procurement challenges in its selected industry and design tailored solutions that address these.

For example, ChemConnect offers a trading center where users can:

- streamline sales and sourcing processes by automating requests for quotes, requests for proposals, and the search for new suppliers;
- negotiate more efficiently with their existing business partners as well as with new companies they meet — in complete privacy;
- selectively invite other users from over 7,500 companies to negotiate — a highly effective way to get the best prices and terms available on the worldwide market;
- access the ChemConnect database containing more than 60,000 chemicals and plastics; and
- identify new trading partners around the world, quickly and cost-effectively.

In 2002, the World Wide Retail Exchange (WWRE) announced that it has saved its members over $471 million through the use of on-line negotiations, its first product offering, and auctions.

Dynamic pricing: auction markets

The auction format is one approach that has become increasingly popular for B2B exchanges, as it enhances efficiency while maximizing the return for the buyer or the seller. In addition, a periodic auction market helps to build liquidity in the early phases of a market by concentrating or "pooling" the available liquidity (that is, all of the buy and sell orders) into one specific point in time when the auction closes.

The ability of multiple buyers and sellers to collectively set prices for a wide range of goods and services creates a dynamic pricing model and represents a radical departure from the fixed-price model of the industrial age.

For example, ChemConnect operates on-line auction and reverse auction products that enable a user to:

- configure the auction to meet its specific needs;
- gather all of its trading partners in the same place at the same time.
- negotiate every aspect of the deal, all at once — from price to specifications, terms, and delivery;
- create competitive bidding dynamics that get the user to a firm market price faster, and take advantage of ChemConnect's proven technology.

By the end of 2001, Covisint had conducted over 1,400 hosted auctions on-line and traded over $50 billion in those auctions. GNX claims to have held over 4,000 auctions with a trade volume in excess of $3 billion, since inception in 2000.

Companies that have started using on-line auctions are consistently reporting cost savings on procurement contracts of between 10%–25%.

Reverse auctions offer the potential for instant ROI in the form of substantial cost-savings. For example, PurchasePro (www.purchasepro.com) advertizes that Owens Corning, a $5 billion world leader in advanced glass and building material systems, has been able to save an average of 10% on the price of direct and indirect supplies and services, using PurchasePro's e-Source technology to run on-line, reverse auctions, and realized a complete return on investment in just 53 days. A reverse auction for bottled water for plants in the Ohio region netted Owens Corning a saving of 60% over the old prices.

Analyzing B2B Exchange Business Models

In another tangible example, A.T. Kearney, the management consulting subsidiary of EDS, recently announced that its eBreviate Internet auction technology has been used to negotiate more than $20 billion in purchases since its launch in January 2000 and, in the process, saved its clients more than $3 billion.

Dynamic pricing: electronic auto-execution systems
Also emerging are electronic trading systems that can automatically match buyers and sellers on a continuous basis and thus create real-time, dynamic pricing.

In effect, such systems are continuous two-way auctions where the seller offers to sell (the ask) and the buyer offers to buy (the bid).

The bid and ask offers must either have a fixed (that is, a limit) price or be priced at "market" (that is, at the best price offered on the other side of the market at that precise point in time). The system checks when an order is received to see if it can be immediately matched against an equal, but opposite, order already in the system. If it cannot be matched, the new order is stored in the system awaiting an equal and opposite offer to arrive.

It is usual for such systems to give first priority to orders which have the best price (the lowest ask and the highest bid order) and for orders with an equal price to be ranked strictly based on time of receipt by the trading engine — what is called "price-over-time priority." These systems, therefore, provide a central "limit order book" system which allows members to trade on an anonymous, equal, and fair (first come, first served) basis. Auto-matching systems provide real-time prices and enable fast trading.

For example, ChemConnect offers a "Commodity Exchange" in addition to, and separate from, the trading center and the on-line auction area, where pre-qualified buyers and sellers can trade standard, high-volume commodity, chemicals and plastics products in real-time.

However, limit order book systems are only effective if you have:

- standardized or "commoditized" products which are fungible (eg, securities or securitized contracts); or
- high liquidity (ie, lots of competing bid and ask orders flowing into the order book).

If there is little liquidity in the product, then a member's limit order is unlikely to be able to find an immediate match in the system and it will sit in the order book waiting for a matching order to come in. For every second that the limit order sits out in the order book, the buyer or seller may be cruelly exposed to changes in the fair market price for the item (because that order can be automatically executed against at any time until he cancels it). This makes traders use a "fill or kill" (FOK) approach whereby they enter an order at a limit price, but remove the order immediately if it is not instantly matched in the order book. (Many electronic trading systems provide a special FOK order type, which automatically flushes the order if it does not match.)

FOK orders reduce the number of orders in the central order book at any one time, and thereby reduce the chances of another order being matched immediately — a vicious downward spiral that intensifies the lack of liquidity. In highly liquid and volatile markets it is important to maintain the anonymity of buyers and sellers, as the buyer's or seller's identity could significantly affect market prices — so-called market impact. Electronic trading systems are, therefore, ideally suited for anonymous trading.

However, most B2B exchanges are not yet trading products that are sufficiently commoditized to be traded on a continuous basis. For less fungible products, knowing the identity of the trading partner is a very important component of a trading decision. As we shall see, in the future, B2B exchanges will trade derivative contracts which are ideal products for auto-execution, anonymous electronic trading.

Trading rules

One of the value propositions of an exchange as opposed to an unregulated telephone market, lies in the standardization of the product, of the legal environment, of the trading and settlement terms, and of the documentation. To enhance trader satisfaction, a B2B exchange must reduce the uncertainty that traders face in completing market transactions. The exchange does this by imposing rules (or encouraging members to adopt existing industry standards) that regulate the quality of the products offered on the exchange, the lot sizes in which they are offered, the way in which they are priced, the acceptable pricing increments (called the tick size), and the standard terms for trading and settlement. Many of these may be varied by agreement between the trading parties, but in the absence of specific terms, every trading member of the exchange should know that the standard terms set by the exchange will apply.

Analyzing B2B Exchange Business Models

Regulating the quality of the products offered on the exchange helps to build trust in the exchange's centralized e-marketplace. Similarly, creating standardized documents and a common legal environment helps to avoid disputes and to

build credibility in the integrity of the exchange. By maximizing the satisfaction of participants, these factors encourage trading and help to build liquidity.

Using Market-Makers to Build Liquidity

Building the volume of trades is more important than numbers of members at the start. This means that you should target the key players who are likely to trade the most and get them to join early, rather than focusing on signing up as many members as possible. In addition, if there are any intermediaries that can "make a market" they are like gold dust at the start. These key players help to create liquidity by smoothing out natural timing fluctuations in the number of buyers or sellers that are available at any particular point in time.

In the securities business, liquidity has always been king. NASDAQ succeeded as a market for smaller company stocks (which are naturally highly illiquid) by providing two market-makers for each stock. These market-makers undertake to quote a bid and an ask price for their designated stocks on a continuous basis. The result is that investors can always trade in those stocks.

EnronOnline (www.enrononline.com) was a good example of how a market-maker can build liquidity for a new market. On EnronOnline, Enron was the counter-party to every transaction. This meant that a potential buyer or seller could always find a trade at EnronOnline — provided they were prepared to take the price that was being offered by Enron.

For a discussion of the sudden loss of credit-worthiness and subsequent demise of Enron see Chapter 8.

Using Restricted Hours to Build Liquidity

All current securities markets use restricted hours to help ensure deep liquidity when the market is open.

For example, the NYSE is not open for 24 hours a day. It is only open from 9:30 am to 4:30 pm EST on each trading day. This concentrates the day's trading into those hours. It is interesting to note that when electronic communications networks (ECNs) started to offer 24-hour trading in NYSE-

and NASDAQ-listed stocks in 1999, the volume of trading at night was negligible compared to the trading during those exchanges' trading hours. This shows that even the most liquid stocks in the US (eg, General Motors, Microsoft, etc.) do not yet support or require a continuous 24-hour market place. By having limited daily trading hours the NYSE and NASDAQ help to ensure that the marketplace is liquid when it is open.

Indeed, the NYSE did not start as a continuous trading market. Rather it started as a "call" market. This means that traders used to gather together at a predetermined time each week and the exchange called over the list of stocks. As each company name was called the traders could shout out their offers and make trades. When trading dried up in one stock the exchange staff called out the next company name for trading. It was more than 50 years after the NYSE started as a call market before it moved to continuous trading.

The London Metals Exchange (www.lme.com) operates a call market in which each contract trades in turn for a five-minute period, starting at a pre-specified time.

Call markets concentrate liquidity for each stock and reduce the participation costs of traders — since they only have to show up at a specified time in order to trade a specific product.

Start up B2B exchanges, therefore, will often find that liquidity is maximized if they restrict trading to a very short period each day, or even once a week to begin with. This is achieved if the exchange starts off with periodic auctions that only run at limited times and for limited durations.

Using a Centralized Clearing and Settlement System to Build Liquidity

Most start-up B2B exchanges have focused on providing a trade matching engine and have let the two parties to each trade sort out the logistics of settling the trade on a bilateral basis.

Exchanges that provide centralized clearing and settlement services, and/or a central counter-party guarantee of settlement, are far more attractive to potential traders. As mentioned above, clearing and settlement costs, plus settlement risks, are part of the overall cost of using a particular marketplace. And the anticipated high settlement risks associated with on-line exchanges reduce trading and liquidity levels in their e-marketplace, as illustrated in Figure 4B. Exchanges that own their own clearing and settlement systems are able to lower transaction costs considerably and reduce settlement risk for users.

Analyzing B2B Exchange Business Models

Efficient clearing and settlement solutions promote confidence in the e-marketplace and reduce transaction costs — thereby helping to generate liquidity.

Figure 4B: The High Settlement Risk Associated with B2B Exchanges Reduces On-line Trading and Liquidity Levels

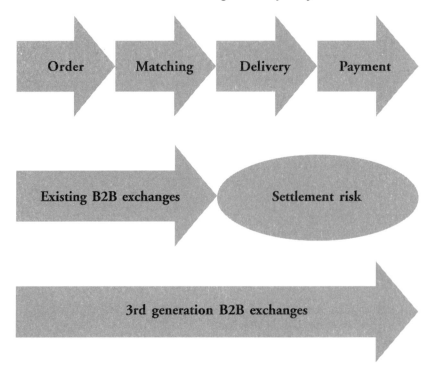

Source: Author

The vertical integration of a central clearing and settlement mechanism with the exchange's trading system is a key networking benefit that can lock users into an exchange and build a sustainable competitive advantage.

See Chapter 11 for more information on clearing and settlement services.

Using Market Aggregation to Build Liquidity

Large stock exchanges have gradually aggregated multiple, competing local and regional exchanges to build their central liquidity. For example, the aggregation of over 17 regional exchanges into one central stock market for the United Kingdom in the 1970s, formed the London Stock Exchange. At one time there were more than 20 stock exchanges operating in downtown Manhattan.

Using today's technology, B2B markets do not have to be physically merged in order to pool their individual liquidity.

This has been proven by the US-based ECNs which agreed common standards for order routing and messaging, so that orders which could not immediately be matched on one ECN could be forwarded on to the other markets for execution, if a suitable counter-party was waiting on that other market. NASDAQ is now seeking to provide a centralized market place for all orders for NASDAQ-listed stocks, including ECN orders, called the "SuperMontage." SuperMontage is an important step forward in the ongoing evolution of the NASDAQ stock market. SuperMontage is intended to be like an electronic "dashboard" which aggregates all the orders for a particular NASDAQ-listed stock, no matter which market (or pool of liquidity) that order comes from. A trader will also be able to see up to five competing price levels for each stock (ie, the depth of the order book) rather than just the best bid and ask as at present. The primary goal of SuperMontage is to centralize liquidity in the over-the-counter market by acting as a large order routing network that routes orders to the market/pool of liquidity that is offering the best price at any given moment in time. Many ECNs have resisted NASDAQ's attempt to consolidate the order information, through fear that it will suck liquidity away from their marketplace, but in April 2002, Island, which is now merging with Instinet to form the leading ECN, decided that it would participate in SuperMontage, which gives NASDAQ's new system a big boost.

In Europe, companies such as RoyalBlue Financial plc (www.royalblue.com) and Teleinvest (www.teleinvest.com) have created order routing software that allows a trader to access multiple pools of liquidity from the same "dashboard." In other words, it is becoming less relevant where a trade is executed, as long as traders have access to all the available pools of liquidity.

Analyzing B2B Exchange Business Models

Similarly, in North America, the Belzberg trading system (www.belzberg.com) offers direct access to the NYSE, NASDAQ market makers, CBOE, Ashton Technology Group's eVWAP market, US regional stock exchanges and various ECNs, the TSE, CDNX, and Instinet as well as some European and Asian stock exchanges. The system provides traders with automated routing to point of best execution or most liquidity.

In the same way, users can access a B2B exchange's e-marketplace from anywhere in the world.

This means that B2B order routing systems will be developed that enable a trader to access multiple B2B exchanges through one common interface. The order routing system will seamlessly route the B2B trade to the exchange with best execution or most liquidity for that particular product.

Using Derivatives to Build Liquidity

Derivatives (such as forwards, futures, swaps, and options) enable users to control the risks associated with market fluctuations. The enormous trading volumes for financial derivatives demonstrates the utility of derivatives.

Derivatives will serve the same functions in B2B exchanges as they do in the established commodities markets. By integrating derivatives transactions with their e-procurement systems, B2B exchanges will build liquidity, pricing data, and enhance the overall value proposition of the exchange.

While e-procurement systems today offer buyers the ability to purchase goods based on current prices, derivative transactions enable users to set contracts for purchases based on prices projected into the future. Derivative transactions offer B2B exchange users the ability to control the price risk of adverse future price swings and market fluctuations.

Derivatives, therefore, enable a wide range of trading and risk management strategies and tactics that effectively complement the e-procurement transactions that B2B exchanges currently facilitate. In addition, by supporting new trading strategies not requiring physical delivery, derivatives bring in new classes of market participants.

Figure 4C: Pools of Liquidity

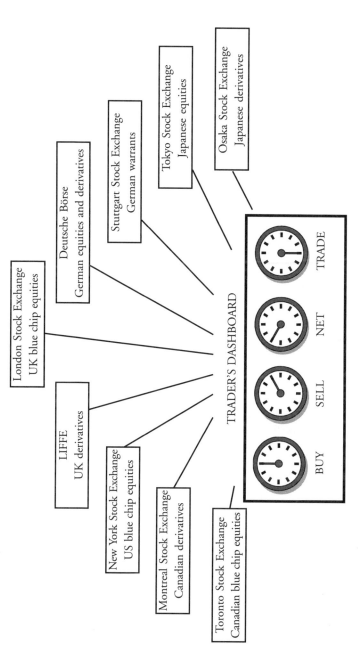

London Stock Exchange
UK blue chip equities

Deutsche Börse
German equities and derivatives

Stuttgart Stock Exchange
German warrants

Tokyo Stock Exchange
Japanese equities

Osaka Stock Exchange
Japanese derivatives

LIFFE
UK derivatives

New York Stock Exchange
US blue chip equities

Montreal Stock Exchange
Canadian derivatives

Toronto Stock Exchange
Canadian blue chip equities

TRADER'S DASHBOARD

BUY   SELL   NET   TRADE

Source: Author

Analyzing B2B Exchange Business Models

New B2B exchange participants that will be attracted by derivative contracts include:

- treasury departments (eg, the chief financial officer and/or corporate risk manager);
- financial institutions;
- hedge fund managers; and
- inter-market traders.

Derivatives will be powerful liquidity drivers for B2B exchanges, since all of these players are significant new liquidity providers for an exchange.

Banks and other financial institutions active in a marketplace will use derivatives to hedge their financial exposure to an industry. In addition, banks and other financial institutions typically use public derivatives markets to hedge highly customized, private derivatives that they write with companies in a particular market sector.

Hedge fund managers can be pure liquidity providers in that they typically use their trading capital to make prices, both bids and offers, based on sophisticated quantitative and/or arbitrage market models. Hedge fund managers are significant sources of liquidity in existing financial and commodity markets. Their models and quantitative skills are readily transferable to new asset classes such as B2B exchanges that offer derivatives.

Inter-market traders typically make bids and offers in one market based on their trading activity in another, related market. For example, a natural gas options trader at a large utility company could make bids and offers for natural gas-derived chemical products. Because these traders can easily lay off their market positions in a more liquid market, natural gas in this example, they effectively transfer the liquidity of the more liquid market to the emerging e-marketplace.

These new uses and users of B2B exchanges can enhance liquidity on markets that are currently just procurement-oriented sites. It is due to the trading of these types of players that trading volumes in established derivative markets are much larger than the trading volumes in the underlying cash or procurement markets.

Derivatives are based on a contract for differences, so the number of contracts that can exist in respect of a given derivative at any point in time is theoretically infinite. Therefore, the size of any given derivatives market depends only on the willingness and frequency with which parties enter into offsetting transactions and not on the size of the underlying cash market. Some derivatives, such as weather or inflation-based derivatives, have no underlying cash traded asset or instrument whatsoever, and exist solely to exchange financial risks.

Since derivative transactions are not limited by the market size of the underlying asset, trading derivatives represents a potentially limitless source of transaction growth for a B2B exchange.

B2B exchanges that are early adopters of derivatives trading will have an opportunity to establish first-mover advantage and improve liquidity so that they can reach a critical mass of transactions first. Also, with longer-dated transactions, the B2B exchange retains contact with its users for longer on each trade and therefore has more opportunity to cross-sell other value-added services to their customers (eg, insurance cover and credit enhancement products, such as credit derivatives).

For example, CheMatch (now merged with ChemConnect), a leading bulk chemicals and fuel products B2B exchange, acquired The Energy Group (TEG) in December 2000. TEG was a traditional petrochemical, feedstock, and gasoline components voice brokerage firm based in Houston, Texas. The press release quotes Larry McAfee, CheMatch.com's president, as saying "TEG will substantially increase the liquidity on the CheMatch platform, particularly in the feedstock products…..With TEG's experience in the financial derivatives market this acquisition should accelerate our OTC derivatives activity and provide our customers with better risk management tools."

See Chapter 8 for greater details on how B2B exchange can introduce derivative products to increase liquidity.

Value-Added Web Services Will Add Liquidity

A web service describes specific business functionality exposed by a company across its firewall, usually through an Internet connection, for the purpose of providing a way for another company or software program to use the service.

Companies now face the choice of either establishing multiple bilateral links with each outside party that they need to integrate with, or establishing one link to a B2B exchange that sets the communications standards and enables users' applications to talk to each other (see Chapter 9).

Analyzing B2B Exchange Business Models

B2B exchanges can act as a "Babel fish" communications hub, through which suppliers, customers and trading partners can connect their systems and obtain access to web-based services.

This is exactly what successful stock exchanges have been doing for years. Successful securities exchanges provide software services such as back-office software and risk management packages for brokers. In many cases the exchange does not own the software packages but it ensures that they are tightly integrated with the exchange's core trading engine and then helps to market the applications. This helps the users of the securities exchange to establish and grow their businesses while simultaneously locking the brokers into using that exchange.

In the B2B world, the equivalent back-end processes are clearing and settlement and supply chain management. B2B exchanges, both private and public, have the capability to tie together a manufacturer with its suppliers (Tier 1) and its suppliers' suppliers (Tiers 2 and 3). This can lead to a collaborative process that generates greater efficiencies in the design of products and significant reductions in the time and cost of manufacturing through collaborative planning, forecasting, and replenishment.

The exchange thus becomes a collaborative trading community. By adding access to these types of web-based services, a B2B exchange drives usage of the exchange and helps build transaction liquidity in its e-marketplace.

Chapter 5

What is a Neutral Exchange? Independent Dot-coms and Industry Consortia Models

"The winner in each industry is likely to be the exchange that demonstrates that it is operated in a neutral way."

A perception of "neutrality" is critical to the success of a B2B exchange. However, neutrality is not a binary state like the state of virginity. Many start-up B2B exchanges fell into the trap of believing that you are either totally neutral or you are not neutral at all.

In reality, you just need to be neutral enough to attract a wide enough membership base and to achieve critical mass.

A successful exchange must get the largest number of buyers and sellers, and ensure that the largest buyers and the largest sellers use its central e-marketplace.

Two business models with two totally different approaches to this issue have been explored — independent dot-com exchanges and industry-led consortia exchanges.

Independent Dot-coms

Many B2B exchanges were developed as "dot-coms". These were independent companies launched by entrepreneurs and funded mainly by venture capital. Some have been launched by pure entrepreneurs. Others were launched by industry professionals, who took the view that their former corporate employer could not launch a B2B exchange, because of the perceived lack of neutrality when a major player owns the market space.

Analyzing B2B Exchange Business Models

Dot-com exchanges have the following advantages:

- automatic perceived neutrality;
- speed in decision making;
- independence from legacy systems and entrenched business practices;
- a dedicated and motivated professional and senior management team; and
- the ability to refine and change business model in real-time.

However, all dot-com exchanges have to raise enough capital to survive through the long build-up phase, during which the exchange integrates its systems with users. Many of them have not made it — the so called "dot-bombs".

Also independent exchanges commonly lack the deep industry knowledge that existing companies in that industry have. Although many dot-coms were founded by individuals with industry experience, they lacked the breadth of relationships with all the major players throughout the industry, and deep vertical knowledge, to quickly obtain industry-wide buy-in to their exchange.

In order for dot-com exchanges to build up sufficient liquidity to make the exchange a winner they have to attract the largest buyers and sellers on to the exchange. In many case, these refused to join unless they were offered special deals — such as reduced fees or a substantial equity stake. This immediately raised some questions about the continuing neutrality of these exchanges, and many dot-coms refused to compromise on this issue.

In reality, as long as the exchange continues to operate as a neutral market and retains the key elements of neutrality that I highlight in Chapter 13 — such as objective standards for new members, fair and equal access to the trading system and an independent compliance team that reports directly to the advisory board — then the exchange can still demonstrate the necessary level of neutrality to attract other players.

Some dot-coms would have had a better chance of survival if they had been more willing to co-opt the existing larger volume traders at an early stage.

Industry Consortia

Not to be left out of the B2B revolution, many large "bricks and mortar" companies decided to form their own B2B exchanges, rather than give a percentage of their business to an independent exchange. Competitive pressures forced even the largest manufacturers to work together to launch B2B exchanges. For example, GM, Ford, DaimlerChrysler, Nissan and Renault agreed to work together to create Covisint.

These types of exchange have been called "industry consortia plays" because they are formed by a consortium of existing buyers or sellers in a particular market space.

An enormous advantage for consortia plays is that they bring tremendous natural liquidity to the exchange — in the form of combined buying or selling power.

Other leading consortia plays include:

- Cordiem — formed by merging MyAircraft and AirNewco for the $500 billion aviation industry. Cordiem's 12 founding aviation members include nine airlines: Air France, American Airlines, British Airways, Continental Airlines, Delta Air Lines, Iberia Airlines, SAirGroup (Swissair), United Airlines, United Parcel Service; and three original equipment manufacturers (OEMs): Goodrich Corporation, Honeywell International Inc., and United Technologies Corp.

- CPGmarket.com — a marketplace for the European consumer packaged goods industry, created by Nestlé, Danone, Henkel, and SAP markets.

- E2open — Acer, IBM, Hitachi, Matsushita Electric (Panasonic), LG Electronics, Lucent Technologies, Nortel Networks, Seagate Technology, Solectron, and Toshiba in the computer, electronics, and telecommunications industries.

- Exostar — Boeing, BAE Systems, Lockheed Martin and Raytheon in the aerospace and defense industries. Rolls-Royce joined in June 2001.

- GlobalNetXchange — Carrrefour Supermarche, Sears Roebuck, Kroger, and J. Sainsbury in the retail supermarket space.

Analyzing B2B Exchange Business Models

- IntercontinentalExchange (ICE) — a marketplace for energy, metal, and other commodity products. Founding participants in ICE include BP Amoco, Deutsche Bank AG, The Goldman Sachs Group, Inc., Morgan Stanley, Royal Dutch/Shell Group, SG Investment Banking, and the Totalfina Elf Group. ICE owns the International Petroleum Exchange in London.

- Omnexus — founded by BASF, Bayer, Dow, DuPont, Ticona, and now representing more than 20 global suppliers in the plastics industry.

- Pantellos — for the utility and energy industries, founded by 20 utility companies including American Electric Power, Duke Energy, and Ontario Power Generation.

- Quadrem — for the mining, minerals, and metal industries. The shareholders of Quadrem include Alcan Ltd, Alcoa Inc., Anglo American plc, Barrick Gold Corporation, BHP Billiton Ltd., De Beers Consolidated Mines Ltd., Glencore International AG, Newmont Mining Corporation, Normandy Mining Ltd., Rio Tinto, and WMC Limited. The estimated spend of the industry as a whole is approximately US$200 billion: Quadrem buyers represent approximately $80 billion of that spend.

- The WorldWide Retail Exchange — a B2B retail store procurement exchange set up by Target, Kmart, Safeway, Walgreen, DairyFarm, and 13 others.

- Transora — a consumer products exchange (food, beverages, and household consumable products mainly) set up by a large number of the leading consumer brand manufacturers.

These consortia plays usually start off as representative of either the buy-side or the sell-side.

However, competitive pressures are driving them to merge. For example, in 2000, Ford's AutoXchange and GM's TradeXchange merged to form Covisint and My Aircraft and AirNewco merged to form Cordiem. In June 2001, ChemConnect merged with Envera.

AirNewco was an airline-led (ie, buyers') initiative and MyAircraft was a manufacturer-led (ie, sellers') exchange. Cordiem, the merged exchange, was therefore the first to represent both buyers and sellers. Similarly, about 40 players, primarily suppliers, in the chemicals industry set up ChemConnect. Envera, on the other hand, was set up by a group of buyers in the petroleum and chemical industries. The merged exchange, therefore, brought together potential willing buyers and sellers in one e-marketplace. ChemConnect then bought rival CheMatch in a stock swap, in February 2002, to help cement its market dominance in chemical and plastics.

Industry consortia have the major advantage that they are usually well funded by their bricks and mortar parents — which reduces the pressure to bring their systems to market quickly in order to be the "first mover." They also have deep knowledge of the intricacies of doing business in the industry and an installed base of users' applications to integrate with.

However, these attempts to start B2B exchanges face some of the same challenges as the entrepreneurial exchanges. In particular, to survive, consortia plays must still ensure that they:

- play to win — the exchange with the most liquidity will dominate;
- operate as a neutral exchange — so that they attract the maximum number of potential buyers and sellers to generate the most efficient prices;
- establish their independence from the founders — so that they can be fast, flexible, and change the business plan quickly;
- secure the transaction volume of their founders;
- retain the financial support of their founders long enough to survive the long growth phase (eg, MetalSite ran out of capital backing from its original founders before it had established a dominant position); and
- develop a fully-integrated suite that establishes the industry standard for business process and data interchange.

Case study: Covisint

Covisint (www.covisint.com) was set up in 2000 by General Motors, Ford Motor and DaimlerChrysler with a mission to become the automakers' global on-line exchange, linking manufacturers, suppliers, and component makers. Since the launch, other major companies like PSA Peugeot-Citroën and Renault of France and its affiliate Nissan Motor of Japan have joined the consortium. Many big suppliers and component makers have also signed up.

Analyzing B2B Exchange Business Models

Key Milestones — Covisint

March 2000 — a "NewCo." planning team is established including executives from DaimlerChrysler, Ford's AutoXchange, and GM's TradeXchange, is established.

April 2000 — French automaker Renault S.A. and Nissan of Japan join the NewCo's planning initiative. In addition to bringing personnel and resources to the project, Renault and Nissan led the development of the European and Asian operations respectively.

May 2000 — NewCo. becomes Covisint.

July 2000 — Several Tier 1 automotive suppliers, including Delphi, publicly voice their support and intent to join Covisint. In addition, the Federal Trade Commission review of Covisint begins.

September 2000 — Covisint receives clearance from the Federal Trade Commission. The German Bundeskartellamt grants unconditional clearance to Covisint 12 days later on 23 September.

September 2000 — Covisint launches the exchange with a mock auction involving ArvinMeritor. Its initial suite of tools includes products for auctions, catalogs, quote management, and product development.

December 2000 — Covisint becomes a legal entity known officially as Covisint, L.L.C. — with DaimlerChrysler AG, Ford Motor Company, General Motors, Nissan, Renault, Commerce One, and Oracle as members.

April 2001 — Kevin English, 48, is named the first Chairman, President and CEO of Covisint. English was formerly the managing director for e-commerce at investment bank Credit Suisse First Boston and prior to that was CEO of the financial news website, TheStreet.com.

May 2001 — PSA Peugeot Citroën joins Covisint.

July 2001 — the European Commission approves Covisint.

March 2002 — Covisint announces that in 2001 more than US$51 billion in automotive industry transaction volume was driven through the exchange.

July 2002 — Kevin English resigns. Harold R. Kutner, 61, former group vice president, worldwide purchasing, General Motors, is named chairman and CEO, succeeding English. Bruce Swift, former vice president of purchasing for Ford of Europe, joins Covisint as President and COO. When asked about his decision to leave, English said "In the past year, Covisint has grown from a sound idea to a solid business with a bright future. With the company near profitability, my goals are accomplished. I leave Covisint on a solid footing and poised for profitability in the fourth quarter of this year."

Covisint's goal is to wire up the auto industry on a global basis. It conducts component auctions, and helps companies shorten supply chains and manage stock using the Internet. It links design engineers across the world to make communications and collaboration simpler. Covisint was created because suppliers approached the original equipment manufacturers (OEMs) like GM and Ford insisting that they did not want to have to join multiple B2B exchanges. They could not support multiple exchanges, each with its own proprietary standards.

In 2001, Covisint's customers contracted for more than $100 billion in raw materials, parts, and components for current and future vehicle programs using its electronic quote management (e-RFQ) product and over $51 billion was contracted through the exchange's on-line auction system. Its founding members represent a total annual procurement budget in excess of $300 billion — so it instantly has critical mass.

Covisint took a long time to get going and over 12 months to appoint its first CEO — reflecting the lethargy and bureaucracy that a large industry consortium can be affected by. However, it fixed the corporate governance issues in 2001, by establishing an independent management team.

Covisint has been steadily developing a clear and independent vision for the automotive industry since the independent management team was appointed and it now anticipates that it will be profitable by the end of 2002. Covisint has over 5,000 registered users and states that more that 1,500 companies are using its supply chain management systems.

Covisint is already a global business with offices in the US, several European cities, and also in Japan.

Analyzing B2B Exchange Business Models

Corporate governance and neutrality

The largest problem that industry consortia face is how to establish the operating neutrality of the exchange. One of the most hotly debated issues in B2B is whether consortia plays can retain sufficient neutrality to attract other buyers and sellers.

The German giant VW has set up its own e-commerce company, Electronic Supplier Link. Luxury car maker BMW believes that joining might jeopardize its trade secrets. Sports car maker Porsche and the leading Japanese companies like Toyota and Honda are not currently interested in the auction capabilities, but are studying the other products Covisint offers.

Kevin English publicly urged VW, Toyota, Honda, and Porsche to join. He put to me "If Volkswagen and Bosch (and others) use their own exchanges we will end up having multiple standards which would take us right back to where we were 15 or 20 years ago when nobody could share information and it became a huge cost burden."

As part of its perceived neutrality, Covisint must show BMW and others that it will not compromise their trade secrets. It must maintain very strict security to make sure that proprietary information is kept proprietary. Covisint claims that it protects proprietary information through the use of encryption, appropriate workflow rules and data segmentation schema.

The key issue is not necessarily ownership — but how the exchange is operated and controlled. Independent ownership and neutrality in operation are not the same thing.

The main things that an industry consortia must focus on to demonstrate its neutrality are:

- establishing objective standards for new members;
- maintaining fair and equal access to the trading system;
- appointing an independent CEO and management team with entrepreneurial incentives to develop the exchange;
- having an advisory board and user committee structure (as described in Chapter 13) which brings representatives from all the user groups into the management of the exchange; and
- an independent compliance team that reports directly to the advisory board and enforces the rules and regulations of the exchange fairly against all members.

Every industry consortium must be staffed with dedicated, independent management. Most industry consortia are set up initially by seconding existing staff into the new exchange. This does not tend to work very well. The seconded staff do not have the right motivation to make the business succeed — when success may be at the cost of some of the owners' core existing businesses. Similarly, seconded staff do not tend to have the "career at risk" or bottom line responsibility that enables them to change the business plan as frequently and as dramatically as may be required to succeed.

The fledgling exchange is then "managed by committee" and those committees place traditionally cut throat competitors alongside each other, until an independent management team is recruited.

For example, as mentioned above, Covisint took just over 12 months to find and appoint an independent CEO. The exchange had been officially launched with seconded staff and initially it had three co-CEOs and multiple committees.

Inherent conflicts of interest

Industry consortia can display some inherent conflicts of interest. On the one hand they clearly have a role to play in reducing costs and improving efficiency for their founder members. On the other hand, they can only be financially independent if they develop business outside of the pool of founding members. These value-added services have to be offered to competitors of the founding members.

The objective of creating a sustainable, independent business may ultimately conflict with the competitive instincts of the founding members.

On the other hand, there is an ancient Chinese saying "keep your friends close and your enemies closer." Working with your main competitors in an industry consortium is one way of keeping a close eye on what they are doing. As we shall see in Chapter 6, Wal-Mart took massive market share away from its competitors by building its own private network exchange called RetailLink. Members of a consortium are unlikely to be able to develop such a competitive advantage outside of the consortia exchange.

Private network exchanges and industry consortia

Several industry consortia are embedding themselves into the very heart of their industry by also helping individual members set up private network exchanges. Such private exchanges are web-based trading applications implemented by a single company with a select group of suppliers and customers.

Building private exchanges leverages off of the sunk costs of the public exchange's infrastructure build-out and is an important revenue source for developing B2B exchanges. B2B exchanges can charge software license fees, customization fees, and transaction-based fees, for use of the exchange's core technology in the private network.

For example, Covisint has built a private supply chain network for Ford, and is now building a supply chain private network for DaimlerChrysler in Germany: both are founding members. Before he left, Kevin English told me "We are developing custom (bespoke) portals for our customers including Ford, DaimlerChrysler, Delphi, Lear, and others. These portals will be developed, managed and hosted by Covisint and, since accessible directly through Covisint, enable a highly secure, single sign-on capability that makes it easier for users to navigate from one site to another."

If the exchange develops numerous users who build private networks on its technology platform it can, over time, start to link those private exchanges together. Because they are all built on the same technology, integration is relatively simple. In this way, purchasers can start to expand their network of suppliers by venturing out into the "public" e-marketplace occasionally to get price and other quotes.

This is most likely to happen initially for the more standardized or "commoditized" products such as MRO supplies.

In February 2002, GartnerG2 issued a strategic report entitled *Evaluating Consortium E-marketplaces Across Industries*. The report suggests that some consortia members may start to develop their own private exchange while still remaining an active member of a public, consortia exchange in order to keep their competitors actively focused on developing the consortia exchange. This may give them the time to take a commanding lead with their private network — as Wal-Mart did with RetailLink.

On the other hand, consortia members can leverage off of the technology investment they have already made in the consortia exchange to build their private network, as Ford and DaimlerChrysler are doing with Covisint. In addition, using a common platform creates the greatest cost savings in the long term as the private exchange can easily be connected to the public e-marketplace when the individual companies are ready.

Setting the standards for the whole industry

One enormous advantage of industry consortia exchanges is the ability to set the standards for connectivity throughout the whole industry. For example, Covisint, the automotive industry B2B exchange, is implementing the ebXML message transport layer and will use the Open Applications Group's OAGIS standards for its XML document payload. Covisint says the technology will give it the ability to exchange Internet-based messages between trading partners wrapped in a standard message framework that is being adopted globally.

By using these common standards, OEMs, automotive suppliers and software providers throughout the automotive industry will be able to improve communication and reduce integration costs.

In major, well-established industries such as automotive manufacture and aviation/aerospace, a relatively small number of large manufacturers are negotiating with substantially the same group of suppliers. If a B2B exchange in that market space establishes common standards for business processes and document exchange, it can squeeze costs out of the supply chain for all the suppliers across the whole industry.

Playing to Win

The GartnerG2 strategic report *Evaluating Consortium E-marketplaces Across Industries* supports my contention that B2B exchanges must play to win. Gartner predicts that no more than two consortia per industry can survive.

I believe that the network effect will mean that only one exchange per industry will survive.

As with securities markets, the more willing buyers and sellers that can be brought together to compete against each other in one place, the more liquid a market becomes, and the more efficient the price-setting mechanism is. This creates a self-reinforcing mechanism whereby the sellers are attracted to the market with the most potential buyers and the increase in sellers makes that market space more attractive to more buyers, and so on — resulting in more transactions in that market.

ChemConnect's merger with Envera and subsequent acquisition of CheMatch illustrates exactly how the "winner takes all" network effect will drive one exchange to dominate each major industry vertical. Since only one exchange will dominate in each market space, there have been bitter fights to the death between dot-com start-ups and industry consortia in the same industry over the last two years.

In most cases, the industry consortia have won — as in the aviation industry, where AviationX succumbed to the power of Exostar and Cordiem. But in some cases nimble independent exchanges such as e-STEEL — now called NewView Technologies — which outlasted the industry-backed MetalSite, have overcome industry consortia.

Case study: AviationX and the Aviation Industry

A good example of a dot-com exchange is AviationX, Inc. (www.aviationx.com), which started out to be the B2B exchange for the whole aviation industry — a $500 billion market place. However, the idea never got off the ground after the major airlines and manufacturers announced their own consortia approaches, called Exostar and Cordiem.

AviationX

AviationX was launched in 1999 based on the expertise and connections of the CEO, Henrik Schröder. Schröder was President of Saab Aircraft, the leading regional aircraft manufacturer and part of the Investor AB group of companies. Schröder spent more than 11 years at Saab. During his tenure, Schröder was President of Saab Aircraft Finance Group and Saab Aircraft Leasing. Prior to Saab, Schröder spent almost 10 years in the global aircraft equipment leasing industry.

AviationX had "first mover" advantage and generated a considerable amount of press publicity from launch. In February 2000, AviationX raised $1.6 million in seed capital from a Bermuda-based venture capital fund called WiredAtlantic and some private investors, including Tim Strojka, one of the founders of PlasticsNet. AviationX attracted three mid-sized airlines to beta test the new e-marketplace, including Express Airlines I Inc., which serves the Memphis, Tennessee hub for its parent Northwest Airlines.

However, AviationX ran into major turbulence in early 2000 after General Electric and Honeywell announced the formation of MyAircraft and six major airlines, including American, Delta, and United, said they were forming their own exchange, called AirNewco, to collaborate with suppliers for replacement parts, fuel, maintenance services and other supplies. Several smaller companies, such as Aerospan.com and TradeAir, also launched aviation-industry e-marketplaces in early 2000, and Boeing, BAE Systems, and Lockheed Martin formed Exostar for the aerospace industry. The multiple start-ups created confusion and a proliferation of choices, and prevented AviationX from building a critical mass of customers. Regional airlines, AviationX's preferred customers, decided to delay joining AviationX to see what the major airlines would do.

AviationX also stalled because it became clear that the amount of data that would have to be stored by the exchange was enormous. Each aeroplane model requires tens of thousands of parts — each of which may be designed differently by any given manufacturer — and each of which may be modified slightly by the airlines (whereupon it is assigned a new part number). To track a fleet of planes, an airline must use hundreds of thousands of part numbers and the airlines continually change the parts' specifications.

The sheer extent of this information made it impossible to simply upload the suppliers' catalogs, in the way that, for example, PlasticsNet had been able to do in the plastics business.

In the heavily regulated aviation industry, AviationX's total neutrality turned out to be a major disadvantage. US regulations require each manufacturer and airline to maintain meticulous records of each part, including serial number and date of manufacture, in case anything goes wrong. It became clear that airlines and parts manufacturers were not prepared to let a totally independent third party manage such critical information for them. Henrik Schröder put to me "It became apparent that a centralized depository of that information was not practicable as the airlines were obliged to retain ownership of that data. We underestimated industry opposition to turning that data over to a private exchange."

Schröder had thought that his first mover advantage and industry experience would enable him to raise $20 million in second-round funding. But by mid-2000, the original $1.6 million was nearly all gone. Starting in March 2000, the stock market began to crash and tech stocks, especially dot-com start-ups, fared the worst. In the face of a tech stock meltdown, the financial community refused to provide additional funding for AviationX at a critical time. AviationX staff dropped from 30 to 20 and the company moved into smaller offices, to cut its "burn rate."

AviationX decided to refocus on smaller regional airlines and change its business plan to make it more of an application services provider for those airlines. Through 2001, AviationX continued to provide consulting services and implementation support in order to help aviation companies meet their B2B, ERP, decision support, and e-business objectives. However, after 9/11/2001 the whole aviation industry was hit very hard and AviationX is now mothballed, like an aircraft in a hangar.

Analyzing B2B Exchange Business Models

Exostar

Exostar (www.exostar.com) was formed in March 2000 by BAE Systems, Boeing, Lockheed Martin and Raytheon, for the $400 billion aerospace and defense industry. Rolls-Royce joined in June 2001. Exostar claims that it is an "independent, global exchange" and it continues to build its capabilities since the first business transactions were conducted on its web-based systems on 29 September 2000.

The founders are among the largest and most significant players in the aerospace and defense industry and they have agreed to buy and sell on a common industry-wide exchange. These initial trading partners represent instant critical mass and worldwide reach since they collectively have a $71 billion annual procurement budget.

Since its inception as an industry consortia-owned B2B exchange, Exostar's goal has been to use the Internet to bring together manufacturers, suppliers and service providers along with airline and government customers in a secure virtual market. Today, Exostar is a full service exchange providing the information, services, and tools that the aerospace and defense industry needs to standardize systems, increase efficiencies and reduce costs. Exostar already has over 7,500 registered users.

Key Milestones — Exostar

March 2000 — Exostar formed.

September 2000 — indirect procurement services launched.

December 2000 — first procurement auction.

March 2001 — mass trading partner adoption begins, executive staff additions.

May 2001 — 4,000 suppliers connected through Exostar.

June 2001 — Rolls-Royce becomes fifth founding partner.

October 2001 — Boise Cascade, an interoperable supplier of office supplies to Boeing, completes 50,000 transactions on Exostar in four months.

November 2001 — 300+ auctions transacted to date through Exostar resulting in over $50 million in throughput.

January 2002 — Donald E. Bielinski selected as first independent President and CEO.

February 2002 — Rolls-Royce Corporation announced that a cross-functional team including Exostar, CommerceOne, and EDS had brought over 180 suppliers on-line in under three months to transact business electronically through Exostar. Documents being transmitted are electronic planning schedules, goods receipt reports, and invoice documents. Rolls-Royce's global supply chain now has a single scheduling system.

June 2002 — Cap Gemini, Ernst & Young, and Exostar form a strategic alliance to offer the worldwide aerospace and defense industry a complete suite of B2B electronic procurement and collaboration services. As part of the agreement, an on-line communications and trading link is established between the UK Ministry of Defence's electronic procurement system, Defence Electronic Commercial Service (DECS), and Exostar. This alliance represents the world's first working model for web-based transactions between governments and the private sector.

Cordiem

Cordiem (www.cordiem.com) was formed in March 2001, by merging MyAircraft and AirNewco. Cordiem was the first B2B exchange for the $500 billion aviation industry to be jointly owned by buyers and sellers. Cordiem's 12 founding aviation members include nine airlines: Air France, American Airlines, British Airways, Continental Airlines, Delta Air Lines, Iberia Airlines, SAirGroup (Swissair), United Airlines, United Parcel Service; and three OEMs: Goodrich Corporation, Honeywell International Inc. and United Technologies Corp.

The founding airlines represent $45 billion in annual purchases, while the three OEMs represent more than $13 billion in aftermarket parts and services.

In October 2001, Cordiem announced a partnership with the Aerospace Hardware Exchange. A total of 11 airlines are now using Cordiem's services which include e-sourcing and e-procurement, auction services, catalog and inventory content listing, inventory collaboration, and supply chain management services. These services support trading in aircraft parts and service, catering materials, fuel procurement, and non-operational materials.

On these exchanges, and some other aviation B2B exchanges such as Airparts, there is now a very active on-line trading in second-hand aircraft parts.

Analyzing B2B Exchange Business Models

Anti-trust Issues

B2B exchanges demonstrate the potential for on-line markets to bring together buyers and sellers from all around the world. The results can be a highly competitive virtual market with on-line auctions creating dynamic pricing, reducing manufacturers' costs of raw materials, parts and supplies. In addition, these net markets have the capability to tie together the manufacturer with its suppliers (Tier 1) and its suppliers' suppliers (Tiers 2 and 3) in a collaborative community. This can lead to greater efficiencies in the design of products and ultimately, to a "build to order" business model that dramatically reduces manufacturing time, inventory levels and distribution costs.

On the other hand, collaborative communities can still create the opportunity for collusion, unreasonable restraint of trade, abuse of market power and — in the case of buy-side led exchanges — the power to drive purchase prices below free market prices (ie, monopsony power). In the worst case, a consortia exchange could become a cartel that indulges in price fixing, market allocation and other anti-competitive actions.

Pro-competitive structural features

However, there are a number of structural features in on-line exchanges that can help ensure that these dynamic new businesses are used to create the significant pro-competitive efficiencies that they promise to deliver.

Trading system design

One feature of B2B exchanges is that they are using the ubiquitous connectivity standards of the Internet to enable companies to connect to each other, to connect to the exchange's central e-marketplace, and to power their electronic trading systems. By definition, no B2B exchange has a physical trading floor.

The direct result of this is that B2B exchanges have electronic pricing mechanisms which provide a full audit trail of all activity in the system and which can be "hard wired" to ensure that anti-competitive activities do not occur on the exchange.

In order to guarantee that the pricing mechanism is a fair system for all qualified members, the systems must ensure that:

- members have equal access;
- rules are established to determine order priority;

- orders are treated on a first-in, first-out basis;
- effective procedures are in place to ensure that each seller's products are posted correctly and that the buyer's bids and orders are transmitted accurately; and
- trades are consistently executed in accordance with the published rules of the exchange.

With a fully electronic, auto-matching system, these rules can be hard coded into the system software using sophisticated algorithms. The rules of a neutral B2B exchange require members to honor the integrity of the exchange's pricing mechanism.

To the extent that the exchange's trading rules cannot be "hard-wired" into the trading system, the exchange must introduce and enforce the trading rules against the members through an internal compliance team.

Ownership structures

Most traditional stock exchanges were set up by stockbrokers and are still exclusively owned by the brokers (eg, the NYSE). This type of exchange operates rather like a "mutual society" or private club.

It was mainly due to the fact that the NYSE is, and has acted as, a private club that the US Government passed the Securities Exchange Act of 1934, which requires all National Securities Markets to be registered by the SEC. For example, in the 1920s the NYSE would protect members who were trading while insolvent, if they were long standing members, rather than kicking them out immediately.

By way of contrast, B2B exchanges are all being set up as "for profit," neutral market spaces. This follows from their objective of bringing as many buyers and sellers together as possible, in order to create dynamic pricing, and to therefore lower the cost of procuring supplies for buyers and expand the range of potential buyers for the suppliers. Successful exchanges are seeking to be neutral and independent markets with open access to all players in that industry.

B2B exchanges that are truly open have objective criteria to determine who may have access to the centralized e-marketplace and provide equal access. Equal access means that every trading member has equal access to the exchange's trading system, irrespective of size or duration of membership.

Analyzing B2B Exchange Business Models

Monopsony power

B2B exchanges can empower buyers by enabling them to contact more potential suppliers and by creating the potential for "reverse" auctions — where the buyer sets a price and the suppliers have to bid on it (with prices falling as the auction progresses).

This is well illustrated by the buy-side led industry consortia which seek to lower the members' procurement costs by creating a central exchange. In these B2B exchanges, the buyers can create cost savings by getting suppliers to bid in on-line auctions for some contracts.

On the other hand, by combining their purchasing power through an exchange and restricting suppliers' access to that exchange, the buyers may be able to exercise monopsony power and force the suppliers that are members to quote prices below those that would prevail in a freely competitive market. This danger is particularly prevalent in industries that are already dominated by a relatively small number of large purchasers, rather than those which are more fragmented.

However, providing these exchanges are set up as "for profit" commercial entities with open access, then these B2B exchanges would be in breach of their financial responsibility to maximize shareholder value if they were to subjectively restrict access to their markets. Imagine if the WorldWide Retail Exchange (the B2B retail store procurement exchange set up by Target, Kmart, Safeway, Walgreens, and DairyFarm among others), decided to restrict access to a limited number of suitable suppliers/vendors. It would immediately be self-defeating.

Initially, the retailers might be able to extract cost savings from those vendors which it admitted, but by limiting access to a small number of potentially suitable suppliers, the retailers would actually be reducing their chances of securing food, drugs, general merchandise and textiles of the right quality at a lower price and with the right after sales service, etc. In such a scenario, the retailers would risk driving their limited number of selected suppliers to depress output and ultimately to go out of business as they forced the prices down. Open market forces therefore dictate that this B2B retail store exchange will be open to the widest range of potential suppliers that prove that they can deliver goods of the quality, in the quantity and with the other service attributes that the retail stores require.

Regulation

For the time being, the Federal Trade Commission (FTC) in the US and the EU have both refrained from premature regulation of B2B exchanges. For example, the FTC decided in 2001 to permit the Covisint industry consortia exchange for automakers to proceed, after conducting a thorough investigation of the proposed exchange including a June 2000 public workshop on *Competition Policy in the World of B2B Electronic Marketplaces*. In July 2001, the EU also approved the Covisint exchange after a thorough review.

When announcing that Covisint could proceed, the FTC Chairman Robert Pitofsky stated, "As we learned at the FTC's workshop in June, B2B electronic marketplaces offer great promise as a means through which significant cost savings can be achieved, business processes can be more efficiently organized, and competition may be enhanced. B2Bs have a great potential to benefit both businesses and consumers through increased productivity and lower prices. Of course, as is the case with any joint venture, whether in the traditional or new economy, B2Bs should be organized and implemented in ways that maintain competition. The antitrust analysis of an individual B2B will be specific to its mission, its structure, its particular market circumstances, procedures and rules for organization and operation, and actual operations and market performance."

In 2001, the FTC started to investigate some of the on-line trading exchanges in the financial services sector. In particular, it has sought information from FXall and BrokerTec about their operations. The FTC's concern appears to be that the Wall Street firms that own these exchanges may be giving them an unfair advantage by directing their own trading onto the exchanges they own, to the detriment of their rivals (ie, acting as a cartel to allocate markets).

In May 2002, the EU gave regulatory clearance to Inreon, which trades insurance capacity/products and is owned by two traditional competitors — Munich Re and Swiss Re — and Accenture. Internet Capital Group is also an investor in Inreon.

A B2B exchange should have no anti-trust concerns if it can show that:

- it is not being used for blatant price fixing or allocation of markets between competitors;
- it produces pro-competitive benefits and efficiencies for the members of the exchange and the industry as a whole;

- any restrictions on new members joining or existing members leaving are reasonable and not designed just to restrict competition;
- it is independent of, and managed independently from, any founding consortia; and
- competitors' confidential data is being kept separate and secure.

In the end, it is free markets, low barriers to entry, and rapidly changing technology — and not governmental regulation — that will ensure that all B2B exchanges preserve open and equal access to their market spaces.

However, regulators are maintaining a watching brief to ensure that successful B2B exchanges do not change their open structures in order to support anti-competitive features.

Looking Forward

B2B exchanges are being judged on how well they serve all their members and how fair and equal they are. The winner in each industry is likely to be the exchange that demonstrates that it is operated in a neutral way so that all buyers and sellers feel comfortable in joining that e-marketplace.

In most cases, the industry consortia are winning because they have greater liquidity and are better capitalized.

However, in some cases this is being achieved by adopting a hybrid approach that combines the strengths of industry consortia with the independence of dot-coms. For instance, both Covisint and Exostar now have an independent, senior management group.

Chapter **6**

Private Exchange Models

"Private networks are providing a way for companies to formalize their existing trade flows and relationships on-line, which will eventually give them the understanding and the e-business infrastructure to be able to link into more dynamic public exchange marketplaces in the future."

Over the last 12 months, large public B2B exchanges have been overshadowed by smaller, private networks that put a single e-business at the center of the B2B network. Such private exchanges, as they are called, are web-based trading applications implemented by a single company with a select group of suppliers and customers.

Private exchanges offer increased collaboration with suppliers and a deeper view into the supply chain and are now fueling new growth in B2B transactions.

With the benefit of hindsight, it is possible to see that many companies were not ready to go straight to public B2B exchanges to begin their B2B efforts because their own business environment was not sufficiently on-line. The result was that many B2B exchanges only offered a novel procurement mechanism and could not deliver on the full potential of an on-line network, since — as we shall see in Chapter 9 — that requires deep integration with the users' internal systems.

Companies are now progressing with the smaller set of B2B processes involved in linking up their existing suppliers and supply chain. As a result, many public exchanges are trying to broaden their services and even host private exchanges. For instance, CATEX, the insurance B2B exchange, is broadening its base of services by assisting in the creation of several private networks. Even big exchanges such as Covisint are building private exchanges for specific users.

Are Private Networks Really Exchanges?

In 1999 I wrote, "…The important point, which differentiates an exchange from other B2B e-commerce companies, is that an exchange involves **multiple** buyers and sellers and it centralizes and matches buy and sell orders and provides post-trade information."

The private network business models that have been developing over the last twelve months are a form of exchange, albeit a private exchange, because:

- they are based on "collaboration," not just a one-way transaction process; these private networks are often called "collaborative supply chain solutions"; and
- they are often being set up and run by, and as part of, a public B2B exchange — and can later be connected to the public e-marketplace of that exchange.

Advantages of Private Exchanges for Users

Behind the trend toward private trading networks is the desire for purchasing managers to have more control over their on-line relationships. Companies can use private exchanges to establish central control over purchasing through contracts with established suppliers.

These private exchanges can prove the effectiveness of the technology and the business model, before a company links into a large public B2B exchange. Existing Enterprise Resource Planning (ERP) systems do not easily allow companies to automate transactions with suppliers and customers because ERP systems are generally internal systems that do not connect the company to outside partners. Legacy ERP systems, therefore, do not currently have:

- the ability (the database records) to keep information that other systems need to have or that others give away as reference; or
- natural repositories for keeping references to other systems (external ERP references). Therefore, they have problems when shaking hands with the external system.

For example, an ERP system can only track a company's own inventory at any given time whereas a private exchange allows a company to monitor its suppliers' inventory, ie, what is being produced on its contract manufacturer's shop floor, and to track products that are in transit to it. In addition, an ERP system does not normally handle sourcing and contracting with suppliers. On the other hand, a private exchange provides an on-line way to aggregate how much a company needs to buy, define specifications, negotiate with suppliers, and establish the contract.

Companies use private exchanges to trade proprietary information like supplier performance metrics and sales forecasts in addition to orders and invoices. This is possible because private exchanges do not force companies to give up sensitive information — such as purchasing patterns — to competitors or to suppliers that are also serving those competitors. By excluding competitors, a private exchange encourages the sharing of sensitive data along the whole value chain. This allows suppliers to make better marketing and pricing decisions regarding their products.

As we have seen, the fear of giving away proprietary information is one of the main reasons that BMW has given for not yet joining Covisint.

Other advantages of private exchanges over public exchanges include:

- they allow companies to integrate their internal applications and re-engineer their business processes before exposing themselves to the dynamics of an on-line public marketplace (this is particularly relevant for small- and medium-sized entities that do not have the resources to take their whole business on-line in one go);
- companies can direct suppliers and customers to use their exchange and encourage them to use it with price incentives; and
- private exchanges can be customized to serve specific projects and customers, unlike public exchanges, which have to be more generic so as to accommodate everyone.

Dell, Cisco Systems, and Wal-Mart are prominent examples of large firms that have built private exchanges. Wal-Mart's RetailLink is a private exchange that is credited with enabling Wal-Mart to expand its market share from 9% to 27% during the 1990s. Wal-Mart uses information technology to keep track of what is selling in the stores, to replenish the products that are selling the fastest, and to keep inventory costs down.

Analyzing B2B Exchange Business Models

The McKinsey Global Institute (www.mckinsey.com) has released a study on US productivity growth 1995–2000, which shows that in general merchandise retailing, productivity growth accelerated after 1995 because Wal-Mart's success forced competitors to improve their operations. McKinsey states that in 1987 Wal-Mart had just 9% market share, but was 40% more productive than its competitors. By the mid-1990s, its share had grown to 27% while its productivity advantage had widened to 48%. Competitors reacted by adopting many of Wal-Mart's innovations, including the large scale "big box" format, economies of scale in warehouse logistics and purchasing, EDI, and wireless barcode scanning. From 1995–1999, competitors increased their productivity by 28%, while Wal-Mart raised the bar further by increasing its own efficiency another 20%.

Wal-Mart has always been a leader in supply chain management. Every store has scanning cash registers that instantly feed sales data to the store's computers, which adjust sales and inventory records. Store managers can watch the inventory of a fast-moving item drop and electronically send replenishment orders to Wal-Mart's distribution centers. Since the early 1980s, Wal-Mart has used EDI to electronically place orders and receive shipping notices. The RetailLink system is now Internet-based and can be accessed through a browser.

RetailLink is really a private B2B exchange that connects Wal-Mart with its 7,500 suppliers, allows suppliers to access Wal-Mart's sales data and projections, and helps Wal-Mart devise ways to drive up sales. RetailLink allows Wal-Mart to instantly see potential stock shortages and launch promotions for substitute products. In the same way, Dell Computers uses its private exchange network with suppliers to spot component shortages and instantly offer promotions on substitutes or free upgrades that maintain sales around the temporary shortage. On the other hand, RetailLink helps Wal-Mart's suppliers make better marketing and pricing decisions regarding their products, access more retail and consumer information, and gain visibility with the company's stores and distribution network.

These types of private exchange are, therefore, collaborative trading communities.

Kmart, which is now in Chapter 11 bankruptcy, has struggled to compete with Wal-Mart and this is due in part to its delay in investing in a comparable electronic supply chain management system.

Private Exchange Builders

Several companies that had hoped to build all the public B2B exchanges are now focused on building private network exchanges, including Ariba Inc, Commerce One, i2 Technologies, and VerticalNet.

Following the acquisition of Atlas Commerce in December 2001, VerticalNet now focuses on connecting suppliers to various buyers in enterprises through private network exchanges that create collaborative supply chain solutions. Atlas Commerce, a privately held software company, specializes in providing private exchange software and strategic sourcing applications, with a client list that includes Wal-Mart. Similarly, Ariba Inc. has bought Agile Software Corp. and allied with Syncra Systems Inc. to boost its presence in the private exchange space.

At the same time, the leading providers of EDI network services, such as GE Global Exchange Services (GXS) and IBM, are now offering to build private Internet-based exchanges, using Internet-EDI. For example, GE GXS recently announced that it has built a private exchange to connect about 5,000 of DaimlerChrysler suppliers through its own hosted Internet-based EDI services.

But many public B2B exchanges are also offering to use their own core technologies to build private network exchanges for specific users (eg, CATEX, Covisint, E2open, and MetalSite).

In doing so, B2B exchanges have to develop an e-business communications infrastructure that enables them to receive and deliver information and documents in a multitude of formats and channels (see Chapter 10).

Advantages of Private Exchanges for B2B Exchanges

Building private exchanges leverages off the sunk costs of the public exchange's infrastructure build out and is an important revenue source for struggling B2B markets. B2B exchanges can charge software license fees, customization fees, and transaction-based fees, for use of the exchange's core technology in the private network. Building private exchanges allows B2B exchanges to:

- extend their customer base;
- increase revenue;
- make great connections with potential users of the public e-marketplace;
- establish integration standards within an industry; and

- provide a single sign-on capability for users accessing multiple networks through the B2B exchange.

Private networks built by B2B exchanges use the core functionality of the exchange (eg, the reverse auction application) but with an on-line interface that reflects the customer's specific requests and branding. The customer's data must also be kept separate from the public exchange.

Although the private network system is based on the exchange's "generic" applications, customization is usually offered and, despite the cost involved in customizing it, these systems provide the user with a tailored, complete e-business solution at a minimal price and with minimal maintenance. Customized private exchanges are similar to stand alone proprietary systems as they are designed to meet a user's specific requirements.

However, they exclude the costs incurred and the long implementation times encountered when outsourcing or building proprietary systems in house.

Case study: CATEX

CATEX (www.catex.com) runs the CATEX Global Market, one of the world's largest electronic exchange for reinsurance and insurance business. CATEX is now also a leading technology company in the reinsurance and insurance sector. With its exclusive focus on this sector, CATEX's technology is used by over 300 companies worldwide.

CATEX has been building its B2B exchange for over four years but, like many exchanges in the last three years, has struggled to develop a critical mass of transactions in its public e-marketplace.

In 2001, CATEX decided to drop transaction fees altogether in the public e-marketplace, to help attract liquidity, and to focus instead on providing IT solutions to the insurance and reinsurance industries.

CATEX's main IT product is a low cost, private network approach termed "Trader Domains." Trader Domains are branded, sub-licensed versions of the CATEX system with full CATEX functionality. CATEX has seen a sharp increase in company specific business being placed through these proprietary and private systems. By using such systems CATEX allows companies to deploy turnkey Internet trading systems under their control and with customized branding and underwriting requirements built in. The systems are connectable to the CATEX Global Market should the client so elect.

Aside from the Global Market, the business transacted on these private trading exchanges is not visible on the main CATEX System, but these companies are utilizing an Internet trading platform closely linked to the Global Market.

With the implementation of private networks, CATEX has moved beyond its initial role as a public e-marketplace of last resort to become a supplier of efficient trading tools and applications for the industry's "core" reinsurance business.

The benefits of a private Trader Domain for customers are:

- companies can maintain their own underwriting standards and access a private market rather than hand over proprietary underwriting data in a public market that requires the data to be formatted to a rigid data standard controlled by others;
- use of an "off-the-shelf" product based upon proven technology;
- the user has complete administrative control;
- the system can only be viewed by the companies that the user specifies;
- non-CATEX subscribers can be granted access to a Trader Domain;
- CATEX will host and maintain the system on the user's behalf;
- the private exchange is accessible via a corporate website and/or the CATEX Global Market;
- a user can set up more than one Trader Domain; and
- further customization is available for a fee.

CATEX offers to maintain the system on a user's behalf, update it as CATEX technology advances, and provide full support and training.

For example, John P. Woods Co., Inc. selected CATEX technology to replace its back-office system. Woods is a reinsurance intermediary founded in 1978. It is a member of the Arthur J. Gallagher Companies (NYSE: AJG) and represents over 100 client companies, which cede in excess of $700 million in reinsurance premium to reinsurers worldwide.

CATEX has implemented a customized, web-based accounting and placement system for Woods that securely co-ordinates back-office functions involving Woods' personnel, clients, and reinsurers. This private network supports facultative reinsurance operations and treaty business.

The CATEX system allows for "real time" negotiation and tracking of contracts, placements, claims and transmittal of accounting information into the fiduciary ledger of Woods. It is a seamless, end-to-end system that is open at the

Analyzing B2B Exchange Business Models

front-end to ceding clients of Woods and integrated at the back-end to reinsurance markets and the company's general and fiduciary accounts. Woods hopes that the combination of placement information, claims management, premium tracking and accounting data offered by the web-based CATEX system will put it ahead of its competitors.

CATEX has also built private networks for SCOR, CNA Re, and others.

In February 2002, CATEX announced that the 1,400th transaction on its trading systems had been completed. The trade was completed in a private network designed and operated by CATEX for a major market. CATEX Chief Executive Officer, Francis X. Fortunato, told me "that over $10 billion in reinsured limit has now been bound on our systems. Our reports indicate that in excess of $900 million in reinsurance premium is accounted for by the 1,400 transactions." Business bound on CATEX systems includes treaty business, facultative coverage, and other lines of reinsurance.

Building Liquidity by Stealth

If the exchange develops numerous users who build private networks on its technology platform it can, over time, start to link those private exchanges together. Because they are all built on the same technology, integration is relatively simple. In this way, purchasers can start to expand their network of suppliers by venturing out into the public e-marketplace occasionally to get price and other quotes.

This is most likely to happen initially for the more standardized or "commoditized" products such as indirect supplies.

The increase in users accessing the CATEX Global Market through CATEX developed private networks is proof that private exchanges can, over time, act as portals to the public e-marketplace of B2B exchanges.

For example, Kevin English told me "Covisint is developing custom (bespoke) portals for our customers including Ford, DaimlerChrysler, Delphi, Lear, and others. These portals will be developed, managed and hosted by Covisint and, since accessible directly through Covisint, enable a highly secure single sign-on capability that makes it easier for users to navigate from one site to another."

Private exchanges also allow companies to become familiar with on-line trading so that they will be more prepared to trade in the more dynamic on-line public marketplace. As private exchanges become more common over

the next few years, the momentum will build to bring business onto the public e-marketplaces — the pendulum will swing back towards the public part of the exchanges.

Networking the Private Networks

If the exchange develops numerous users who build private networks on its technology platform it can, over time, start to link those private exchanges together. Because they are all built on the same technology, integration is relatively simple.

Private networks are providing a way for companies to formalize their existing trade flows and relationships on-line, which will eventually give them the understanding and the e-business infrastructure to be able to link into more dynamic public exchange marketplaces in the future.

Buyers in private exchanges already have ongoing business partnerships with the sellers connected to that network, so both parties keep each other up-to-date on products, pricing, and other important information. The public B2B exchange, on the other hand, is ideally suited for integrating buyers and sellers that may not have done business together before. The public B2B exchange provides an opportunity for vendors who seek to extend their market base by finding new buyers and for manufacturers to find new suppliers.

Private exchanges cement existing relationships and reinforce long-term commitments between suppliers and a manufacturer. By putting these relationships on-line, the manufacturer will realize efficiency benefits but is unlikely to see major price reductions. Once a manufacturer has a private network established it will eventually seek price reductions through public B2B exchanges, where competition between a larger number of participating companies involved in auctions or group purchasing activity creates downward price pressure.

Ultimately, large public B2B exchanges will have a new role as a connector between private trading exchanges, as well as a facilitator, that will have the clout to create and enforce standards for data creation and document exchange. That will make things easier for suppliers, once they have connected to one or two private networks, to then extend those connections into one or more public exchanges. The private exchange also brings greater value by providing a secure, single sign-on capability through which users can access private networks, web services and the public e-marketplace.

Analyzing B2B Exchange Business Models

In addition, private exchanges are not well suited to integrating a wide range of web services. As we shall see in Chapter 9, integrating related web-based services significantly increases the value proposition of a B2B network.

However, private exchanges face the arduous task of creating bilateral relationships with each web-based services provider. A public B2B exchange, on the other hand, can establish relationships with all the necessary web service providers and the private exchanges can then access all of those services through one connection to the B2B exchange.

Figure 6A: Network of Networks

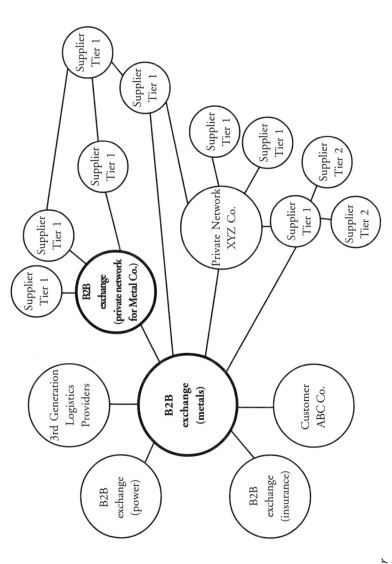

Source: Author

Chapter 7

The Hybrid Model: Combining Clicks and Mortar to Build Liquidity

"Right now we are in a transitional phase where the old 'voice broking' models are gradually transforming into on-line trading."

The rush to use the "on-line" trading systems of B2B exchanges has in many cases been under-whelming. B2B on-line trading systems, particularly those that allow counterparties to interact anonymously with each other, face the issue of trying to completely change the traditional way of trading by phone and fax. Often the traditional way includes using brokers as intermediaries and procurement managers develop strong personal relationships with those brokers over time. It is, therefore, a major cultural challenge to get procurement managers and their existing voice brokers to migrate their trading to an on-line system. Some people may feel that their job is threatened by a move to on-line trading and they stick with voice broking to preserve their position.

Many B2B exchanges that faced this cultural resistance to change simply ran out of money before they could build sufficient trading volume to survive.

Key issues raised in respect of trading through new on-line systems are:

- the initial lack of liquidity;
- the lack of standardization of deals;
- poor design — making systems difficult to use;
- lack of transparency and color; and
- a perception that trading on-line is inferior to voice broking.

Analyzing B2B Exchange Business Models

The relationships that develop among traders, their counterparts in the market, and their clients are sometimes considered critical, both to getting a deal and then to ensuring a successful trade. When prices change suddenly, investors currently rely on their voice brokers to interpret the move and the market trends. The best trading technology in the world cannot yet replace a relationship and the voice broker's ability to elicit a quote from a relationship.

However, I believe — and many market participants agree — that the move to on-line trading of all fungible financial products is inevitable. Right now we are in a transitional phase where the old "voice broking" models are gradually transforming into on-line trading.

US Financial Services Market

The Bond Market Association (www.bondmarkets.com) published a survey in December 2001 entitled *eCommerce in the Fixed-Income Markets* which revealed that, from a list of 68 fixed-income systems in the US at the end of 2000, 21 (about one-third) had merged with other partners or gone bust. The survey reported that there were still 49 fixed-income systems in the US at the end of 2001. The survey identified 24 systems in Europe, up from 5 in 2000. The survey also reports that six electronic loan trading systems had been identified. Including derivative trading platforms, the survey reports a total of 79 electronic trading platforms operating in the US and Europe for all fixed-income products.

The Bond Market Association concludes its 2001 study as follows:

"The consolidation in the number of US trading systems is attributable to several factors. First and most important is an overcapacity that existed in 2000. There were simply too many systems launched for the volume of trading taking place. Second, the overall contraction in the Internet economy has taken its toll on the electronic fixed-income trading sector. Start-up platforms have found it increasingly difficult to obtain continued capitalization, and investors have become less patient with money-losing ventures. Finally, some systems were based on business models that failed to take into account investors' desires for liquidity and market-making commitments from the dealer community. For these same reasons, continued consolidation among trading platforms is likely. However, this should not be taken as an indication that electronic trading and e-commerce in the fixed-income markets are unworkable. There are some key success stories among trading system vendors, and strong platforms will continue to thrive as electronic trading brings efficiencies and cost reductions to the market. In addition, the appeal of electronic trading will

continue to grow as the industry completes its transition to straight-through processing of securities transactions and as participants finalize and implement common communication protocols for the electronic marketplace."

The Hybrid Model

For the time being, therefore, a combination of traditional voice broking and on-line services is necessary to make a B2B exchange successful. This is a "hybrid" model, in which the exchange seeks to offer the best of both worlds. The full service voice brokerage is supported by on-line documentation, data, analytics, and real-time information. The more standardized deals are traded on-line while the more complex deals continue to be voice-brokered. In each case, electronic tools that cut costs and improve efficiency support the trading.

For example, CheMatch (now merged with ChemConnect), a leading bulk chemicals and fuel products B2B exchange, acquired The Energy Group (TEG). TEG was a traditional petrochemical, feedstock, and gasoline components voice brokerage firm based in Houston, Texas and was acquired to substantially increase the liquidity on the CheMatch platform, particularly in the feedstock products.

ICAP plc (LSE: IAP.L), which owns Garban-Intercapital, is also a good example of the hybrid model between a voice brokerage and an electronic trading platform, this time in the wholesale financial markets. Garban-Intercapital is the world's largest inter-dealer broker in the over-the-counter (OTC) financial markets, with daily transaction volumes in excess of $300 billion. These markets include interest rate derivatives, fixed income securities, money markets, futures, commodities, and equity derivatives. Technology is now playing a critical role in the rapidly evolving OTC derivative and bond markets. ICAP is, therefore, increasingly committed to the application of technology to the wholesale broking business to provide improved price discovery, deal execution and straight through processing. ICAP is gradually moving its highly liquid and generic products on to electronic broking platforms, initially in the fixed income markets. By creating a hybrid of electronic and voice broking, ICAP aims to cover the entire spectrum from highly liquid to highly illiquid markets.

On-line support tools

The on-line systems can support voice brokers and move them toward automated execution and straight through processing, in several ways by:

- enabling more cost effective, efficient, and wider distribution of real-time prices to dealers and their clients;
- providing enhanced data capture, retrieval, and presentation capabilities; and
- facilitating instantaneous market or price specific communications between dealers and with clients (eg, instant messaging).

Instant messaging

Instant messaging services, based on web protocols, provide a fantastic on-line support service for voice brokers. The basic consumer versions of instant messaging (IM) offered by AOL, Microsoft, and Yahoo are not secure enough for business applications and do not archive conversations for users. In response, several secure versions of IM have been designed which give corporate users control over what information is sent and how it is stored. In the financial services area, Communicator's IM Hub (www.communicatorinc.com) is proving popular after Salomon Smith Barney, J P Morgan Chase, Merrill Lynch, CSFB, Goldman Sachs, Lehman Brothers, Morgan Stanley, and UBS Warburg signed up to use it for their employees and institutional clients. IM Hub secures IM messages by sending them using Secure Socket Layer encryption.

IM services allow dealers to negotiate deals in real time in conjunction with a simultaneous telephone conversation with another dealer or a client. IM therefore represents a perfect "hybrid" technology as it is an on-line service that supports voice broking and it allows dealers to migrate the deal making on-line in an evolutionary manner. IM also allows dealer indications of interest and securities research to be instantly transmitted to a firm's client list. By replacing short e-mails and phone calls, IM can make sales people more efficient.

Communicator Inc. worked with the eight financial institutions to develop an address book that encompasses each institution's employees as well as their customers and partners. The address book is only open to members of the community, and strict access and authorization tools control who can access the application and the content.

Case study: CreditTrade

To understand how this hybrid model works in practice, let's look in more detail at the development of the credit derivatives market, and specifically the success of CreditTrade in that market.

The credit derivatives market

Essentially credit derivatives allow a party to transfer its credit risk to another, for hedging or speculative reasons.

A credit derivative contract generally provides that in the event of a "trigger event" (ie, if a company defaults on its bond or goes bankrupt) a buyer of credit risk protection receives payment from a seller of that protection. Therefore, it works like insurance, with the seller of the derivative only paying the buyer after a trigger event. The most popular contracts are credit default swaps, collateralized debt obligations, and total return swaps.

The role of credit derivatives in managing default risk and pricing debt securities is now recognized as central to the efficient working of the debt markets. The International Monetary Fund has noted that credit derivatives have the potential to enhance the efficiency and stability of credit markets overall and improve the allocation of capital.

In 1998, the British Bankers' Association estimated that the global credit derivatives market was $350 billion. Since then, the notional amount of credit derivatives outstanding has grown about fivefold to $1.6 trillion. While credit derivatives only account for about 1.6% of the global OTC derivatives market, which is currently estimated to be $100 trillion, they are the fastest-growing part of the market.

CreditTrade anticipates strong momentum toward broader and more robust use of credit derivatives in the near future. Liquidity in this market is also improving.

In a classic "virtuous circle," as the usage of credit derivatives grows, the products become increasingly useful, more institutions use them, and usage continues its growth. Credit derivatives are used for hedging bond credit risk. For example, in early 2002, the pre-sale of credit protection before the launch of a major bond issue by the troubled mobile phone company, MM02, indicates growing acceptance of the credit default swap as a protection instrument. CreditTrade has used key trigger events such as Enron's bankruptcy to illustrate that credit derivatives can also act as a leading indicator of credit quality. CreditTrade's data shows that, in this case, the credit default swap price moved in advance of the bond price, indicating a downshift in credit quality. Another reason for the growing popularity of credit derivatives is that investors also now see them as useful for seeking incremental returns. In the last couple of years, credit derivatives have been marketed more actively and purchased by investors nearly as much for profit as for hedging purposes.

Financial strains and significant credit market events in 2001, such as those surrounding the failure of Railtrack plc in the UK, the Argentine currency crisis, and the collapse of Enron, have been a real test, which arguably have proved that the credit derivatives market is maturing quickly and becoming increasingly important. Due payments were made by credit risk protection sellers (excluding Enron) to protection buyers, even though in some cases this occurred only after arbitration.

Many market participants believe that the credit derivatives market will continue to expand rapidly in 2002/3 as global economic growth slows, boosting demand for protection against bankruptcies and bond defaults.

Overview of CreditTrade

CreditTrade is a leading provider of transaction, data, and information services to the credit markets. The company's transaction services are supported by an electronic trading platform (www.credittrade.com) designed to bring together buyers and sellers of credit quickly and efficiently. Founded by CEO Paul Ellis, the CreditTrade platform was initially launched on a trial basis with simulated trading on 30 June 1999. The official launch with live trading was on 26 July 1999. Major products traded through CreditTrade include: credit derivatives, secondary loans, and a variety of structured products, such as collateralized debt obligations and asset swaps. CreditTrade serves the world's leading financial institutions from offices in London, New York, and Singapore.

The credit derivatives marketplace is currently hindered by a lack of transparency and a shortage of standardized documentation. CreditTrade aims to deliver solutions to these problems by dramatically improving the ease, transparency, and efficiency of institutions to exchange documents, negotiate, trade, and manage credit risk. For example, CreditTrade provides credit data subscription services such as "CreditTrade Benchmarks" for mark-to-market pricing and "CreditTrade Market Prices," which comprise a comprehensive set of intra day market prices.

Market opportunity

The credit derivatives marketplace is not commoditized; the details of each trade must be individually negotiated. Because of this, it is less easily understood and solutions are less easily implemented, which results in a less crowded marketplace.

There are two primary reasons why CreditTrade believes that credit trading is well suited for the Internet — documentation and transparency. Because the Web can be used to automate the processes required to define and close credit transactions, sharing occasionally extensive documentation between business partners can be streamlined. The CreditTrade website provides a mechanism to upload, download, share and forward documents involved in negotiating and closing a deal. An example of where this model has succeeded is the foreign exchange market where electronic trading is commonplace.

In addition, the Web offers the promise of transparency which is an improvement over the traditional system where voice brokers intermediate between different market players. At the moment, not everyone has access to all the information that might be available at any given time. When trades are done, brokers have privileged information that is valuable when they talk to another market player — so called "color" which can present problems of decreased market transparency. Players who do not feel they have access to prices, or are "in the loop" are less likely to take risks, participate in the market, and consequently increase liquidity. However, CreditTrade's platform is designed to ensure anonymity. Therefore, traders can ensure their prices remain private to selected counterparties. All telephone deals are captured and reported on CreditTrade's website. This means that the on-line platform is gradually increasing transparency in the marketplace — as originally envisaged.

CreditTrade has positioned itself wisely. CreditTrade's website provides an efficient, transparent, and neutral way to execute trades (both on or off-line) with the ability to access a range of data services to support and inform trading decisions. The most important thing that on-line trading can bring to the credit trading market is greater transparency, with the goal of increasing overall volume.

Original trading model

CreditTrade launched its on-line trading platform in February 1999, with the aim of providing traders with greater access to real-time data, improved trading information and enhanced liquidity via the Internet. Originally, CreditTrade was exclusively a web-based trading system. The system gives brokers and traders the ability to post real-time prices. The system is enhanced and automated with the use of templates designed for different users, locations, and types of credits. Each price or market also carries supporting information about the reference credit, rating, sectoral classifications, and price histories.

If traders see a trade that interests them, they can correspond electronically with their broker, through CreditTrade, and initiate a trade. If the counterparties reach an agreement, then, provided each party agrees, CreditTrade will affect a simultaneous exchange of names allowing completion of the trade directly. The parties then "lock" the deal on the system and clear credit and/or finalize the documentation off-line. Once a trade has been executed, the trade information is collated and published on the site, to provide a price reference for other participants.

The new trading model — combining clicks and mortar

However, CreditTrade quickly recognised the need to adopt the "hybrid" model. In 2000, CreditTrade formed an agreement with Prebon Yamane, a leading global credit derivatives intermediary, which saw Prebon move its global credit derivatives team (the bricks and mortar) and historical default swap database to CreditTrade in return for a substantial equity stake. In all, 13 credit derivatives brokers in London, New York, and Singapore joined CreditTrade's on-line credit sales desk to form a single global team. The agreement highlights the potential benefits to all market users of combining the personal attention provided by traditional voice brokers with the speed, efficiency, and cost effectiveness of an on-line B2B exchange.

At the moment, CreditTrade is dealing almost totally by phone, but is increasingly using the on-line platform for supporting data and information services, rather than as an execution platform exclusively. Paul Ellis told me "The migration to trading on-line will be driven by the provision of powerful supporting data and services available through our Internet platform. It is naïve to assume that you can simply put an electronic execution service on people's desktop and expect people to start trading on it. The on-line business is now, and will remain for the near term, a supporting service. In the medium term I see it as a potential execution mechanism, but even in the long term I do not believe, certainly in our market, that you will ever completely replace the telephone broker."

CreditTrade's platform supports voice brokers in the following ways:

- it enables more cost effective, efficient, and wider distribution of real-time prices — between desks, offices, and clients;
- the customized application provides enhanced data capture, retrieval and presentation capabilities — a vital tool for monitoring market activity;
- it facilitates instantaneous market or price specific communication with clients; and
- it is a step toward automated execution and straight through processing.

Market perceptions

In 2001, CreditTrade commissioned an independent research survey into various aspects of the credit derivatives market. In addition to evaluating the enormous growth potential for the market, CreditTrade was also interested in assessing market opinion about on-line trading of credit derivatives. The main research was based on detailed interviews with a wide range of market practitioners and the information obtained was compiled into a detailed report.

The report shows that key factors such as lack of liquidity, pricing, lack of transparency, and an absence of standardization of deal documentation inhibit the acceptance of on-line trading in the short-term. However, over the long-term, market participants believe that the migration of credit derivatives to on-line trading is inevitable. This migration is expected to acquire critical mass in the next two to five years, as specific market issues cause the business to transfer.

However, a significant proportion of people interviewed in the study believe that on-line trading platforms for credit derivatives are ahead of their time. They believe that electronic trading mechanisms still require additional qualities to elevate them to "must use" status. They also criticised on-line sites for being difficult to access, hard to navigate, poorly designed, lacking in color, and inferior to conventional voice broking.

These negative perceptions go beyond mere functional issues. At present, electronic platforms lack sufficient liquidity and critical mass. Documentation issues are difficult to resolve on-line and, although many interviewees noted that their resolution would benefit the market, the market for credit derivatives has flourished despite general concerns about the lack of standardized documentation. Unrealistic pricing — "fictional offers" that are posted on-line to attract a contact but which evaporate when pursued — were also quoted as a source of deep frustration.

Today at least, the market seems to favor voice brokers as the preferred method of trading. The following advantages give some insight as to why this voice broking prevails.

The Advantages of Voice Broking

- Voice broking is at present considered to be "instinctively better" because "it offers color, speed, and the confidence of a tried and trusted working relationship."

- A high proportion of people contend that "most trades are brokered — and will continue to be brokered — by voice until the on-line market eventually achieves critical mass."

- In the absence of standardized documentation, electronic platforms will find it hard to compete against voice brokers.

- Voice brokers appear reluctant to persuade clients to adopt new electronic platforms that currently offer few clear advantages.

- There remains widespread concern over documentation, lack of liquidity, counter-party credit limits, etc. — critical elements of the business that are not presently well handled on-line.

- There is a widely-held belief that more complex, non-vanilla deals will, for the foreseeable future, continue to be brokered or handled directly with principals.

Source: Market Research Survey, 2001 — CreditTrade

Disadvantages of Managing the "Mortar"

Managing a team of traditional voice brokers is not an easy task. First, talented voice brokers are expensive and have significant bonus expectations if they are successful. Second, retaining talented brokers becomes a major issue since the broker "owns" the personal relationships with the clients.

Third, the exchange can become dependant on the voice brokers. A tragic example of this occurred on 11 September 2001, when the horrendous terrorist attack on the World Trade Centre almost destroyed the firm of Cantor Fitzgerald after nearly their whole New York broking team was lost. Cantor Fitzgerald was the largest inter-dealer voice-brokerage in the US Treasuries market. Since that time, Bloomberg has reported that Cantor lost about 40% of its business to BrokerTec, a fully electronic rival based in Jersey City that was unaffected by the World Trade Centre tragedy.

Even before 11 September 2001, Cantor was moving its clients' bond-trading business onto its electronic trading platform, operated by a subsidiary of Cantor Fitzgerald, and called eSpeed. That process is now being accelerated. eSpeed reported total electronic volume for the fourth quarter 2001 was $7.2 trillion versus $9.9 trillion for the same period in 2000. The decrease in total electronic volume was attributed to significant declines in voice electronic volume, as a direct result of the tragic loss of life in Cantor Fitzgerald's voice brokerage business on 11 September.

Fourthly, it can take a long time to persuade dealers to give up their personal relationships with voice brokers and trade on-line. It is a major cultural challenge to get existing voice brokers in bank dealing rooms to migrate their trading to an on-line system. Many sales people feel their job is threatened by a move to on-line trading and they stick with voice broking to preserve their position. In the future, as the on-line platform becomes a major reason why people choose to trade with a particular B2B exchange then special broker relationships will become somewhat less relevant.

Market dynamics moving trading on-line

Although voice broking is so important today, there are several market trends that are moving the industry towards on-line trading.

Analyzing B2B Exchange Business Models

First, credit derivatives are a major growth sector — with annual growth rates of 40–50%.

The average volume of trading done by European institutional fixed-income investors in credit derivatives nearly tripled in 2000, while the proportion of product users in the market nearly doubled. Such growth will dramatically improve the liquidity of the whole market; build a critical mass of users and force volumes up. Liquidity attracts more liquidity in the exchange business in a virtuous circle.

In a developing market, the enormous scalability of electronic trading platforms makes them uniquely qualified to absorb rapidly increasing liquidity. On-line systems can efficiently support more players and also feature more products and more credit risks.

Other drivers of growth in the credit derivatives markets are:

- the changing quality of credit and the increasing need for protection;
- the growth in regulatory hedging;
- the rise in third-party trading of distressed debt (eg, by hedge funds);
- the emergence of more commoditized products; and
- the expected resolution of documentation issues.

All these will accelerate the pace of growth.

Increased trading leads to increased costs in a conventional voice-broker model — which is not easily scaleable. Increasing costs will, therefore, also drive people towards technology-based trading solutions.

Within this process a high proportion of market practitioners believe that the credit derivatives market will continue evolving as a hybrid market. Single name "vanilla," credit default swaps will become exclusively traded on-line; more complex trades and deals with a "basket" of credits will remain the province of voice-brokers.

While at this stage in its development the market for credit derivatives still consists of a relatively small group of participants operating in a highly segmented way, in the short term, broking activity will remain dominated by telephone/voice broking relationships. However, significant technological

advances, coupled with document standardization and increasing liquidity makes exchange trading of credit derivatives inevitable long-term.

Adding services to the basic trading mechanism

CreditTrade market research identified the following key requirements platforms should develop:

- create indices/benchmarks with detailed information on risk and implied volatility;
- introduce voice recognition;
- make it easier to post trades on the site;
- update the site regularly; and
- make it quicker, cleaner and easier to use.

Not all of these can be easily incorporated into an on-line site but the list illustrates how electronic platforms are perceived as mechanisms to further the transparency of the market.

In response to market demands, CreditTrade is adding value to its on-line site by:

- making the site quick and easy to access, navigate, and use — constantly aiming to improve user experience;
- introducing customizable pages that show real-time market movements;
- including access to extensive historical data, time series prices (or benchmarks) for mark-to-market purposes and research, on a wide range of global credits, for eg, when and where it last traded, where it was last priced, and the latest news pertaining to that credit name; and
- providing hotlinks to other information suppliers.

Perceived Advantages of On-line Trading for Credit Derivatives

- Clients get a fast, flexible, scalable, and user-friendly way of doing business — combining the strengths of cutting edge technology with the personal chemistry of traditional broking.
- There is a strong belief that, in time, electronic platforms will become an effective alternative to voice broking.
- There is general agreement that on-line sites would make the market more liquid and transparent.
- Some believe that electronic platforms reflect the greater appetite from the buy-side — people searching for cheap prices. This gives impetus to the view that on-line trading will drive down margins.
- Most people believe that second-tier banks, insurance companies, and other "virgin" players will be increasingly attracted by on-line sites to access prices and monitor market interest.
- There is a fair degree of confidence that electronic platforms will handle increasing volumes of plain vanilla, credit default swaps, even though the majority believe that complex deals will remain the domain of voice brokers.
- Ability to provide in-depth color and data.
- Provision of an interactive (text and/or voice based) networking options for direct dialogue while remaining on-line.
- Can be individually tailored for specific client requirements.
- Value-added services/information feeds can be added or linked to that are unavailable through conventional voice-broking channels.
- Build in hotlinks with other information suppliers.

Source: Market Research Survey, 2001 — CreditTrade

Lessons to be Learned from the Credit Derivatives Market

Traditional voice brokered markets will take some time to adopt on-line trading, and so B2B exchanges need to "prepare for the long haul."

Securing the promise of on-line trading

One of the challenges for electronic platform growth is how to incorporate some of the intelligence that participants in voice broking enjoy. This intelligence is difficult to capture and display on-line.

The issue of whether the market is willing to pay for color, trading data and other types of information is not yet resolved. The clear demand for color and its recognised (but undefined) value, indicates that such information would be a welcome addition to electronic exchange platforms. Such information can either be provided directly by the participants in the market or be grafted on to an on-line platform from a number of external sources.

If on-line sites are to seize market share, they must add value or provide services and information feeds that are not available through conventional voice broking channels.

Adopt a hybrid model

To build liquidity and accelerate the transition to on-line trading, B2B exchanges need to adopt the "hybrid" approach. This means combining the clicks — on-line trading — with bricks — the traditional voice brokers.

B2B exchanges need to accept that not all products will be traded on-line. On-line trading is ideally suited to fungible products — like "plain vanilla credit default swaps" — but more complex products may always require some level of human intervention.

Initially, the on-line site can enhance and complement the traditional voice-brokers by providing additional information, standardized documentation, and greater transparency.

In the end, however, the credit derivatives market is an example of a market where the market participants understand that the movement towards on-line trading is inevitable.

Analyzing B2B Exchange Business Models

Chapter 8

B2B Securities Exchange Models: The Introduction of Risk Management Products such as Derivatives

"Enron notwithstanding, derivatives are in the future of many B2B exchanges."

Many B2B exchanges have started by providing simple on-line trading mechanisms for physical products such as plastics, chemicals, and metals with spot buying and on-line price catalogs. Others are already focused on trading more sophisticated financial products such as forward contracts or securitized derivative instruments. For example, CreditTrade is trading credit derivatives and ChemConnect trades forward contracts on chemical products such as benzene. The introduction of dynamic pricing and auctions by B2B exchanges has led to greater price transparency and created the conditions and elements of a full trading market similar to traditional securities and commodity markets. As they develop, many B2B exchanges will seek the appearance and operational standards typical of full securities trading exchanges.

Having multiple competing buyers and sellers leads inevitably to market volatility. Because market volatility can involve adverse price moves it substantially increases market risk.

Analyzing B2B Exchange Business Models

B2B exchanges can be considerably enhanced if the core price discovery function for cash products is supplemented by the availability of financial derivatives, which can be used to hedge exposures or arbitrage price differences in the underlying cash markets.

Many B2B exchanges will, therefore, seek to introduce financial products that allow their customers — the buyers and sellers — to manage these risks, hedge their exposures, and speculate on future prices. This will also enable them to expand their universe of participants to include players previously "unknown" to the original community of buyers and sellers of the physical products traded in the cash market. As the users of successful B2B exchanges search for new tools to effectively improve risk management strategies, the exchanges must move quickly to introduce products, such as derivatives, to meet that demand and to increase transaction volume on the exchange.

B2B exchanges that develop to the level where they can introduce these sophisticated securities products will be B2B Securities Exchanges (B2BSX).

What are Derivatives?

Derivatives can be defined as "a financial instrument, traded on or off an exchange, the price of which is directly dependent upon (ie, derived from) the value of one or more underlying securities, equity indices, debt instruments, commodities, other derivative instruments, or any agreed upon pricing index or arrangement (eg, the movement over time of the Consumer Price Index or the Dow Jones Industrial Average Index)."

Derivative transactions include futures, forwards, swaps, and options and are used primarily to transfer price risk between two parties. Originally developed for agricultural products, derivatives expanded into the financial arena with bond and equity index futures and then into metals and the energy industry. More recently, derivative products have been created to transfer many forms of risk including credit risk, weather risk, and risk based on economic variables such as inflation and unemployment rates. According to some commentators, non-agricultural futures now represent about 85% of the total market.

Derivatives involve the trading of contractual rights or obligations based on an underlying product or reference asset, but do not themselves directly transfer physical property. Rather, the derivatives contract is designed to capture the economic effects of a real transaction in the underlying product or reference asset, without having to make or take delivery of that asset.

For an excellent guide to derivatives generally, I would recommend *Derivatives: A Manager's Guide to the World's Most Powerful Instruments* by Philip McBride Johnson (McGraw-Hill).

Derivatives can be structured as private, bilateral agreements or standard term contracts. Standard term contracts are ideal for trading on a regulated, centralized exchange. Private agreements, such as forwards, swaps, and options, are more often traded in the over-the-counter (OTC) market. OTC markets are generally not regulated, or are exempted from regulation, provided that all of the market players are qualified participants (ie, sophisticated entities and individuals with a high net worth).

Private contracts have the major advantage that they can be customized to meet the precise risk transfer requirements of the two parties involved. On the other hand, private agreements are difficult to value over time and cannot easily be traded. Each party is reliant on the credit worthiness of the other party to ensure that the contract is completed. As Enron has vividly demonstrated, an apparently strong counter-party can turn out to be a hidden credit risk in the OTC market.

Standardized contracts cannot, by definition, be customized, but they can be traded — which creates a market price at any given time and enables one or other party to get out of the contract by executing a counter-trade with the original counter-party or with a third party (called "offset"). Where a standardized instrument is traded on a regulated commodity exchange there will usually be a central clearing system, which acts as a central counter-party and guarantees the performance of every contract (therefore reducing counter-party risk).

Why B2B Exchanges are Introducing Derivatives

Derivatives serve the same functions in B2B exchanges as they do in the established commodities markets. Derivatives are traditionally used to hedge risk or to exchange a floating rate of return for a fixed rate of return.

As we saw in Chapter 4, by integrating derivatives transactions with an on-line marketplace, B2B exchanges will help build liquidity and enhance the overall value proposition of the exchange.

While e-procurement systems today offer buyers the ability to purchase goods based on current prices, derivative transactions enable users to set contracts for purchases based on prices projected into the future. Derivative transactions, therefore, offer B2B exchange users the ability to control the price risk of adverse future price swings and market fluctuations.

For example, in most companies the procurement activities are closely co-ordinated with the manufacturing schedules. Take a fictitious company, Metal Co. Inc., which makes rolled steel. As a manufacturer of steel it uses a significant quantity of coal to power the furnaces. The procurement manager's primary task is to purchase the coal supplies as they are needed to meet production requirements. Metal Co.'s treasury department will buy and sell coal derivatives to manage the price exposure of the company to fluctuating coal prices.

As B2B exchanges develop new e-marketplaces and displace traditional procurement systems, treasury departments and risk managers will manage price exposure of critical production inputs through associated derivatives, as they do today in respect of basic raw materials through commodity exchanges.

For example, ChemConnect already offers "paper trades" on certain aromatic products such as benzene. Because some ChemConnect users are locked into long-term contracts on products with price volatility, such as benzene, they are constantly seeking ways to limit the exposure created by holding physical inventories or having cargoes in transit. ChemConnect provides paper trades on its Commodity Exchange which do not require the delivery of physical product and are linked to the average price in a particular month, based on a standard reference point (eg, Platt's reported average price for benzene in the month of August). Members can buy on the spot market at the best price available, and can hedge their physical position through a paper trade. ChemConnect reports that the paper market can be 2–4 times the size of the physical market. In addition, ChemConnect has a partnership with the Chicago Mercantile Exchange through which it offers its users the ability to trade futures contracts on benzene and xylene products.

An enabling aspect of derivatives is that they rarely result in an actual delivery of the underlying commodity. Therefore, risk managers can manage price exposure without concern that they will be required to deliver the underlying asset.

The enormous trading volumes for financial derivatives demonstrates the value of derivatives: the dollar volume of financial derivatives transactions is many times that of the underlying cash markets. In mature commodity and financial markets, the dollar volume of these derivatives transactions is five to 10 times that of the underlying cash market. On the Chicago Board of Trade, it is generally the case that less than 5% of all derivatives trades actually result in a physical movement of goods to settle the transaction.

Size of the derivatives market

Record trading levels in 2001 at several of the largest futures exchanges — including CME, LIFFE, and Eurex — led to a huge rise of 57.4% in global trading volume for derivatives over year 2000 figures. The Futures Industry Association (www.futuresindustry.org) has released world futures and options volume figures for January–December 2001 which show total world trading on futures and options exchanges at 3,183.3 million contracts (excluding options on individual equities).

The total volume on global exchanges surged thanks to a substantial increase in trading of financial futures. The FIA's figures show that financials surged 75.3% globally in 2001, rising from 1,568.8 to 2,749.8 million contracts traded. Trading of equity indices jumped 117.9%, up to 1,470.3 from 674.8 million contracts, while interest rate contracts gained 44%, rising from 844.3 million to 1,216 million. Non-financial contracts, however, experienced a 4.5% decline to 433.5 million from 453.6 million. Agricultural and metal trading dropped 15.7% and 2.3% respectively, while energy trading rose 7.8%.

See Figure 8A over the page: Size of the Derivatives Market.

Introducing Derivatives on B2B Exchanges

First and second generation B2B exchanges have mainly provided trading mechanisms for products that are required to be delivered immediately, or as soon as practicable after the trade is made — the so called "spot market."

It is a natural progression for spot markets to evolve into transactions with future delivery dates. These can take the form of forward contracts or other derivatives such as swaps or futures. Third generation B2B exchanges are well positioned to host such derivatives trading and to be the issuer of certain types of derivative contracts.

If a B2B exchange introduces derivatives it enables the existing buyers and sellers to directly integrate their daily business activity with risk management instruments in one centralized location.

Using futures contracts and other risk management tools as part of their automated purchasing processes allows market participants to mitigate the

Figure 8A: Size of the Derivatives Market

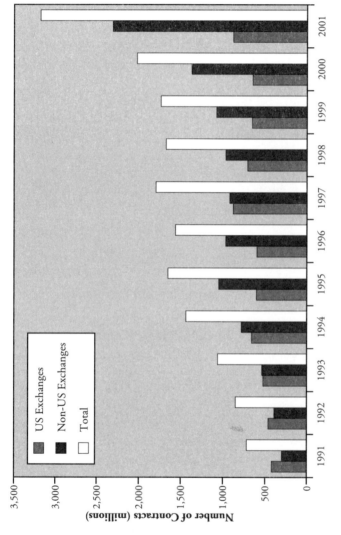

Volume on futures, options on futures, and options on securities indexes and foreign currencies (excluding options on individual equities)

Source: Futures Industry Association

risk of future purchases. For example, procurement networks today offer buyers the ability to purchase goods based on current prices, while derivatives transactions enable users to set or float prices to lock in future purchases. In essence, derivatives transactions offer B2B exchange users the ability to control the price risk of adverse future price swings, as well as the variability of critical market factors.

If the B2B exchange introduces standardized derivatives contracts, then the contract terms (or "specifications") will be designed by the exchange's product design experts. The exchange may design and calculate its own underlying reference asset (eg, an index based on the cash prices paid for a good or service that is traded in the exchange's own spot market), or license a reference asset from another party (eg, an index published by Dow Jones or a reference price for a commodity published by a third party like Platts). The exchange provides a market for those contracts on its electronic trading platform. A derivatives contract is created every time a buyer and a seller make a trade together on the market. The overall number of contracts in existence (the total "open interest") fluctuates as new contracts are created (increasing the open interest) or as new contracts offset existing contract positions (reducing the open interest).

Electronic trading platforms facilitate the design and low-cost distribution of new, innovative, and flexible derivatives products that regulated, bricks and mortar exchanges cannot support because of their fixed infrastructure costs and technological limitations. A B2B exchange can introduce derivatives products that are specifically customized for its users' risk exposures and business needs.

For example, in November 2001 BrokerTec — a leading B2B exchange for trading US Treasuries and Euro sovereign bonds — expanded its mission to modernize and innovate the fixed income marketplace by launching BrokerTec Futures Exchange (BTEX). BrokerTec aims to replicate the advantages of its cash and repo markets — low cost, liquidity, transparency, and straight through processing — in the futures market for fixed income products. Since the launch, BTEX has fostered steady growth and liquidity in US Treasury futures, including: US Treasury Bonds (30 year), US Treasury Notes (10 year) and US Treasury Notes (five year). Other US interest rate futures and options will soon follow.

However, the processes required to manage forward trading grows dramatically in complexity when compared with spot trading. Trading derivatives requires three key facilities, which are lacking in virtually all B2B exchanges today:

- sophisticated order matching technologies and trading systems — providing optimized outcomes for participants;
- a clearinghouse and central counter-party — to address concerns about counter-party credit risk by guaranteeing trades (see Chapter 11); and
- some measure of regulatory oversight — as a pro-active measure to allay fears of inappropriate price action and market manipulation.

Electronic trading systems for derivatives

The trading system must become much more sophisticated to deal with the automated matching of competing bids and offers, and the clearing and settlement system must be exponentially more complex. The system must also be capable of handling a much larger volume of transactions than the spot market.

Like other securities, the derivatives contracts are fungible and require continuous auto-execution. The electronic trading system must, therefore, support a central limit order book with flexible ranking rules. The system must support integrated multi-leg combinations (strategies) in the order book, thus providing the ability to trade standard combination orders and spreads (eg, butterfly spreads). The best systems also enable users to create customized baskets and spreads and options or futures on them for pre-defined and ad hoc strategy trading.

The system must provide parameter driven product design so that new products can be designed on-line by the exchange's officials. Good systems have open APIs for integration of third-party trading and back-office applications.

Clearinghouse and central counter-party

A critical component of any market that seeks to expand its community of participants and facilitates automated and anonymous trading of derivatives is an efficient clearing system that offers a central counter-party (CCP) guarantee (see Chapter 11).

Derivatives contracts are designed by the B2B exchange to capture the economic effects of a real transaction in the underlying product or reference asset, without the buyer or seller having to make or take delivery of that asset. Unlike goods and services, therefore, derivative securities do not usually result in a physical delivery of any goods or services. Instead, most derivatives are "cash settled." This means that the derivative contract is settled at maturity (or before maturity at close out) by a closing cash payment from one party to the other party, based upon the change in the market value of the underlying product or reference asset.

In the options and futures market, listed options with the same strike prices and expiration dates, and futures contracts for the same asset and delivery month, are fungible as the contracts have standard specifications. By virtue of this fungibility, it is possible for buyers and sellers to close out, or "offset," their positions by buying or selling equal but opposite offsetting transactions. In the same way on a B2B exchange, even if the contract calls for delivery of a specified amount of the underlying reference asset at a specified date in the future (eg, a forward contract), because the contract can be traded on the B2B exchange, either party can get out of the contract by executing a counter-trade with the original counter-party or with a third party . As with a closing payment, an offset is settled in cash.

Clearinghouse functions

A clearinghouse for B2B exchange-traded derivatives fulfills the following functions:

- acts as the issuer of the exchange's derivative contracts;
- confirms all matched derivatives trades at the end of each trading session;
- keeps a complete record of all derivatives trades;
- acts as a central counter-party to all derivatives trades made on the exchange;
- provides a central guarantee for all derivatives trades made on the exchange; and
- makes closing cash payments to settle derivatives contracts at the end of the contract.

Central counter-party

To be successful in derivatives a B2B exchange must introduce a CCP because as forward delivery dates move out into the future, it becomes more difficult to sustain bilateral credit risk arrangements and any bilateral credit lines between the trading counter-parties are rapidly used up.

The CCP provides stability to the marketplace by assuming the cash settlement obligations of a defaulting member towards other members. A CCP ensures the integrity and stability of the derivatives market through its guarantee. To ensure its ability to fulfill its obligations under this guarantee, the CCP must maintain a rigorous credit risk management process.

All derivatives exchanges set minimum margin requirements for brokers. The initial margin requirement is for the broker to deposit an amount into an account before trading for that account. The initial margin is used to absorb subsequent losses that may arise from trading in that account. The initial margin requirements should be designed to provide the CCP with sufficient resources, based on industry-accepted margin methodologies, to ensure an orderly liquidation of each member's positions in the event that a default occurs and liquidation becomes necessary. The main industry standard margin methodologies are TIMS, first developed by the Options Clearing Corporation and SPANS, developed by the Chicago Mercantile Exchange.

If trading losses reduce the initial margin below a level set by the exchange, the broker must deposit additional or "maintenance" margin to top up the account.

The role of the clearinghouse is to monitor each account's positions and calculate the projected losses on at least a daily basis. The clearinghouse can then make margin calls for the maintenance margin on an intra-day basis. The margin system must be able to project a liquidating value for each account, based on multiple projected market moves. The difference between the current market value and the worst projected liquidation value represents the market risk of the portfolio. Maintenance margin represents the difference between a position's current market value and the projected worst liquidating value. Maintenance margin protects the clearinghouse to the extent that it is only exposed to the change in value of positions since the previous day.

In addition, fully electronic B2B clearinghouses can monitor price changes from the B2B's e-marketplace in real-time and require a trader to post additional intra-day margin during periods of increased market volatility. Such additional margin must be deposited within a short period (say one hour) of the time the trader is notified of the requirement.

The B2B exchange's rules must require that the broker is responsible for all losses in its accounts. This means that the broker will pass margin calls straight on to its clients and retains the legal right to close out open positions in an account if the margin call is not met in time. In order to ensure that brokers can normally meet this financial responsibility, the B2B exchange should require brokers who are clearing members to maintain a sensible level of net capital in the business at all times (a capital adequacy standard) and monitor the financial strength of traders on a day-to-day basis.

In summary, the CCP's credit risk management process must include:

- a requirement for clearing members to be approved for membership, so that the clearinghouse can perform an initial evaluation of the creditworthiness of each member;

- maintain well-defined capital adequacy standards as a requirement of membership;
- settlement of all trades and mark-to-market of all positions on a daily basis;
- a requirement for members to deposit initial margin to cover the projected risks associated with their derivative positions;
- a requirement for members to post additional intra-day margin during periods of increased market volatility;
- monitoring the financial strength of traders by subjecting the portfolios of each member to daily stress tests and requiring a member who fails to meet established criteria to deposit additional stress margin;
- a requirement for each member to contribute to a clearing fund: the fund is a shared obligation of all members, and provides coverage for residual risks (eg, the risk that market conditions may prevent an orderly liquidation of a defaulting member's positions within the timeframe contemplated in the calculation of margin requirements);
- default procedures to ensure that a member's obligations are satisfied in the unlikely event of a member default;
- processing of all cash settlements through an irrevocable electronic payment processing system;
- maintaining a standby credit facility with a designated clearing bank to ensure immediate access to liquid funds to make settlement payments; and
- catastrophe risk insurance to cover the unlikely risk that the capital requirements for clearing members, the margin held by the clearinghouse and the clearing fund all prove inadequate in the event of a catastrophic market melt down.

Risk-based portfolio margining systems that can do all of these things are obviously very complex and sophisticated products.

Regulatory Issues

B2B exchanges still face significant regulatory barriers when introducing derivatives. Until 2000, the US Commodity Futures Trading Commission's (CFTC's) requirements effectively prohibited any electronic system that was not a regulated board of trade from allowing trades to be "closed out" or offset before delivery. In other words, all forward trades made on a B2B exchange had to be satisfied with a physical delivery.

Analyzing B2B Exchange Business Models

This limitation impeded the usefulness of B2B exchanges because traders knew they could not change their position once an order was executed. This requirement, therefore, limited participants' ability to effectively manage their procurement and trading needs because they were limited in their ability to modify or reverse transactions.

On the other hand, privately negotiated OTC derivatives never had the same regulatory restrictions as futures. However, for a party to modify or reverse an OTC transaction, it must renegotiate the contract with the other party, which is not always possible. In addition, OTC trading is based on bilateral credit agreements that can rapidly consume market participants' credit lines. If a B2B exchange relies on this bilateral credit line structure, it constrains the number of market participants that will be eligible counter-parties to any given transaction and thereby restricts the growth of the market.

Some B2B markets were able to obtain exemption from the need for CFTC registration in the US on the basis that their products had low volumes and were mainly traded by industry players — eg, the oil and natural gas forward contracts markets.

Regulatory changes in the US made in December 2000 — by the Commodity Futures Modernization Act (the US Modernization Act) — now mean that qualified participants can trade in futures contracts through their established B2B supply chain channels and exchanges in real-time. The US Modernization Act was passed, in part, to streamline and eliminate unnecessary regulation of commodity futures exchanges and derivative products regulated under the Commodity Exchange Act. The new Act provides for electronic trading facilities to be set up under an exemption from the requirement to be registered as an organized market (ie, a full commodity exchange like the Chicago Board of Trade). The exclusion provided by the Act is for transactions in excluded commodities (essentially non-agricultural products) that are conducted on an electronic trading facility between eligible contract participants trading on a principal-to-principal basis. The principal-to-principal requirement reflects the way institutional OTC trading has developed in derivatives and other markets, such as foreign exchange, and now permits financial institutions and high net worth individuals to trade derivatives with each other through electronic systems.

The benefits of self-regulatory oversight

Where a B2B exchange becomes dominant in a market place and starts to introduce financial products for hedging, risk management, and speculative activities, public pressure may arise for regulation of the operations of that market place. This is particularly likely in the wake of the fallout from the collapse of Enron.

Following the Enron scandal, some US lawmakers are already calling for the deregulation of energy derivatives trading set out in the US Modernization Act, to be reversed — even though the CFTC has publicly stated that it does not need any additional regulatory authority due to Enron's collapse.

Securities and commodity futures markets worldwide have been a classic example of such calls for regulation in the past. B2B exchanges which take proactive steps to operate in a proper self-regulatory environment and provide oversight of their members, in the manner recognized by regulators such as the SEC, CFTC, and European Commission will better avoid calls for legislation to regulate and license their activities as organized markets once they become dominant in their industry.

Even if a B2B exchange can operate its derivatives trading within an existing exemption from regulatory oversight, the exchange should ensure that the features and facilities provided by the exchange's systems and the use of the technology provided by the exchange at least meet the "Principles for the Oversight of Screen-Based Trading Systems for Derivative Products" developed by the Technical Committee of the International Organization of Securities Commissions (www.iosco.org).

The Sweet Spot for B2B Securities Exchanges (B2BSX)

Cash products that can be traded in a simple spot market are usually unregulated. On the other hand, the more sophisticated derivative products require a very sophisticated trading mechanism and will usually fall within the definition of a "security" or "commodities contract" and, therefore, are regulated as securities, unless an exemption is available.

This relationship can be depicted in a matrix as illustrated in Figure 8B over the page. A B2BSX is an exchange that supports the continuous, auto-executed trading of sophisticated derivatives contracts and which meets the highest regulatory standards.

Figure 8B: B2BSX Sweet Spot

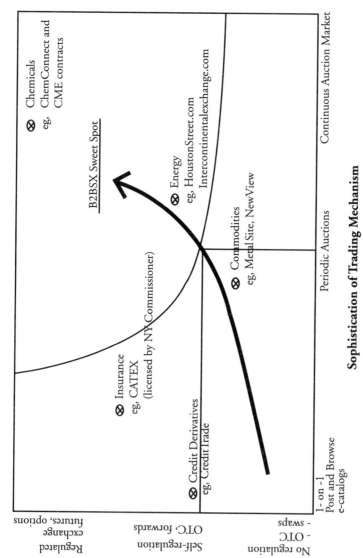

Source: *Author*

Time to Market

Different markets are at different stages and will be able to introduce derivatives at different rates, as illustrated in Figure 8C.

Figure 8C: Adoption of Derivatives

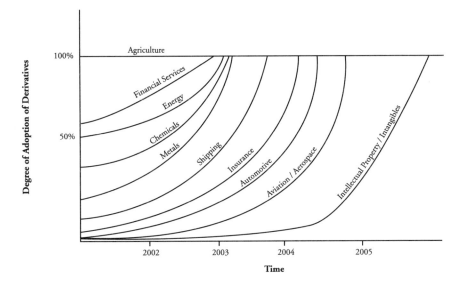

Source: Author

Markets that already support derivatives are financial services, energy (natural gas, coal, oil) power (electricity), freight (shipping), telecommunications bandwidth, credit risk, non-ferrous metals (eg, copper, tin, aluminum), some chemical products, and weather risk.

Markets that are only just moving towards derivatives include insurance, ferrous metals (steel), plastics and petrochemicals, pulp and paper, palm oil, aviation, automotive manufacturers, and intellectual property/intangibles.

For example, it was only in late 2000 that EnronOnline started to offer financial swap contracts in respect of commercial grade steel products to help companies mitigate price risks without altering their physical operations. In addition, Enron started to develop a transparent spot market and a liquid forward market for base, commodity grades of steel.

Analyzing B2B Exchange Business Models

The Structure of a B2B Securities Exchange

The ideal structure for a B2BSX that offers derivative securities is set out in Figure 8D.

Figure 8D: Structure of a B2BSX

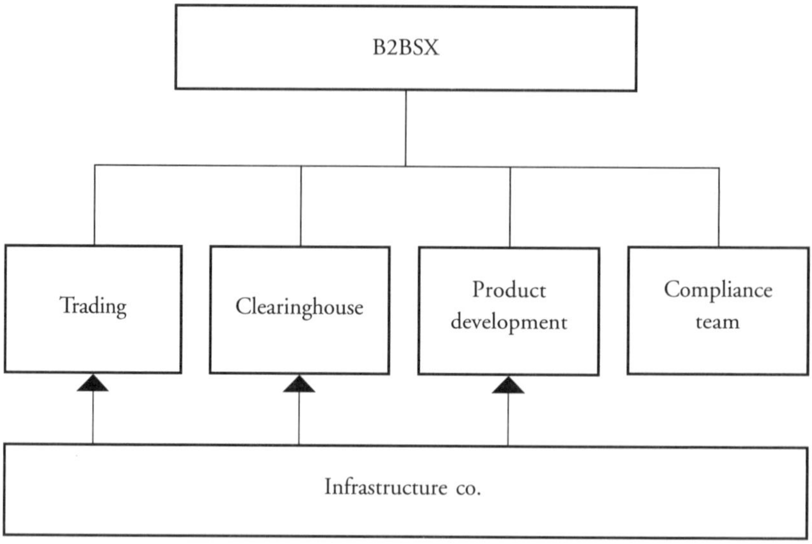

Source: Author

A separate technology company provides the trading system, the clearing system, the risk management modules, and the information dissemination systems. This company can also license the technology to other, non-competitive exchanges and develop back-office systems for trading members to expand the exchange's revenue sources.

A separate product development group is responsible for developing contracts that can be traded on the exchange and that are specifically customized for its users' special risk exposures and business needs. This may involve licensing third-party indices or other benchmarks.

System Challenges When Introducing Derivatives

Few B2B exchanges have the expertise or resources to redesign their processes for efficient forward trading. Even those that have the expertise face significant systems implementation challenges that may restrict them from expanding into large scale derivatives trading in the near term.

Build your own

One option is for the exchange to build its own trading and clearing system. The cost is likely to be around $5–10 million and the project will take at least 18 months.

License an existing system

An alternative is to license an existing, proven system. One advantage is that development costs of the system have been amortized over many clients and those other clients form invaluable reference sites for the exchange to approach. The licensing exchange can also benefit from upgrades made for other clients. The main disadvantage of existing systems is that competitors can usually get hold of the same system from the vendor. The main vendors in this space are: EFA Software (www.efasoftware.com), ePIT software (www.epit.com), OnExchange (www.onexchange.com), and OM AB's CLICK trading system (www.om.com).

Partner with an existing derivatives exchange

An alternative approach is to partner with a separate exchange that provides the derivatives trading and clearing capabilities. This may be one of the major commodity exchanges or one of a small group of new players that offer to act on an outsourced basis — or effectively as Exchange Systems Providers (ESPs).

One potential disadvantage of this approach is that the derivatives exchange (or ESP) may choose to work with competing markets or products. Another issue is customer retention. If the derivatives trading is done on another system that is not linked to the spot market on the B2B exchange, then the B2B exchange will not be providing a tightly integrated value proposition.

Analyzing B2B Exchange Business Models

Case study: CheMatch and the Chicago Mercantile Exchange

In October 2001, the Chicago Mercantile Exchange Inc. (CME) and CheMatch (now merged into ChemConnect) launched a CME-CheMatch benzene futures contract and a mixed xylenes futures contract. These contracts were the first futures to be traded on a futures exchange with an electronic link to a B2B exchange. They are also the first futures on chemical products in the US.

Each CME-CheMatch futures contract on benzene or mixed xylenes represents 42,000 gallons of the chemical and is cash settled at contract expiration to an index of monthly contract prices compiled and calculated by DeWitt & Company, a Houston-based international petrochemical consulting firm. Contracts are quoted in US dollars per gallon, with a minimum price increment (tick size) of $0.001 per gallon valued at $42 per contract.

The contracts are traded on the CME's GLOBEX 2 electronic trading system from 8:30a.m. to 2:15p.m. (Central Time), Monday-Friday. Contracts are offered in all 12 calendar months, with six consecutive months listed for trading at all times. Members of CheMatch are able to enter trades on GLOBEX 2 through the B2B exchange's website (now at www.chemconnect.com). The new products trade exclusively on GLOBEX 2 and clear with CME clearing firms through the CME's clearing system.

This deal enables ChemConnect's members to trade both physical and derivative chemical products through one website, to manage price volatility, and receive a better return on their capital.

Other exchange services providers (ESPs)

OnExchange, Inc. (www.onexchange.com) provides comprehensive derivatives exchange and clearinghouse capabilities to regulated and OTC marketplaces. OnExchange also provides regulatory expertise, product design, marketing, and professional services to its partner marketplaces. In addition to its technology solutions, OnExchange operates a US CFTC-designated futures exchange and clearinghouse.

OnExchange was the first new exchange to be approved under the US Modernization Act of 2000. By partnering with OnExchange, B2B exchanges are able to offer integrated access to regulated futures as well as spot, forwards, and swaps instruments on a single, straight through processing platform, and gain competitive advantages in terms of credit management, financial and market integrity, liquidity, and price transparency.

Outside of the US, the Bermuda Stock Exchange (www.bsx.com) offers similar capabilities.

EnronOnline

Enron realized early the trading opportunities that were raised by the deregulation of commodities markets.

EnronOnline, Enron Corporation's on-line trading system, provided an Internet-based trading platform for about 1,800 contracts on products ranging from pulp to weather derivatives to electricity. The "notional" value of all contracts traded by Enron from November 1999 to November 2001 was over $1 trillion. Enron stated in November 2001 that EnronOnline then handled about 60% of its trading business, or about $2.8 billion a day.

Enron was very successful in transforming the natural gas and power markets. At its height, EnronOnline was reported as representing 25% of the gas and power trading market. Enron helped define product standards and contracts, developed a comprehensive physical distribution system and became a premier market-maker in these markets. Enron's market-making capabilities and EnronOnline's trading platform resulted in increased market liquidity and protection for customers from volatile commodity prices in those markets. Based on its success in those markets, Enron sought to expand its influence and expertise into trading freight (shipping), telecommunications bandwidth, credit risk, steel, metals, pulp and paper, plastics and petrochemicals, and weather risk.

However, EnronOnline was not like a traditional exchange that brings together competing bid and ask offers from multiple parties. Rather, EnronOnline was a billboard for Enron to publicize its own bid and ask offers to the market.

In other words, every third party that traded through EnronOnline was trading with Enron as its counter-party. These are known as bilateral trades since they are made directly between two parties and not through multiple competing orders from different parties. There was no central counter-party in the middle of trades made on EnronOnline (see Chapter 11).

This structure enabled EnronOnline to avoid any form of regulation by the CFTC. As we have seen, the US Modernization Act enabled electronic trading facilities to be set up just by notification and reporting to the CFTC, but with an exemption from being regulated as an organized market. In addition, the US Modernization Act provides that the term "trading facility" does not include

Analyzing B2B Exchange Business Models

"an electronic facility or system that enables participants to negotiate the terms of, and enter into, bilateral transactions, as a result of communications exchanged by the parties and not from interaction of multiple bids and multiple offers within a predetermined, non-discretionary automated trade matching and execution algorithm." This so called "Enron exemption" ensured that EnronOnline did not require the approval of the CFTC.

Enron began to unravel in October 2001 after it said shareholders' equity was reduced by $1.2 billion and it had to restate its earnings for the last five years. The accounting adjustments became necessary because of the way in which the company had previously accounted for outside partnerships it created — in which it had concealed losses or debts not shown on the balance sheet of Enron. The subsequent filing for bankruptcy prompted lawsuits and numerous investigations, including a probe by the SEC.

As its shares plunged, Enron faced a cash crunch because lenders and some trading partners lost confidence that the company would have the cash to pay bills. Trading partners either demanded more collateral to trade, or restricted trading altogether, with the Houston-based company.

In other words, the market lost all confidence in Enron as the sole counter-party for trades made on EnronOnline.

EnronOnline stopped allowing trades and quit posting bids and offers on-line around 28 November 2001. It was Enron's perceived credit worthiness and trading acumen that drove the trading business up. And it was Enron's total loss of credit worthiness that brought the trading business crashing down.

It subsequently came to light that Enron had invested and lost over $600 million in its bandwidth trading ventures because it had purchased massive amounts of bandwidth capacity itself, in order to ensure that it could never be squeezed by short selling of bandwidth.

In January 2002, a US bankruptcy judge approved the sale of the Enron trading business to UBS Warburg after UBS won a bidding war for the business. The sale and purchase agreement entitles Enron to a third of the profits of a new trading entity, UBSWenergy (www.ubswenergy.com), to be run by UBS. Under the terms of the deal, UBS hired about 630 Enron traders and support staff, and acquired Enron's proprietary trading software and office space.

Enron's chief witness, Steven Zelin, a senior managing director with the Blackstone Group, stated that Enron stood to make "substantially less than $50 million" by liquidating the trading business.

The trading unit was responsible for 90% of Enron's $101 billion revenue in 2001, and was formerly Enron's largest and most profitable division. This is because most of the trading entity's value is tied up in its traders, who were free to leave after 1 March 2002, when their retention clauses expired. According to Zelin, that only left the software, which could be re-licensed for about $25 million, and a limited amount of furniture and fixtures.

UBSWenergy seeks to combine the trading acumen of the former trading powerhouse with UBS' AAA credit rating and thereby regain its prior market dominance. This remains to be seen as, post-Enron, trading in the energy markets has been slow .

See the lessons that B2B exchanges can learn from the fact patterns in EnronOnline's case, over the page.

Lessons for B2B Exchanges from EnronOnline's Collapse

Fact Pattern	Lesson
EnronOnline was exempted from regulation as a Board of Trade or even registration with the CFTC as an "electronic trading facility."	More regulation of bilateral electronic trading platforms may be forthcoming in the US and elsewhere. Some US Democrats are already proposing new legislation to roll back the US Modernization Act 2000 so as to have the CFTC regulate all trading of energy futures.
EnronOnline traded forwards, swaps, and other derivatives in non-agricultural commodities.	More regulation of non-agricultural products (currently called exempted commodities in the US) is probably coming.
The rapid collapse of EnronOnline and its low liquidation value illustrates that the main asset of a proprietary trading business is its voice brokers/traders.	Hybrid markets that provide voice brokers must focus on ways to retain key traders as much as on ways to develop their trading technologies.
Lack of an independent central counter-party for trades made on EnronOnline ultimately caused the demise of the system after its parent company lost its credit-worthiness.	See Chapter 11 on why a central counter-party is so important to the integrity of a market.

Part III:

Infrastructure Issues for B2B Exchanges

Chapter 9

Integrating a B2B Exchange with an Enterprise's Internal Applications

"B2B exchanges are the perfect 'Babel fish' communication hubs through which to connect federated e-business applications and web services in a loosely coupled environment."

Companies are increasingly managing their business across an array of networks: extranets, B2B exchanges, intranets, private networks, and the public Internet. The Internet offers an unrivaled vehicle for information exchange. But despite its promise of increased collaboration, lower transaction costs, increased revenues, and mass customization, e-business also raises a completely new set of technology issues and has actually added to the complexity of doing business.

In addition, to realize the full benefits of e-business, it is critical that a seamless flow of information is achieved, not only internally within a company's systems, but also between a company's customers, its suppliers, and all the parties associated with a transaction. For this to be achieved, all the parties involved must be included in the information flow, which requires the sharing of information and the sharing of the underlying networks conveying that information.

In today's network-based e-business environment B2B exchanges cannot be islands on the Internet.

Infrastructure Issues for B2B Exchanges

Unfortunately, many B2B exchanges are still just that — islands that are isolated from the infrastructure of the companies that use them. They host functionality and information that in many cases is also needed within the user's secure applications ("across the firewall") and need to be integrated into the user's internal systems.

Achieving integration is one of the biggest challenges facing B2B exchanges. Over the next two years, B2B exchanges will struggle with systems integration and e-business communication as their users replace existing business processes with networked alternatives. It is the complexity of the technology issues raised by integration that has prevented many B2B exchanges from delivering on their promise and achieving their full potential so far. In many cases, B2B exchanges have failed because they ran out of cash before they could achieve their true value proposition of fully integrating with users' internal systems.

However, open access to, and the ubiquitous nature of, the Internet will ultimately address this issue and provide the optimal framework for integrating B2B exchanges with internal enterprise systems.

EAI versus B2B Integration

Enterprise Application Integration (EAI) is the process of getting all internal applications of an enterprise to talk to each other (eg, ERP, CRM, accounting etc.). Currently, these applications are deployed across various enterprise systems, using differing databases, repositories, and legacy applications. The challenge in EAI is to integrate these "vertical silos" of activity and information.

B2B integration, on the other hand, is about getting an enterprise's internal applications to talk across the firewall, to the outside systems of customers, suppliers and web service providers. Instead of a monolithic interface to applications, applications have to become service-oriented, whereby existing application functionality can be leveraged and exposed to outside applications over the Web, using standard interfaces.

EAI and B2B integration are therefore fundamentally different in approach and objective.

B2B integration is focused on handling transactions between businesses, which mainly comprises handling documents like purchase orders, invoices, requests for quotes, requests for proposals, etc. Where a B2B exchange sits in the middle, it must be able to accept these documents and immediately transmit them onto other users in a usable form. This may involve a multitude of unconnected systems such as purchase order creation, inventory control, production management, ERP, invoicing, shipping, and financial accounting. Many of these back-end systems may be legacy systems such as mainframe applications. When that integration is missing or weak it creates problems. Functionality overlaps, information has to be retyped or recaptured, separate databases can get "out of sync," and document version control is lost.

The document-centric processes for B2B exchanges therefore include:

- connectivity across corporate firewalls and with various message storage and delivery architectures;
- the management of various communication channels, with varying levels of efficiency and reliability;
- validation and transformation of a document into one or more back-end systems;
- processing rules that determine which users receive a document or where a document arrived from and how it should be processed;
- interfaces into back-end applications or into an EAI backbone; and
- security information, including using digital certificates for authentication and encryption.

Companies now face the choice of either establishing multiple bilateral links with each outside party that they need to integrate with, or establishing one link to a B2B exchange that sets the communications standards and enables users' applications to talk to each other.

B2B exchanges therefore play a critical role as the communication hubs through which suppliers, customers, trading partners, and web-based services providers can connect their systems.

This hub-and-spoke concept enables the numerous communications protocols to be "translated," so that different systems can talk to each other and avoids the need for companies to establish a large number of bilateral links to all other partners. It also enables a single sign-on to all the systems connected through the B2B exchange.

Some people claim that, after EAI, business process integration is the "promised land." Many independent software vendors claim the ability to directly integrate an organization's business processes with its suppliers, customers and other trading partners. But that is an elusive dream, for the simple reason that many companies are unwilling or unable to support business process integration. With the exception of organizations like Wal-Mart and General Motors, both industry giants, companies will not be able to force data standards onto their trading partners. The only practical solution is to connect through a central hub — a B2B exchange.

The Tower of e-Babel

There are five main specifications gaining importance as the concept of program-to-program integration develops. These are eXtensible Markup Language (XML); Simple Object Access Protocol (SOAP); Web Services Description Language (WSDL); eXtensible Stylesheet Language Transformations (XSLT) — a language to specify how to transform an XML document of one type to another document type — and Universal Discovery, Description and Integration (UDDI).

To understand how these protocols work together, imagine the computer-to-computer conversation as an ordinary phone call. In a web-based application, XML represents the conversation, SOAP describes the rules for how to call someone, and UDDI is the phone book which acts as a directory of services available. WSDL describes what the phone call is about and how you can participate. XSLT lets you convert the voice conversation into, say, a fax transmission.

As I described in Chapter 2, the complexity involved in implementing these new standards creates an enormous opportunity for B2B exchanges to act as the "Babel fish" communications hubs that translate and map information between all the different parties.

EDI

Electronic Data Interchange (EDI) has been used by businesses for more than 30 years as a mode of communication with trading and fulfillment partners. EDI was originally proposed as the solution to achieve full integration, but implementation of EDI among all but the largest organizations has been disappointing.

For example, only an estimated 200,000–300,000 trading partners worldwide use EDI today. This compares with the millions of businesses that have been waiting for a lower-cost EDI alternative. EDI's weak adoption has been due to its rigid nature, high cost, and difficult implementation. More recently, XML has been used for new applications due to its low cost, flexibility, and enhanced functionality.

Integration with an Enterprise's Internal Applications

XML is a core enabling technology for B2B exchanges. The inherent cost advantages of web-based integration versus EDI will bring about rapid market penetration in the coming years.

The automotive industry is often held out as the best example of an early adopter of industry-wide standardized document exchange via EDI. Contrary to perception, EDI was only utilized between the automotive manufacturers and their Tier One or largest suppliers. EDI was too costly and complex for small- and medium-sized suppliers (Tiers 2 and 3).

However, despite its shortcomings, EDI will remain a business communication vehicle that many companies will need to support. The important point is that companies have significant investments in EDI and will need independent software vendors to support that investment. It is naïve to believe organizations or value chain partners are going to rip out EDI systems. These systems represent multi-million dollar investments in time, resources, and effort, but more importantly, they work. For those organizations that have already made the investment in EDI and a value-added network (VAN) infrastructure, EDI still represents the lowest cost, secure transaction processing infrastructure.

GE Global Exchange Services (GXS), the largest independent EDI VAN operator, reports that its EDI business experienced 5% growth in 2001 and is still growing in 2002. GE GXS connects over 100,000 trading partners and handles about 1 billion transactions worldwide, with a total value of over $1 trillion.

According to eMarketer[1], EDI networks will probably be with us for another 10–15 years. However, all the main providers of EDI services are now also offering Internet-based networks and EDI/XML translation services. For example, GE GXS also builds private exchanges networks and recently announced that it had connected up about 5,000 of DaimlerChrysler's suppliers through its Internet-based network.

The Internet and XML — the solution?

Internet-based networks are now able to connect trading partners at considerably lower cost than EDI networks. Small and medium size companies, who could not afford the major services work of EDI or application integration, can now participate in the network economy.

Internet-based B2B e-business will increasingly grow, therefore, at the expense of EDI.

Infrastructure Issues for B2B Exchanges

Although GE GXS's business is still growing, its future growth is tied to building Internet-based networks and using pure XML. In that area, GE GXS will face intense competition from the large B2B exchanges. Facing that prospect, GE decided in June 2002 to sell GXS to Fransisco Partners, a large technology buyout fund.

While the Internet does provide a low cost communication channel, the document standards that need to be supported are complex and daunting.

XML is a technology that enables businesses to exchange structured information. It has been highly touted as the e-business communication and integration panacea. XML, being a text-based language, travels over the same Internet communications channels as traditional web browser traffic.

However, XML is not a platform, it is a standard and it does not provide one universal standard for building and exchanging documents, it only provides a blueprint. The XML standard has been established by the World Wide Web Consortium, known as the W3C. The current standard, 1.0 was approved in February 1998. So far, the efforts of developers to use XML have fragmented some of the data definitions and tagging so that XML, while promising a great deal, is still very much in its infancy.

There is a common saying "The wonderful thing about standards is that there are so many to choose from." And XML could fall into this trap. If 20 companies use XML to build a purchase order for their business, then 20 different XML-based purchase orders will emerge, reflecting the individual needs of the respective businesses. This is similar to what has happened with the Society for Worldwide Interbank Financial Telecommunications (SWIFT) in the financial services area. As SWIFT expanded beyond its core banking message sets (ISO 15022) it has had to develop new message series to deal with the individual requirements of stock broking (buy and sell orders) and mutual funds (subscriptions and redemptions).

XML is fragmenting across four groups:

- Standard bodies: The W3C — which developed the XML 1.0 standard, the Open Application Group (OAG), and the XML/EDI organization are three of the open standards bodies each defining XML document type definitions and schemas.

- Application vendors: Microsoft's major initiative is BizTalk, SAP is developing XSF, an XML document exchange standard, Commerce One and Ariba have developed their own XML schemas, xCBL and CXML, respectively.

- Industry consortia: RosettaNet is the defacto XML standard in the information technology and electronic component sector. Electronic business XML (ebXML), sponsored by UN/CEFACT and OASIS, is gaining acceptance in the global retail sector and automotive industry, and the chemical industry has established the Chemical Industry Data Exchange (CIDX) standard. In the financial services environment there are already 18 different emerging standards and in the insurance area an industry group called ACORD (www.acord.org) is working to set standards.

- Large companies: Major companies, like Wal-Mart and General Motors, who can force XML standards up and down their value chains, have been building their own XML standards.

Covisint, the automotive industry B2B exchange, is implementing the ebXML message transport layer and will use the OAG's Integration Specification standards for its XML document payload. A message transport layer is a set of electronic protocols that contain such information as who sent a document and where to deliver it. The XML payload is the document itself. Covisint says the technology will give it the ability to exchange Internet-based messages between trading partners wrapped in a standard message framework that is being adopted globally.

By using these common standards, OEMs, automotive suppliers, and software providers will be able to improve communication and reduce integration costs.

What does this mean for B2B exchanges? If an exchange's users are suppliers to more than one industry, it may need to support more than one XML standard. If the exchange's users include the largest players in the industry, it may need to support EDI, XML/EDI, and an XML standard mandated by that company for the exchange of business documents with it. It will be important for the exchange to have local repositories of appropriate schemas and document type definitions, XML mapping tools, transformation tools, and a vehicle for ensuring guaranteed delivery of XML documents.

Infrastructure Issues for B2B Exchanges

In this way, the B2B exchange acts as a "Babel fish," translating the different XML standards and helping to set a common industry standard.

Despite the current fragmentation, XML is here to stay because it is a very efficient way to transfer structured data between applications, since XML supports "structured" data, is "flexible" and, by definition "extensible" (ie, it is everything that traditional EDI is not).

XML adoption will be rapid in some industries, like high-technology and financial services, slower in others, but XML will become a component of document exchange in most supply chains.

As a result, industry participants are beginning to come together to set more formal standards:

- The Business Internet Consortium (BIC) was formed in 2001 in order to create an over-riding standard that ensures that each industry specific XML standard is interoperable with the others. In other words, an architecture for B2B integration that crosses all industries. BIC's founders include Intel Corp., Hewlett-Packard Co., SAP AG, Ford Motor Co., and Pennzoil-Quaker State Co.

- UN/CEFACT (www.unece.org/cefact) is the UN body whose mandate covers worldwide policy and technical development in the area of trade facilitation and electronic business. Headquartered in Geneva, it has developed and promoted many tools for the facilitation of global business processes including UN/EDIFACT, the international EDI standard. It strongly supports the development and implementation of open interoperable, global standards and specifications for e-business.

- OASIS (www.oasis-open.org) is the international, not-for-profit consortium that advances electronic business by promoting open, collaborative development of interoperability specifications. OASIS operates XML.ORG (www.XML.org), the non-commercial portal that delivers information on the use of XML in industry. The XML.org registry provides an open community clearinghouse for distributing and locating XML application schemas, vocabularies and related documents. OASIS serves as the home for industry groups and organizations interested in developing XML specifications.

- The Interactive Financial eXchange (IFX) Forum is a forum for business and technology professionals to develop a robust XML framework for the electronic business-to-business exchange of data among financial service institutions around the world. ACORD, an insurance industry group, currently works closely with the IFX Forum in the development of XML standards for the banking and insurance industries. ACORD also participates in the ebXML initiative with OASIS.

UN/CEFACT, OASIS, and W3C have agreed to work together to create an over arching architecture for web services. The relevant BIC workgroup hopes to gain the co-operation of UN/CEFACT, OASIS, and W3C in its efforts too.

E-Business Communication Issues

Even so, it is important to realize that XML, while very promising, will only facilitate a portion of business communications and transactions. Organizations will still need to support other document channels and formats — such as EDI, e-mail, hard copies, faxes, and wireless messages. To illustrate this, let's look again at the hypothetical metal company — Metal Co. Inc. — which does business with hundreds of customers and suppliers, as shown in Figure 9A. How will these companies exchange information?

Figure 9A: Metal Co. Inc.

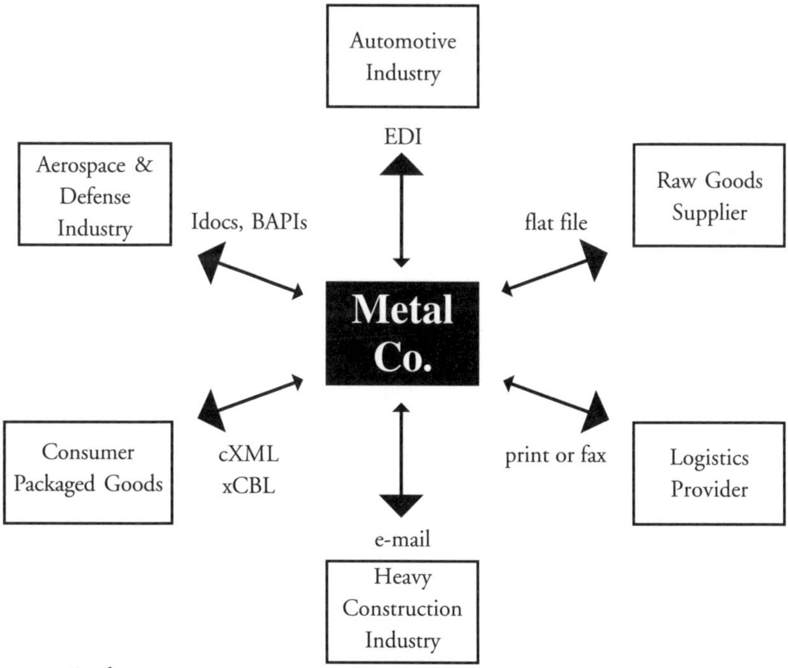

Source: Author

Infrastructure Issues for B2B Exchanges

Each of Metal Co.'s trading partners has its own internal information systems and business processes. Metal Co. supplies rolled steel for auto body panels to automotive manufacturers. Large companies already use standard EDI documents to exchange shipping schedules, purchase orders, invoices, and logistics information. Big automotive manufacturers like General Motors or Ford will, therefore, require Metal Co. to support their existing EDI infrastructure.

Metal Co. also supplies cold rolled steel to the aerospace and defense industry, to companies like Boeing and Raytheon. Raytheon, an SAP shop, needs support for SAP's IDOCs, proprietary EDI documents or Business Application Programming Interfaces (BAPIs). Boeing, which standardized on BAAN and Corba, needs support for Business Object Interfaces (BOIs) and Object Request Brokers (ORBs).

The situation is intensified as we look at other potential customers' needs. Delmonte and Dole, two consumer packaged goods vendors, procure metal from Metal Co. for canned goods. The companies may have settled on an XML standard, such as ebXML, CXML, or xCBL to distribute their requests for proposals.

Metal Co. must also address communication issues with its suppliers. Only its Tier 1 suppliers are likely to have EDI. Many mills procure raw materials from scrap consolidators for use in converting into new, shiny steel rolls and bars. Metal Co. will need to connect to these small- and mid-sized suppliers through an Internet-based EDI network using XML/EDI. Or the required mode of communication might be as simple as a flat file transfer. Metal Co. will also need to submit shipping documents to its logistics providers using the old fashioned fax machine or e-mail.

Metal Co.'s situation exemplifies what many companies and B2B exchanges will be struggling with in the coming years, ie, how to support the communication and integration needs of a diverse e-business community? XML and the Internet will only comprise a portion of business communications since many industries are not abandoning traditional processes, such as EDI.

In the near future, no one data channel or format will encompass all of a B2B exchange's communication needs. Businesses will need the exchange to support both traditional and new means of communication. EDI, EDI/XML, HTML, XML, e-mail, hard copies, fax, and wireless will all play a significant role.

Integration case study: ShipyardXchange handles RFQs automatically

In order to illustrate the complexity inherent in integrating B2B exchanges with internal enterprise systems, let us analyze one example in some detail. In this example, a request for quotation (RFQ) originating in the Enterprise Resource Planning (ERP) system of a shipyard is processed by a B2B exchange and forwarded to the internal systems of a potential supplier. The supplier then prepares a quote and the quote is returned through the B2B exchange to the internal systems of the shipyard.

In the maritime industry, many Internet companies provide procurement support, engineering collaboration, project management, and document exchange facilities. One web-based procurement solution is called ShipyardXchange (www.shipyardxchange.com). ShipyardXchange's mission is to support the complex processes of requesting and quoting for sophisticated products and systems in the shipbuilding industry.

During January 2002, more than 200 RFQs were distributed through ShipyardXchange, while orders for over $2.4 million were awarded to participating suppliers. Many suppliers received more than one RFQ, and several received RFQs from yards that they had not previously done business with. Quite a few also received pre-qualifications to deliver products to new yards. This demonstrates how a B2B exchange can make a significant contribution to the procurement process in the European shipbuilding industry.

The success of ShipyardXchange as an on-line procurement portal derives from the successful integration of the B2B exchange's systems with over eight ship building yards and more than 120 suppliers. To achieve this level of integration took a major development project followed by a long pilot program. With several yards and more than 100 suppliers actively participating in the pilot, ShipyardXchange was able to prove that it worked as originally intended before it was officially launched.

The development project was undertaken by ShipyardXchange with StreamServe (www.streamserve.com), a leading systems integration provider, and sought to establish tight integration with two types of user, a shipyard and a maritime supplier. The project proved that an RFQ originating in the ERP system of the shipyard could be processed by the B2B exchange and forwarded to the internal systems of the supplier. The supplier then prepared a quote and the quote was returned through the B2B exchange to the internal systems of the shipyard.

Infrastructure Issues for B2B Exchanges

The aim was moderate in its ambition: to reuse information across applications that are involved in requesting and tendering equipment for ships. In a sense, the project only involved the copying of information from one source to the next, not a very ambitious goal in the overall context of program-to-program integration over the Internet, but the challenge was, in effect, to automate such copying — and it illustrates why true integration takes so long to achieve.

The fictitious project contained three commercial actors:

- a shipyard that sets out to procure a diesel auxiliary engine by distributing an RFQ;
- a B2B exchange that sells services to assist in procuring these kind of strategic goods; and
- a supplier that quotes on this RFQ.

This kind of complex maritime purchase is not normally achieved by searching in a catalog — it is an elaborate process involving negotiation and a detailed document exchange between the parties.

In practice, some small- and medium-sized shipyards and suppliers might be comfortable with procuring a diesel-engine through a separate third-party web-based application, but most large companies prefer that the information residing on the external system is made available to their internal applications. ShipyardXchange's objective was, therefore, to make the relevant information available to all the users' different systems in the most practical manner.

The participants in the project included:

- IFS, a provider of the ERP system used in this project (but it could equally have been an SAP, BAAN, or Oracle system);
- Lindhard, also a provider of an ERP system called Multi+;
- ShipyardXchange, the provider of web-based services for RFQ procurements; and
- StreamServe, a provider of integration and distribution software.

IFS played the role of the shipyard's ERP system. Multi+ was set up as the prospective supplier's ERP system, and ShipyardXchange acted as the B2B procurement exchange provider. StreamServe had several roles: mapping data between alternative data representations, receiving and unpacking messages, and monitoring in/out folders.

The project emulated the complete cycle from when an "RFQ" is defined as a draft in the shipyard's ERP system until the quote from the prospective supplier is represented back in the same ERP system. The first stage involved establishing XML schemas to be used for representing an RFQ and a quote. Then the processes described below, and illustrated in Figure 9B, were shown to work:

1. An XML representation of a draft RFQ was extracted from the IFS **system** in the shipyard's internal format.

2. This representation was wrapped inside a SOAP message and became a payload there.

3. This SOAP message was posted to **ShipyardXchange** in a mailbox polled by **StreamServe**.

4. **StreamServe** picked up and opened the message and unpacked the XML payload.

5. **StreamServe** then transformed the XML message into a "standard" MindNet format using a proprietary application based on XSLT mapping.

6. The converted XML message was then stored as a file in the *SYX RFQ In* folder.

7. From inside the application, **ShipyardXchange** picked up and parsed the XML file, and used the data to fill in an RFQ.

8. After having completed and published the RFQ, **ShipyardXchange** then exported the completed RFQ as an XML file to the *SYX RFQ Out* folder.

9. **StreamServe** monitored the *SYX RFQ Out* folder, picked up the file and moved it to the *Multi RFQ In* folder.

10. **Multi+**, the supplier's internal system, then picked up and parsed the XML file using SOAP as an internal means of establishing an RFQ in the system.

11. After having created and filled in a quote, **Multi+** then used a SOAP-based Java application to export an XML file representing the quote to the *Multi Quote Out* folder.

12. **StreamServe** monitored the *Multi Quote Out* folder, picked up the file and moved it to the *SYX Quote In* folder.

13. **ShipyardXchange** then picked up and parsed the XML file and used the data to establish a Quote in the system.

14. After having completed and sent the quote, **ShipyardXchange** then exported the completed RFQ as a file to the *SYX Quote Out* folder.

15. **StreamServe** monitored the *SYX Quote Out* folder, picked up the file and sent it as an SMTP message to **IFS**.

Figure 9B: Automating the RFQ Process on ShipyardXchange

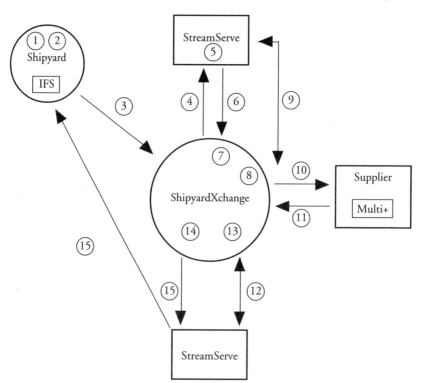

Source: Author, StreamServe

In brief, the project employed a variety of resources and tools:

- Use of XSD schemas as the basis for an XML message in a scenario with multiple players.
- Mapping between two XML representations using XSLT.
- Use of SOAP both as wrapper around an XML payload, and as an access protocol for establishing records in databases.
- Automated message handling, unwrapping, processing, and distribution.
- Reuse of XML data to generate a PDF document representing a formal RFQ document.

In reality, the possible variations and alternatives to this scenario are numerous. The fact that different resources and tools can be combined in several different ways also means that you can have different levels and depths of integration — from simple file transfer to automated communication, from asynchronous to synchronous.

Complex integration issues analyzed and lessons learned

Use of Schemas: On a mundane level, the project confirmed that using schemas to represent the content, structure, and format of business documents carries with it some difficulties. First of all, in order for schemas to be useful they need to describe less than all but more than nothing of the world. In between, there are many choices to make. The project might have established one business document schema to cover an RFQ, quote and purchase order. The reason why they did not do that was that what is mandatory in a quote (for instance price) simply has no meaning in an RFQ. So in this project, they decided to use two schemas: an RFQ and a quote. Had the project covered the purchase order as well, they would have had three schemas.

But this was not a simple process either. Remember that a schema may have four distinct functions:

1. It defines the scope of information that is associated with the message, or business transaction, to which the schema relates.
2. It defines the vocabulary/syntax, or defines and names the tags, which are to be used in generating the XML message.
3. It defines which elements and attributes are to be considered mandatory or optional (or not allowed).
4. It defines the data type (format) that has to be used when using the different elements and attributes.

Infrastructure Issues for B2B Exchanges

The problems with using one schema in several contexts are most prevalent in points 1 and 3.

In point 1, obviously the number of elements and attributes increases with the number of contexts for which the schema is to be used. Arguably, the more contexts and larger the schema, the more complex its usage becomes. However, the delimitation is subjective — there is no clear objective basis to use when establishing the schema hierarchy.

In point 3, the problem is more fundamental. Something that is mandatory in one context, or one usage of the schema, may be optional in another. For instance, the tag <price> is not relevant when requesting, but highly relevant when quoting. Thus, what would be desirable would be some conditional rules — that the schema had different qualities depending on the context. This is not easily supported, and to do so would increase the schema complexity significantly.

In this project they established two variants of both the RFQ and quote schemas; draft (or minimum) and published (or maximum). So, from the initial desire to establish one "purchase process schema" they ended up with two schemas and two sets of schema for each transaction in this process. This is a good example of unforeseen complexity arising in the course of an integration project.

The team ended up agreeing to establish a business process schema that defined the syntax and the typing of the different elements and attributes. From this, they could then derive the specific document schemas adapted to the different contexts. This reduces the value of using schema.

Legacy Issues: The project highlighted two major obstacles to integration, which are:

- that different systems don't necessarily have the ability (the database records) to keep information that other systems need to have or that others pass across as reference; and
- that existing enterprise systems do not have natural repositories for keeping references to other systems (external ERP references). Thus, they have problems when shaking hands with external systems. It is as if the internal system is asking; "Which of my database records are you talking about?"

Security: This type of integration requires two types of security. First, the corporate firewall. Most enterprise firewalls pose a major problem when information is to be taken into the enterprise through that wall. This is not so much of a problem when companies simply exchange messages through e-mail, but is a big problem when trying to implement a more complex integration of data as in this project. Once the corporate firewall has been opened up the company has to secure its internal networks. Second, the corporate information sent out over the network (whether EDI or the Internet) must be secured using a public key infrastructure to encrypt data.

Remote calls: The security issues grow exponentially when an enterprise firewall owner not only needs to let information, untouched by human hands, pass through the wall, but also needs to allow that same information to trigger a process within the internal system. Whether SOAP wrapped or not, there is an understandable resistance to allowing some externally generated message to manipulate the content of a critical, internal database system such as an ERP system.

Resilient Networks: Deep integration requires that the two systems communicate and exchange information without human intervention, and a robust integration requires that these systems agree on what they talk about before processing the information. That normally means they both have to be on-line at the same time and that they exchange information synchronously in real-time. In other words, the systems have to be connected to a highly resilient infrastructure where the Internet connection is always up. This can be a problem given the current instability and capacity of ISP vendors, the Internet infrastructure, message queues, and web-based applications.

And this is just a list of the main problems encountered; there are of course many more issues to resolve in each integration effort.

OAG's B2B vendor challenge

ShipyardXchange's pilot program was a relatively simple integration exercise. StreamServe recently participated in the Open Application Group's (OAG's) B2B Vendor Challenge. The OAG Vendor Challenge consisted of three different scenarios for B2B transactions using OAG's open standards-based XML Business Object Documents (BODs). Lockheed Martin, Lucent Technologies, and Ford Motor Company each presented real life scenarios for the challenge. The B2B Vendor Challenge's objective was to show how customers could operate more efficiently using vendor-implemented BODs for B2B transactions.

Infrastructure Issues for B2B Exchanges

StreamServe played the role of the customer in Lockheed Martin's purchasing scenario. It successfully demonstrated its ability to support interoperability between internal systems, Product Data Management (PDM), and ERP, as well as with the vendor's external systems.

StreamServe began with the customer's PDM system to pick up the purchase orders (POs) containing a fixed price for the known product and a not-to-exceed price for the newly modified unit. StreamServe transformed the PDM POs from the original OAGI BOD format to the ERP system's required SAP IDOC (Intermediate Documents) message format by mapping it to SAP XML. From the customer's ERP system, StreamServe prepared a "complex" PO to include both the standard and new items. It mapped the document back into OAGI BOD format for the vendor to process. StreamServe then passed the PO to the vendor and waited for the vendor's acknowledgement response, advance shipment notice, and invoice from the vendor.

The OAG example demonstrates the additional levels of complexity that arise when B2B exchanges seek to enable companies to collaborate across their whole value chain.

Web Services

Web services are the latest tool for program-to-program integration of software between businesses "across the corporate firewall." Unlike previous component integration frameworks, web services build upon an existing set of communications protocols that have been spectacularly successful — the Internet — and attempt to use it for function-based computing. Web services simply leverage the Internet infrastructure, formats, and protocols to let diverse applications interoperate in a simple, standard way.

A web service describes specific business functionality exposed by a company across its firewall, usually through an Internet connection, for the purpose of providing a way for another company or software program to use the service. Web services thus extend the usage of the Internet to allow direct access to programs by another software application, not just through a web browser.

Web services comprise providers: who publish the availability of their services; brokers: who register and categorize the services of these service providers; and users: who use brokers to find a provider's service. In order for these three parties to communicate, a common language is required — XML. Providers use WSDL to describe the service that they offer. Users use SOAP to target messages to the providers, and brokers use UDDI to list the services that are available.

Integration with an Enterprise's Internal Applications

Let us use ShipyardXchange again for an example of how a B2B exchange can leverage web services to increase the value proposition of the exchange. In the example above, the prospective supplier that provided a price quote over the Internet is a web service provider. In the future, ShipyardXchange will also be linked to a logistics web service provider. This provider will offer a shipping service for the completed diesel engine and it will provide shipping information. Another provider will be a credit service that provides a credit rating on the shipyard asking for the quote. Yet another provider will be an insurance company that offers to insure the shipment of the engine and provides freight insurance prices.

ShipyardXchange will get information about the web services offered by each provider from that provider's private UDDI directory. ShipyardXchange's systems will then automatically invoke the necessary web service from each provider, based on the WSDL binding information posted in the UDDI directory of that provider. Let's say that the engine supplier can automatically give a more favorable price to a shipyard with a better credit rating. So, for example, when a shipyard requests a quote through ShipyardXchange, the exchange will obtain a credit rating on that shipyard using the credit agent's web service. This information will be attached to the RFQ and elicit the more favorable quote.

From the shipyard's point of view, once it has selected a supplier it needs to arrange the transport and freight insurance for the engine. This can all be achieved through the B2B exchange, which invokes the relevant web services of the logistics provider and insurance companies on behalf of the shipyard.

Each user obtains access to all the necessary web services through just one connection to the B2B exchange and a "single sign-on." By linking all these web services together, ShipyardXchange will therefore create additional value for its users.

Applications such as these, created by stringing web services together, are known as "federated applications." Through the use of WSDL, the B2B exchange knows the specific type of XML document to send to each web services provider (for example, the credit rating agency in order to obtain the credit rating request), and the credit rating agency knows what type of XML document to send back to the B2B exchange. This software architecture is known as "loosely coupled," because it allows for dynamic application integration depending on what combination of services is required by each user.

Infrastructure Issues for B2B Exchanges

B2B exchanges are the perfect "Babel fish" communication hubs through which to connect federated e-business applications and web services in a loosely coupled environment.

Implementing web services, however, is going to take longer than many people anticipate. Companies will have to open up their corporate firewalls to let external systems interoperate with their internal systems in real-time. SOAP 1.0 is still only a basic standard and, as with XML, there will initially be many different implementations of it. There is also a shortage of programmers with the skill and experience to code in these new standards and build complex applications with a sustainable business case.

Again, B2B exchanges are the perfect forums to concentrate web services development and, by reducing the number of external connections that enterprises need to make, to act as catalysts for the development of web services.

End Note:

1. *The E-commerce Trade and B2B Exchanges Report*, Steve Butler eMarketer, March 2002.

Chapter **10**

Messaging Systems: The Exchange's Communications Layer

"Communication processes with exchange users cannot be implemented individually for each user's legacy application...all communications must be managed as a single, independent entity."

As we have seen in Chapter 9, the greatest technology hurdle for B2B exchanges is how to integrate the exchange's systems with the user's internal systems. The largest part of this issue is how will companies exchange business documents and information over the web? Since Internet standards such as XML will not immediately replace all other document formats, e-business exponentially intensifies a company's integration problems.

The Metal Co. situation described in Chapter 9 exemplifies what many B2B exchanges will be struggling with in the coming years; how to support the communication and integration needs of a diverse e-business community? XML and the Internet will only comprise a portion of business communications. In addition, many industries are not abandoning traditional processes, such as EDI.

In the near future, no one data channel or format will encompass all of a B2B exchange's communication needs. Businesses will need support for traditional and new means of communication. Successful e-businesses will need flexible support concerning document formats and channels. EDI, EDI/XML, HTML, XML, e-mail, hardcopies, fax, and wireless will all play a significant role.

Infrastructure Issues for B2B Exchanges

EDI/XML, XML, HTML, PDF, and e-mail are the most common documents transmitted over the Internet. Companies must support each of these document types, especially e-mail.

E-Business Communication: One Size Won't Fit All

E-mail will continue to play a dominant role in e-business communications. E-mail is inclusive; it is available on the desktops of all employees within an organization. It provides a way to deliver information directly to the appropriate user. In addition, e-mail is more compatible with wireless technology. Bandwidth issues limit wireless technology. For personal digital assistants and mobile telephones, e-mail provides a user friendly interface versus a scaled down browser.

The Metal Co. scenario illustrated in Chapter 9 does not even take into account the advent of wireless applications and devices. Wireless is a technology in search of a business value, but soon it will add another communication channel that B2B exchanges will have to support. Companies will have to deliver business information — such as a revised bid, offer, or auction price — remotely to employees, trading partners, and customers via short message service (SMS) or wireless application protocol (WAP). In addition, at least for the near future, traditional communication vehicles such as print media and fax will remain a staple of doing business. The predictions of a paperless office have always been unsound and it is clear that the Internet will not be the harbinger of a truly paperless workplace in the near future. It takes time for companies to re-engineer old habits and business processes and B2B exchanges will have to support all of the various document formats and channels.

Case study: FundNexus — e-business communications for the offshore fund industry

There are at least 10,000 offshore funds of which at least 3,000 could be classified as "hedge funds" — or alternative investment funds. Industry estimates suggest that there is already more than $500 billion invested in offshore hedge funds and that amount is growing rapidly.

The hedge fund industry has traditionally been based on direct relationships between alternative fund mangers and individual high net worth investors (HNWIs) — and has been described as a "cottage industry." But as the industry grows, more and more institutional investors are moving a part of their overall investment portfolios into alternative funds and some hedge funds are now targeting retail investors through fund of funds structures.

It is estimated that the assets managed by hedge funds will increase from approximately $500 billion today to $1.7 trillion in 2005 and that at least half of this $1.7 trillion will come from institutional investors.

Source: The Journal of Alternative Investments

Hedge fund data shows that the growth rate in the number of hedge funds is currently running at 15–20% per annum. The vast majority of hedge funds established and administered offshore are non-retail funds. These funds are targeted towards institutional and HNWIs and require a fairly significant minimum investment ($1 million or more is quite common). Hedge funds are generally restricted to accredited investors, by regulations and/or tax issues. Some funds exclude US investors altogether.

The fund usually has no employees and engages a fund administrator to value the fund's portfolio, usually on a monthly basis, and to process subscriptions and redemptions of the fund's shares to its investors. In order to ensure that potential investors meet its qualifications, the fund, again usually through its administrator, has to conduct a detailed due diligence review of each applicant. This process is repeated each time that an investor applies to subscribe to an offshore fund.

However, the subscription and redemption process is currently all paper based and not electronic.

It is clear that the current business processes and infrastructure will not support the anticipated growth in the industry. Some third parties are seeking to automate this process such as FundNexus (www.fundnexus.com, formerly FundXchange), and some of the large fund administrators are building their own systems. However, the industry is currently very fragmented with funds being domiciled in several different jurisdictions (Cayman, Bermuda, and Dublin are the leading ones) and with many different administrators.

FundNexus is an independent B2B exchange that provides the first on-line execution and tracking facility for transactions in offshore mutual funds. Its primary goal is to electronically link fund managers and administrators, and to link both of them to their investors — institutional, advisory, and qualified investors — and to automate the transactions between them. As an independent, third-party service provider, FundNexus is not in a position to mandate business process re-engineering across the whole offshore fund industry and so it has been designed to support users' existing business processes as much as possible.

Infrastructure Issues for B2B Exchanges

FundNexus was set up by a group of entrepreneurs and subsequently funded by Zurich Capital Markets (part of the Zurich Financial Services group). The system is available to fund managers, transfer agents, and administrators and institutional, advisory, and qualified investors.

Investors — trading desk

FundNexus offers an investor the ability to preview all the funds in the system. The system makes available superior historical performance statistics. FundNexus's prices (ie, the offshore fund's net asset values) are input directly by the fund's administrator. Once an investor selects a fund, the system holds all the information necessary to make an investment decision — for example, the latest prospectus, the latest financial statements, and any interim reports from the manager — all in Adobe's .pdf format. Once the investor has made an investment decision he can prepare the subscription form or the redemption request in respect of an offshore investment fund on-line through an XML document. The completed information is electronically transmitted to the administrator of that fund.

However, the industry is not yet fully electronic and funds require the investor to submit a print copy of the form, with a wet ink signature. To accommodate this, the FundNexus system prints off a copy of the form, with fax information, for the investor to sign and fax to the fund's administrator. An investor gets a real-time transaction confirmation once the administrator has processed the request — by e-mail and on the system. In the future, investors may wish to receive these confirms on their mobile phones using WAP or SMS.

The investor's portfolio of fund investments is available on-line at any time and includes a valuation based on the latest fund prices. For financial advisers who invest in offshore funds on behalf of investors, the system provides portfolio management and adviser commission reporting across funds.

Fund administrators

Fund administrators, who calculate issue and redemption prices for funds, can upload fund prices at any time. Whenever an investment request is prepared by an investor it is automatically transmitted to the administrator who can view it on-line and download it into his systems, using the XML format or as a comma separated value (CSV) file. Once the administrator has processed the transaction he can confirm it in the FundNexus system on-line and then an e-mail confirm is automatically issued to the investor.

FundNexus is looking to move the industry towards full integration in incremental steps. The next step will be to eliminate the hard copy of every subscription or redemption form by introducing encrypted .pdf forms that contain the investor's digital signature. These electronic forms will be sent to the administrator and will be archived by FundNexus.

In the future, the system will enable investors to digitally sign the forms using XML Digital Signatures and XML Encrypt (see below), so that administrators can take the forms directly into their existing accounting and transfer agent systems. However, no fund administrators are currently in a position to achieve that level of integration yet. In addition, FundNexus has to co-operate with a large number of offshore fund administrators in order to achieve critical mass. Some of these players are small- and medium-sized businesses and some of them still use spreadsheet programs to calculate fund values, prepare fund accounts and/or maintain fund share registers. FundNexus cannot force them all to use XML right away, so it has to continue to offer other ways to get the data out of its systems — including the basic CSV format.

Fund managers

For fund managers the system provides an enhanced distribution system for their funds. FundNexus has conducted an exhaustive review of the legal and regulatory requirements for marketing hedge funds into each of the major jurisdictions. The system allows a fund manager to select which jurisdictions and which types of investor are permitted to invest in his/her fund and automatically screens eligibility for the manager.

The manager can also use the FundNexus system to track payments and commissions due, and to access up-to-date information on-line about subscriptions and redemptions in his/her fund.

Community features

To grow the FundNexus community the site also offers an industry-specific news desk, with regular updates.

The example of FundNexus illustrates how many B2B exchanges will have to support print, fax, and .pdf as well as XML, until the users are sufficiently sophisticated to use XML forms in a truly integrated way.

Infrastructure Issues for B2B Exchanges

Building A B2B Exchange's Communications Infrastructure

Based on the examples of Metal Co., ShipyardXchange, and FundNexus, it is evident that e-business communications pose many complex business and technology challenges. In most cases, B2B exchanges will need professional expertise to assist in developing the right infrastructure.

The following six points detail the major factors that need to be considered by a B2B exchange when building its communication infrastructure.

It must support the users' existing business processes

The integration task is monumental in its own right without another round of business process re-engineering — and in any event, B2B exchanges cannot always mandate process re-engineering. The business communication framework must, therefore, be able to support the existing relationships and workflow intra- and inter-enterprise. At the same time, the framework should allow for innovative new processes, such as wireless communication.

It must provide business process integration

Larger organizations doing business are actively moving towards program-to-program integration. SAP-to-SAP, I2 to Oracle, and Commerce One to SAP are only a few examples. A strong B2B exchange communication platform will offer support for application programming interfaces (APIs), remote procedure calls (RPCs), and electronic documents.

It must leverage existing business applications and legacy applications

Businesses spent billions of dollars in the past 10 years implementing ERP systems, accounting systems, and other internal applications. Companies are not going to walk away from their multi-million-dollar investments. They are now tasked with extending the capabilities outside the organization's four walls. A B2B exchange's communication infrastructure must offer strong back-end integration into these systems.

It must be flexible and inclusive

To standardize customer and supplier relationships on hard coded application integration or one data standard is not feasible or a smart business decision. As usual, the organizations that will feel the greatest growing pains will be small- to medium-sized companies. Inclusion means understanding that some valuable users may not be able to rapidly adopt new standards. For example, it would be counterproductive and unrealistic for a B2B exchange to force its users to standardize on XML immediately.

It must support customization

Business-to-business customization involves delivering information in the format needed by the intended recipient, at the correct time, whether it is delivered in real time or on a publish and subscribe basis, and through the desired channel (however basic that channel may be).

It must be secure

B2B exchanges handle high value transactions and highly confidential business information. Security must therefore be a priority. Security means ensuring that only authorized users can access the exchange systems and restricting access to sensitive functionality by user. It also means encrypting all data and authenticating who sends data through the exchange. In addition to standard user name and password controls a B2B exchange should use a public key infrastructure (PKI) so that users have digital certificates that control access and enable encryption and digital signing of data.

The Exchange's Communication Layer

As we have seen, successful B2B exchanges need to adapt their services to effectively support the broad range of formats and distribution channels demanded by users.

Communication processes with exchange users cannot be implemented individually for each user's legacy application or business management system; they must be managed and maintained as an integral component of the exchange's computing infrastructure. To do this, all communications must be managed as a single, independent entity.

This requires a specific platform to handle communications — the exchange's communication layer (see Figure 10A over the page).

The exchange's communication layer is a middle-tier layer that makes it possible to link new e-business enabled systems and multiple legacy systems to the exchange, so that information can be shared without changing the data or modifying the applications.

Figure 10A: Exchange Communication Layer

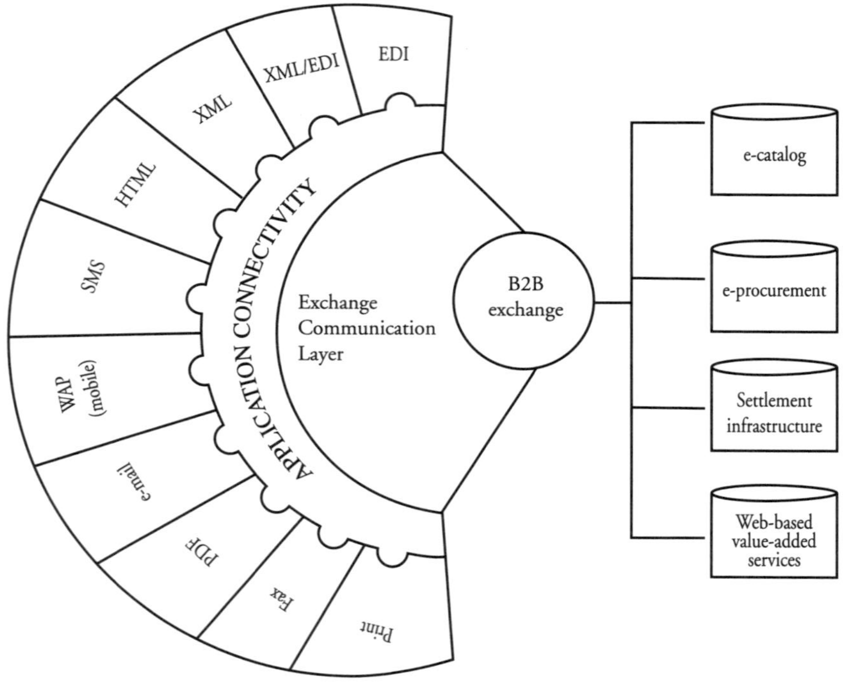

Source: Author

Case study: StreamServe

StreamServe was started in Sweden in 1995 and has expanded its presence throughout Europe and Asia with offices in Denmark, Finland, France, Germany, the Netherlands, Norway, Singapore, and the UK. As part of a growing focus on the American market, StreamServe began its US operations in 1998 and currently has its US headquarters in Boston. In May 2002, *TIME* magazine listed StreamServe as one of the 50 hottest technology companies in Europe. StreamServe provides business communication software. StreamServe's solutions enable B2B exchanges to manage document exchange, personalize interactions, and automate processes. It helps B2B exchanges share critical business information among users, suppliers, and other trading partners. StreamServe's business communication platform represents a flexible communication layer that helps integrate, automate, and personalize communication processes. StreamServe processes multiple incoming documents and prepares them for output in a structured data stream to the receiver, based on pre-determined communication rules.

StreamServe's platform is the flexible product that B2B exchanges need to set up their "exchange communications layer" and meet these communication challenges.

Figure 10B: StreamServe's Communications Platform

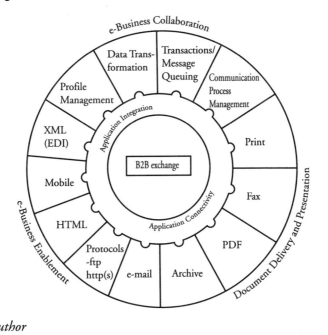

Source: Author

Infrastructure Issues for B2B Exchanges

B2B exchanges constantly have to share information with users, business partners, and employees. StreamServe's platform addresses this need for document delivery and presentation, by offering a comprehensive approach for distributing personalized documents through various channels of communication. It allows exchanges to expand existing output capabilities found in business application systems like SAP, Oracle, BAAN, IFS, and QAD, to produce, automatically distribute, and archive documents such as order confirmations, invoices, and delivery status reports.

StreamServe's platform helps companies exchange electronic documents by transforming data into required formats and enabling wireless and Internet technologies. The communications layer enables e-business by allowing organizations to share electronic documents, such as XML files and e-mail, internally and over the Internet, with trading partners and customers.

StreamServe's solution utilizes communication protocols including the Hyper Text Transfer (HTTP/HTTPS), Internet (IP), File Transfer (FTP), and Simple Mail Transfer (SMTP) to expand document exchange channels. It can send and receive business documents sent by wireless devices or web services via standard XML-based service transport protocols, including SOAP and ebXML. The application also supports EDI transactions, which can be translated into XML for integration with non-EDI systems.

B2B exchanges can therefore use the StreamServe platform to communicate with multiple business partners and users.

Securing E-business Communications

Program-to-program communication between businesses has been occurring for many years, most notably using EDI. Before the Internet, a value-added network (VAN) or virtual private network (VPN) was the only effective way to carry B2B e-business communications. For example, most EDI solutions use VANs. However, as we have seen, only a limited number of large businesses and their trading partners could afford the VAN/EDI solution. But e-business has been slow to move beyond closed networks because of two obstacles. The first obstacle was the lack of common data format standards — this has been addressed by XML and its related technologies. The second obstacle is the lack of security on the World Wide Web. This issue is now being addressed.

By using a VAN, companies could be assured that information passing between the two trading parties remained secure. The VAN authenticated both sender and receiver; verified data was actually exchanged, and archived messages to facilitate problem resolution. The Internet is now replacing VANs, because the Internet supports technology that handles the security needs of business-to-business and it is cheaper.

While EDI remains a viable format for e-business into the foreseeable future, the VAN era is coming to a close. As we have seen, e-business document standards based on XML standards are replacing EDI. VANs do not support XML. VANs are ill equipped to quickly handle and "understand" the full range of new data formats that are developing — a limitation that will restrict their use in B2B exchanges.

The only security VANs offer is limited and based on passwords. VANs do not provide data security or encryption of any kind — indeed the VAN itself must look into every document in order to handle it correctly. VANs rely on store and forward technology. Since transmission is not instantaneous, it can be compromised as well as slow. Since VANs cannot support digital signatures they do not provide secure, non-repudiatable records of origin and receipt.

However, if businesses are to use the Internet instead of VANs, encryption is crucial — so that a third party cannot spy on the information being sent between two businesses — but encryption is not enough for B2B transactions. Authentication — the process of determining whether someone or something is, in fact, who or what it is declared to be — is also crucial.

With all e-business, the standards for operation from a practical, legal, and technological perspective need to be set so that all trading partners can trust that:

- their transactions are only with the intended party;
- the transactions will be protected in transit over the Internet;
- on-line transactions are legally binding; and
- they will have financial recourse should something go wrong.

Without that level of trust there may be no deal.

B2B transactions are heavily document based. If electronic records, which can easily be altered or copied, are to replace signed paper documents, the trading parties need total assurance that the electronic records are authentic. And when data is stored electronically, the parties need to be sure that it is secure but also accessible only by authorized persons.

Infrastructure Issues for B2B Exchanges

E-security is therefore critical to creating enforceable and trustworthy e-business transactions.

The Internet can provide a secure communications channel by using one of several protocols that operate as a layer above the standard Internet TCP protocol. The most popular of these protocols, secure sockets layer (SSL), provides a range of security services for communications between companies. All items sent over an SSL channel are automatically encrypted using a public key system. This provides for the security of the network. But the security of the data must also be assured. And SSL does not provide secure records of what data was received or at what time the data was received.

Secure/Multipurpose Internet Mail Extensions or S/MIME is a popular message format that handles data security and ensures the privacy of communications. It involves sending an encrypted message and transmitting a message in a form that cannot be opened or read by parties who do not have the right private keys. Users can exchange signed and encrypted e-mail messages with other e-mail clients that support S/MIME. E-mail messages encrypted by the user's public key can be decrypted using only the associated private key. When a user sends an encrypted e-mail message, the recipient's certificate (public key) is used to encrypt it; likewise, when a user reads an encrypted e-mail message, the user's private key is required to decrypt it.

The Internet Engineering Task Force (IETF) EDIINT Working Group has defined Applicability Standard 1 and 2 (AS1 and AS2) as security standards to make it possible for companies to perform secure B2B e-business using the Internet. AS1 and AS2 describe methods for sending a message using the S/MIME, HTTP and HTTPS formats with encrypted data, signed or unsigned messages and use of a receipt or message delivery notice, which may or may not be signed. Combined with secure FTP, these protocols address the issues of privacy, integrity, authentication, and non-repudiation, and provide security and transaction volume support comparable to a VAN or VPN in these critical areas, but using the Internet to send and receive data.

In addition, to these protocols, the PKI system of digital certificates provides secure time stamping to prove when data was transported and to prove who sent the data. The newly-issued XML Digital Signature standard defines a means of rendering a digital signature in XML. Any type of digital content can be signed with an XML Digital Signature.

By using both SSL and digital signatures, a complete security framework for B2B exchanges and web services can be constructed. Initiatives such as XML

Key Management Specification (XKMS), and Security Assertion Markup Language (SAML) are specifically focused on integrating digital certificates, certificate authorities and registration authorities into web services.

XML Encryption is a technology that is being co-ordinated by the W3C. Like XML signatures, it is not limited to processing XML, but rather is designed for any digital content. However, this digital content must be represented within an XML document. The functionality of XML Encryption meshes with XML Signature because a document may be both signed and encrypted. XML Encryption allows for certain elements in an XML document to be encrypted (ie, hidden), depending on the viewer's profile and access authorization.

These new technologies mean that the Internet is now superior to VANs and VPNs in protecting high-value, sensitive B2B transactions and will gradually replace EDI networks over the next few years.

A robust PKI deployment for a B2B exchange will usually consist of a certificate authority (operated by the exchange or outsourced to an independent certificate authority) and a registration agency. The certificate authority creates the unique public and private keys that are required to issue the digital certificates and maintains a public directory of valid certificates, so that relying parties can perform an on-line validation of those certificates. The B2B exchange will act as the registration authority and, in that capacity, carry out the due diligence on the users of the exchange to whom the digital certificates are to be issued.

Chapter 11

The "Back-end": Logistics, Fulfillment, and the Clearing and Settlement of B2B Transactions

"Efficient clearing and settlement solutions promote confidence in an e-marketplace and reduce transaction costs — thereby helping to generate liquidity."

Every trade — whether made on-line or not — needs to be completed. One party — the buyer — will normally make a payment and the other party — the seller — will normally deliver a good or service.

Different Product Types: From Widgets to Financial Products

The way in which a trade is completed or settled varies depending on the nature of the product or services traded.

Physical assets, such as widgets, have to be delivered to the buyer — or to the buyer's agent. This physical delivery process requires a logistics exercise to arrange timely transportation, delivery, and recorded receipt of the product.

By way of contrast, securities are normally delivered by book-entry settlement. The buyer's account is credited with securities in the same way as the seller's account is credited with cash, and there is no physical delivery of a stock certificate. Derivative securities are normally "cash settled." This means that the trade is settled by the payment of cash from one party to the other depending on which way the underlying reference asset has moved in value.

A Three-layered Cake

A successful B2B exchange should resemble a three-layered cake — representing the three layers along the value chain in a transaction: trading, clearing, and settlement.

The trading layer covers all the steps in preparing a transaction to the point of execution. The clearing layer is concerned with the process of determining accountability for exchange of cash and the goods or services between the parties, by confirming the trade. The settlement layer involves the final conclusion of the transaction by delivery of the goods and services and finality of payment.

Figure 11A: Exchanges Generally Consist of Three Layers

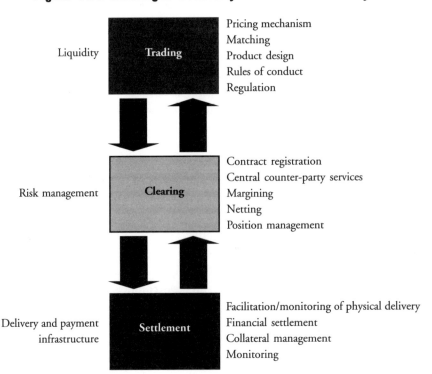

Source: Author

Clearance and Settlement Cycle

The B2B exchange must set the standard settlement period and other settlement terms for the goods or services traded on the exchange. To minimise risk and to avoid tying up users' capital for too long, the exchange should seek to keep the settlement period as short as practicable (see Figure 11B over the page).

So, for example, in international securities markets the current standard is a rolling "trade date plus three days" settlement cycle — called "T+3." However, the US and other markets are committed to moving to a T+1 settlement cycle over the next few years. In the US, T+1 is currently planned for June 2005, although there is now a debate about the high costs for the industry associated with achieving that goal. The ultimate goal is same day settlement — or T+0.

Efficient Clearance and Settlement is Critical to the Success of On-line Trading

A key goal of all B2B exchanges is to build liquidity and obtain a sustainable competitive advantage in their business environment. The creation and operation by an exchange of an efficient clearing and settlement system will enable it to achieve just this.

B2B exchanges have used the Internet to dramatically reduce the front-end costs of trading (eg, searching for trade partners and negotiating the deal) but not, as yet, to reduce the back-end costs of clearing and settlement.

The efficient central clearing and settlement infrastructure run by the Depository Trust & Clearing Corporation (DTCC) for the NYSE, NASDAQ and AMEX has undoubtedly assisted in making the US securities market the most liquid capital market in the world.

Clearing and settlement costs, plus settlement risks (eg, principal risk, market risk, and credit risk) are part of the overall cost of using a particular marketplace. As we saw in Chapter 2, the anticipated high settlement risks associated with on-line exchanges reduce on-line trading and liquidity levels.

Efficient clearing and settlement solutions promote confidence in an e-marketplace and reduce transaction costs — thereby helping to generate liquidity. A good clearing and settlement system is an integral part of the mechanisms required to protect trading entities from the risk of contractual default.

Figure 11B: Clearing and Settlement Cycle for Physical Goods

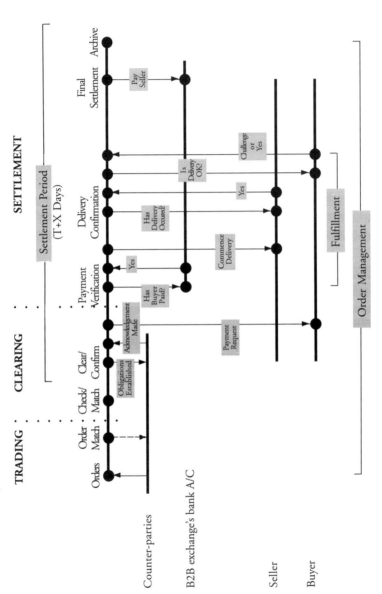

Source: Author

A central clearing and settlement entity acts as a receiving and distribution center that facilitates the processing of trades. It simplifies the process of confirming trades, netting settlement positions, and settling those net positions, after a trade is executed on a B2B exchange. The system holds the trade data and has one common reference database about the products, which all users share. This enables trade data to be verified and tracked by users right through the process from trade to settlement — thereby reducing errors and inconsistencies in the trade data between the trading partners.

In addition, as companies seek to mitigate the risks associated with their core businesses, it is critical that a seamless flow of information is achieved, not only internally but also between customers, suppliers, logistics providers, and all parties associated with the settlement of a transaction. For this to be achieved, all the parties involved in a transaction must be included in the information flow, which requires the sharing of information and the underlying networks conveying that information. The efficiencies provided by a completely seamless clearing and settlement network is called straight through processing (STP).

STP serves to minimize operational risks by reducing the extent to which trades are processed manually.

In the securities industry, STP has become the latest mantra. The Global STP Association (GSTPA) and Omgeo (a partnership of software developer Thomson Financial and the DTCC) are two organizations that have been developed to tackle the problem of post-trade, pre-settlement automation in the securities industry.

Both the GSTPA and Omgeo aim to create a post-trade, pre-settlement information-matching engine that matches trade data communicated among broker/dealers, investment managers, and global custodians. Currently, an error-prone and time-consuming sequence of confirms and affirms passes between the parties during the three-day settlement process, in batch mode. Shortening the settlement cycle to trade date plus one (T+1) requires faster communication of trade data, as batch processes simply cannot handle the necessary operations in a suitable amount of time. Without moving these operations to real-time, which will be facilitated by the central-STP engines being developed by GSTPA and Omgeo, it is impossible for STP to happen.

In the B2B exchange area, FXall is a good example of a financial services exchange which is focused on delivering STP — in this case for foreign exchange traders. FXall states "STP is a cost-saving option that lets FXall users take full advantage of electronic trading. STP's chief advantage is the reduction of manual trade input, greatly lowering the error risk of FX transactions…", and claims that its trade input and trade capture tolls already provide STP.

An efficient clearing and settlement regime (which moves the industry towards STP) is therefore critical to the success of a B2B exchange.

Fulfillment — for Physical Goods

The process of physically or virtually delivering goods and services to buyers is called fulfillment.

The Internet is driving demand for outsourced fulfillment solution providers with web-based logistics systems. The first phase of e-business emphasized developing the front-end of sourcing orders and resulted in the emergence of several first and second generation B2B exchanges. The next logical phase will be increased focus on the management of back-end processes and on ensuring that transactions are linked from the front-end to the systems of all relevant parties required to fulfil a transaction.

Term	Definition
Fulfillment	The process of physically or virtually delivering goods and services to buyers. Encompasses the use of information technology to make the delivery of goods and services as efficient as possible.
Order management	The process of translating, routing, tracking, and executing an order from origin through matching to fulfillment.
Logistics	Includes all of the back-end processes surrounding fulfillment, including warehouse and transportation management. Effective logistics requires integrated XML-based messaging between internal company systems and third-party logistics providers.
Web-based logistics	The use of information technology to optimize the logistics of fulfillment.

Logistics

The need to automate back-end fulfillment processes like warehousing and transportation management has arisen from the real-time demands created by e-business. The complexity in fulfillment often comes from the fact that it typically requires a third party to handle the act of fulfillment, introducing additional risk into the transaction. To ensure that the goods can be tracked in transit, close co-ordination between the shipper, fulfillment provider, and recipient is essential, and to keep the transaction flow as seamless as possible, communication and information management is critical.

With the advent of B2B exchanges, a new challenge has emerged to create web-based solutions for managing the logistics of fulfilling an on-line order. The traditional logistics market, consisting of warehousing and transportation, is nearly 10% of the US's GDP and already approaching $1 trillion per year, according to industry analysts. The back-end logistics of fulfillment is a rapidly growing market space, and there are already many third-party logistics providers who manage that today. As e-business and third-generation B2B exchanges develop there will be attractive opportunities for a new wave of logistics providers to manage and streamline the back-end fulfillment process for B2B transactions, using web-based platforms.

Fulfillment is an integral part of supply chain economics from the time an order is captured to the point of delivery. In addition, the successful delivery of a finished or unfinished good is often the result of a series of fulfillment events between multiple trading partners and logistics providers. As in a relay race, the baton must be passed on seamlessly from hand-to-hand in order to win the race. To achieve that, timely and complete information must be seamlessly communicated to all parties — the goal of STP.

Every transaction requires some form of fulfillment, either digital or physical. In B2B and B2C e-commerce, a series of processes take place behind the scenes to fulfil a purchase transaction. For example, once a purchase is initiated on the front-end (assuming inventory is available), a message is sent to the nearest warehouse holding the inventory to begin packing the order. Simultaneously, a message must be sent to the delivery service provider (eg, FedEx, UPS, etc.) to arrange pick-up and delivery, and advanced shipping notice must be sent to the purchaser while an invoice is prepared. Next, the delivery service provider must pick up the order and provide proof of pick-up and tracking services to manage the order. Upon delivery, the delivery firm must establish proof of delivery for the sender and the end user. The buyer must then inspect the goods and accept them on the basis of quality, quantity, or timeliness of delivery.

The Future Shape of B2B Exchanges

Sometimes a third party is used to monitor performance and notify completion (eg, customs agents, logistics companies or quality inspection firms). Sometimes the buyer rejects the delivery and the goods are returned before final payment, reversing the entire process (known as reverse logistics). Assuming the buyer accepts the delivery, final payment is made.

Clearly, the back-end logistics of fulfilling a transaction can be highly complex. Tight integration of these steps will maximize efficiency in the supply chain and speed up fulfillment.

B2B transactions commonly involve multiple suppliers and distributors, further complicating the fulfillment process. For instance, logistics providers can provide transportation management services to pick the optimal mode and time of transportation. In addition, planning, selecting, and connecting to freight forwarders might be necessary to deliver goods from the point of origin to the delivery service provider, for delivery to a distribution center with separate invoice creation and handling. To achieve maximum efficiency and full transparency for a transaction, these interactions need to be automated, which reduces the time it takes to begin shipping an order once it is placed, which ultimately accelerates the time to delivery and final payment.

Fulfillment is so important because the timeliness of delivery is the most immediate measure of customer satisfaction. As e-business becomes more commonplace, the need for businesses to expedite these processes will grow. The problem for many companies is that they find it difficult to manage the logistics of fulfillment because it falls outside of their core competency. As we saw in Chapter 9, there are serious technological hurdles to integrating internal systems and associated file formats with those of trading partners and shippers.

Until recently, EDI, faxes, phone calls, mail, and proprietary data transfers were the primary methods of communication — particularly for order tracking. However, with the open access of the Internet and XML standards, faster fulfillment is now achievable. But logistics processes must be integrated along the entire supply chain and automated to minimize human error in order to achieve optimal efficiency, improve customer service, and profitability. The speed of fulfillment can be limited by the speed with which order data can be transmitted between all the relevant parties.

This creates an enormous opportunity for B2B exchanges to act as the "Babel fish" communication hubs that translate and map information between all the different parties — and that assist to create STP.

Companies are willing to outsource the management of these processes as businesses seek to rid themselves of the burden in order to focus on their core competencies.

Companies cite real-time order tracking and carrier scheduling as areas where technology can help streamline logistics processes. Providing services like order tracking requires suppliers and carriers to open and integrate their internal systems. In the logistics world, this means enabling a supplier's system to seamlessly communicate with a carrier's system to not only track an order once it leaves its origin, but to better co-ordinate delivery times, modes, pricing, billing, payment, resources, etc.

Linking fulfillment systems to a business greatly enhances visibility in the supply chain. Knowing where an order is in transit across a network strengthens a company's ability to forecast demand and schedule shipment. B2B exchanges can be the co-ordinators of this information and the distributors of it. Ultimately, a B2B exchange's ability to link into and co-ordinate an enterprise's supply chain gives the supplier, manufacturer, carrier, and end user superior visibility in its inventory, delivery demands, and availability. This compares with the legacy method of operating in the dark with visibility gained only through phone calls or faxes.

Booksonbiz.com: A new logistics paradigm

The publishing business is a good example of how integrated logistics can significantly improve the efficiency of the business.

In a traditional publishing model, a publisher produces the end product — a book. However, to get that product to market currently involves a series of middlemen and no straight through logistical process. Even the largest publishers use distributors to store, catalog and market their books to the sales channels. The sales channels are physical bookstores and, since the launch of Amazon.com, on-line bookstores. This means that bulk supplies of newly published books are delivered from the printing press to a warehouse managed by a wholesale distributor such as Ingrams. Bookstores and on-line book sellers then place orders with the distributor, who arranges to supply smaller numbers of books to each sales channel. In the case of an on-line bookstore, the bookstore also has to arrange delivery of the book from its own warehouse to the final consumer. (See Figure 11C over the page.) As you can see, this process involves enormous inefficiencies and a total lack of transparency. The middleman/distributor takes an amount in the range of 35–50% of the sales price of the book and the publisher has no idea of who actually buys its books. If books are unsold there is a reverse logistics process to return them to the publisher.

Figure 11C: Booksonbiz.com E-logistics

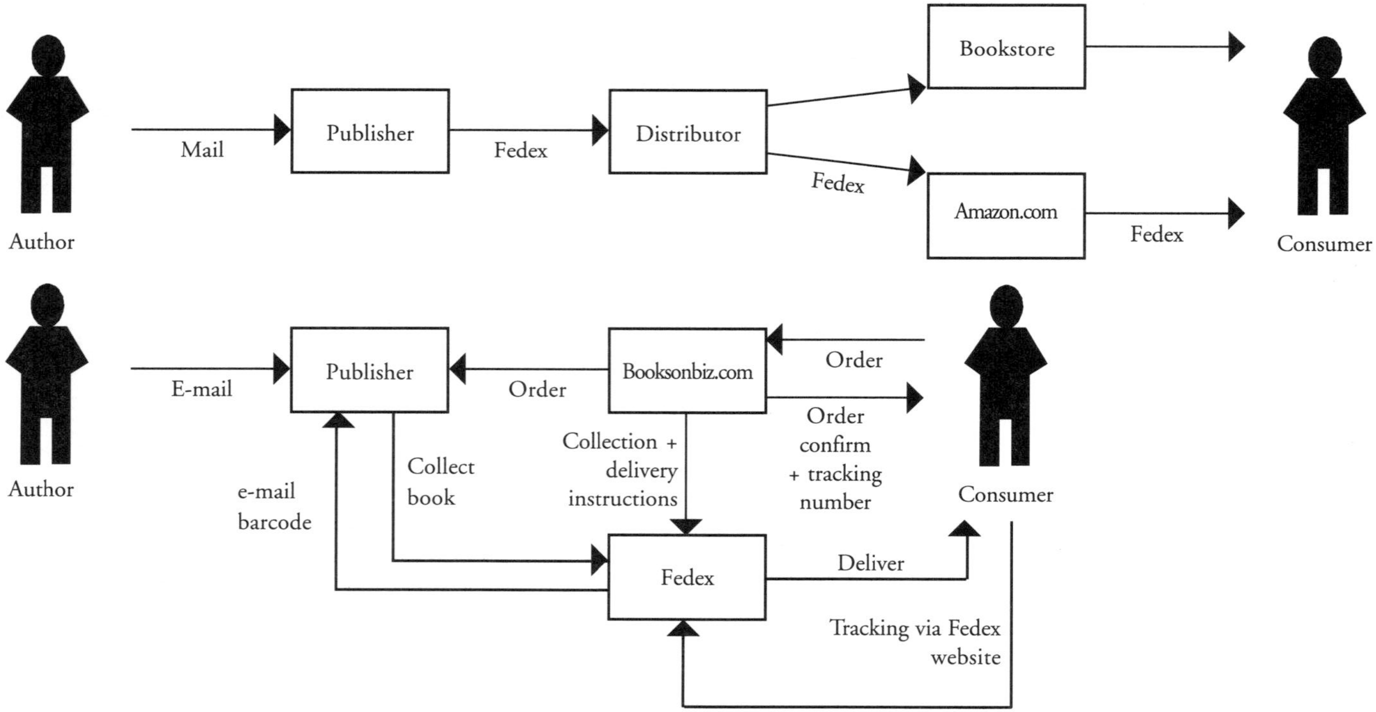

Source: Author

Booksonbiz.com is a specialist on-line bookstore for financial publications. Established by ISI Publications Limited, the publisher of this book, it has created a new "direct from publisher to consumer model." The automated logistics behind the website substantially reduces costs and increases transparency for the publisher. I hope that you acquired this copy of my book from Booksonbiz.com as I get more royalty if you did!

Figure 11C illustrates the new model. The Booksonbiz.com site has a tightly integrated logistics platform. As soon as an order is made on-line and the credit card issuing bank approves the payment, the site sends out several messages. One message goes to the staff at Booksonbiz.com to alert them that a sale has occurred. One message goes to the publisher, informing the publisher that a sale has been made, details of who ordered the book, and full delivery instructions. The third message goes to the delivery service provider — in this case, Fedex to obtain a quote. The Booksonbiz.com website is tightly integrated with the Fedex engine so that Fedex's internal systems calculate the shipping cost in real-time — based on the publisher's location and the delivery address — and adds that amount to the Booksonbiz.com shopping cart. Fedex's system then assigns a tracking code and issues a unique barcode by e-mail to the publisher, to be attached to the shipment. The final message goes to the consumer, by e-mail, to report the sale is complete and provide him/her with a Fedex tracking number. Fedex is currently working on upgrading its system to automatically issue a "pick up" instruction to the Fedex office that is closest to the publisher's dispatch site.

In this model, Fedex's on-line logistics system enables all members of the supply chain to view where the shipments are in real time. This leverages Fedex's core business of having to know where its deliveries are in the first place to manage the delivery of a product. Furthermore, thanks to wireless technology, a Fedex delivery person can update Fedex's internal system the moment a package is signed for through a remote hand-held device.

The result of this automated process is as follows:

- Fedex arrives at the publisher's dispatch location to collect the book;
- Fedex delivers the book to the consumer who is able to track the shipment on-line at Fedex's website using the tracking number;
- the publisher knows exactly who bought the book; and
- the publisher and the author stand to make more money from the whole process of publishing the book — since the middleman has been removed.

The Future Shape of B2B Exchanges

This level of e-business integration thus creates greater richness and increased profits for the publisher and the author by "dis-intermediating" the wholesale part of the publishing business.

Fulfillment — derivatives

Derivatives involve the trading of contractual rights or obligations based on an underlying product or reference asset, but do not themselves directly transfer physical property. Rather, the derivatives contract is designed to capture the economic effects of a real transaction in the underlying product or reference asset, without having to make or take delivery of that asset (see Chapter 8 for a fuller definition of derivatives).

Unlike goods and services, therefore, derivative securities do not usually result in a physical fulfillment. As mentioned above, most derivatives are "cash settled." This means that the derivative contract is settled at maturity (or before maturity at closeout) by a closing cash payment from one party to the other party, based upon the change in the market value of the underlying product or reference asset. Alternatively, in respect of an exchange-traded derivatives contract, either party can get out of the contract by executing a countertrade with the original counter-party or with a third party (called "offset"). As with a closing payment, an offset is settled in cash.

Cash Payments

Cash settlement is the end goal of every transaction, and typically involves the movement of money from the buyer to the seller to complete a purchase transaction. Bills or invoices summarize the details of any purchase transaction, and initiate the settlement process. With the growth of e-business, trading partners have increasingly adopted electronic billing and payment technologies to decrease the time it takes to get paid for a transaction and to improve workflow by minimizing the need to manually process paper checks.

While the existing financial settlement networks are well developed (eg, credit cards), the use of these networks to settle electronic B2B transactions is still limited. Less than 25% of B2B bills in the US are paid electronically. There is, therefore, plenty of scope for technology providers to enable businesses to send and receive electronic payments and payment-related information, particularly as more procurement activities move on-line. This opportunity includes the movement and presentation of an electronic invoice and remittance information that matches invoices to payments.

Puchasers see reduced costs as the primary reason to implement electronic invoicing and payment. The most tangible benefit for business sellers is to reduce the time that sales receivables are outstanding, thereby improving cash flow and reducing the strain on working capital. Based on the benefits that can accrue to both parties, B2B payments initiated over the Internet are likely to grow quickly.

Driving this growth will be the continued integration of payment services with internal systems. As B2B exchanges and other e-business applications are more broadly adopted and linked over the next couple of years, it will become increasingly important to automate the cash payment process so that it moves as fast as the other processes.

Letters of credit

International cross border B2B trade is currently dependent on Letters of Credit (LCs). An LC is a document issued by a bank at the buyer's request in favor of the seller, promising to pay the agreed amount of money to the seller within a specified period of time, provided that the seller conforms to the product specifications, delivery schedule, and documentary requirements of the buyer.

LCs are provided to secure payment for a cross border transaction by inserting a bank as a trusted third-party as assurance for both trading parties. With an LC there is a defined time frame for the coverage and payment, and coverage is dependent upon the presentation of predefined, compliant documents.

The shortcomings of LCs include costs, complex document logistics, and time delays. The costs of an LC include charges for LC issuance, amendments, presentations, bank drafts, commissions and wire transfers. Currently, LCs and the documentation required to prove good delivery and release final payment, are all paper based.

Payment systems

In B2B payments the following methods are prominent:

Checks. Good old fashioned, hand written checks — slow to arrive and slow to clear.

ACH or equivalent: ACH or the Automatic Clearing House system is a batch-oriented electronic payment delivery network connecting over 12,000 financial institutions in the US, to provide for the clearing of electronic payments. To a business, an ACH transaction looks and functions like an electronic check. Other countries have similar systems (eg, CHAPS in the UK).

The Future Shape of B2B Exchanges

Financial EDI: Financial EDI, or FEDI, is the electronic exchange of payments, payment-related information, or financial-related documents in standard formats between business partners. Large corporations use EDI to exchange purchase orders, invoices, bills of lading, etc. When FEDI includes a payment, a financial institution is used to facilitate the fund transfer over the ACH network. With financial EDI, the remittance information typically accompanies the payment; that is, the money and the pre-formatted data stay together.

Wire transfer: Wire transfers are typically used for large value payments between businesses. The most commonly used systems in the US include the Federal Reserve Bank's Fedwire system and the Clearing House Interbank Payment System (CHIPS) administered by the New York Clearing House. Internationally, wire transfer systems include NACHA, BACS, the European Banking Association (EBA), VisaNet, and RTGS. Banks throughout the world also use the SWIFT network to pass secure payment messages between banks. Wire transfers offer real-time transfers and have higher fees than ACH transfers, but the remittance information is usually lost in the process.

The cash settlement of B2B transactions is ready for automation.

A B2B transaction is generally more complex than a B2C transaction — which means that the parties can derive greater benefits from automating it.

For example, a B2B invoice needs to be presented to the buyer with line-item-by-line-item information in order for the customer to allocate and authorize charges to departments, projects, or individuals within a firm. Next, the seller must electronically present the bill in a format that is readable by the recipient. Ideally, the electronic bill and remittance information is integrated with the seller's accounts receivable system, and similarly tied to the buyer's accounts payable system. This requires both parties to decide on standardized file formats (eg, EDI, e-mail, XML) to make sure that they can exchange information. The electronic invoice must also be reconcilable with the purchase order and shipping documentation.

In addition, the system needs to enable a buyer to enter a transaction with the confidence that payment will only occur if agreements regarding quality, quantity or timeliness of delivery are met — currently the role of the traditional LC. The system needs to be able to connect with any independent, third party that is being used to monitor performance and notify completion (eg, customs agents, logistics companies, or quality inspection firms).

When a party's bank account details change, the system must provide a way to forward the changed information to all relevant trading partners to maintain the system.

Finally, in order for businesses to extract maximum efficiency from e-business, the system must provide electronic forms of payment to speed up the actual cash settlement process. Paper-check writing is clearly inconsistent with the speed of e-business. Settling a transaction by paper check can take well over two weeks, while using electronic settlement methods reduces the settlement time to two or three days or less. Also, the use of electronic payments aids in reducing credit and fraud risks as the seller is typically receiving "good funds."

One method of effecting payments electronically is with credit or purchasing cards or through PayPal, which leverages the existing credit card networks. Credit card payment systems provide "good funds" but are not very efficient or cost effective for payments in excess of $2,000 — so they are rarely used for B2B payments.

The current method of making an electronic B2B payment is as follows:

1. **The trade.** The buyer browses the seller's on-line catalog at the B2B exchange and places an order or participates in an on-line auction.

2. **The settlement process begins with delivery of an invoice with payment instructions.** By using an electronic invoice, a business improves receipts management by speeding invoice delivery to customers and eliminating the cost of producing, processing, and mailing paper invoices.

3. **The parties mutually agree upon a form of payment.** The most popular forms of electronic payments are those that leverage the ACH network like e-checks and financial EDI. Credit cards can be used for smaller payments but have higher fees relative to ACH, and rely on proprietary file formats. In traditional inter-bank clearing and settlement networks — like ACH — the information that goes with the transfer is often lost or severely truncated, meaning sellers have to reconcile incoming funds with orders and invoices. In our example, let us assume that the buyer states it will execute payment over the ACH network.

4. **Buyer initiates payment.** The buyer instructs its commercial bank to make payment to the seller's bank.

5. **Seller receives payment.** The seller receives payment some days later. The seller's accounting function struggles to reconcile the payment with the invoice, print out ACH receipt information, and manually file it with the invoice. Often the seller also has to re-key information into their systems.

Clearly a better mechanism must be, and is being, developed.

In the ideal scenario a payment gateway service/technology is used to capture and translate orders into a form in which they can enter and travel across the existing inter-bank financial settlement networks (eg, EBA, RTGS, SWIFT, the ACH system and the credit card networks). A financial institution or third-party processor initiates the payment. Funds are verified and remittance information is electronically delivered to the seller's and buyer's accounts receivable and accounts payable cash application systems to settle the transaction.

A prominent third-party provider in this space is TradeCard, Inc. (www.tradecard.com), which aims to automate the steps necessary for purchase order approvals, payment decisions and settlement.

With the potential for independent, third-party payment gateways such as TradeCard to dominate in B2B e-payments, many of the world's largest banks realized that they faced being "dis-intermediated" out of the process. To defend their position, a group of leading banks joined together to create Identrus (www.identrus.com), a global trust system that permits buyers and sellers to conclusively identify one another using Identrus Global IDs issued by their financial institutions. Identrus is analogous to VISA and MasterCard networks as it is a globally uniform, closed contract system. Identrus has designed an advanced e-payments solution called Project Eleanor, which is currently the subject of pilot activity by a diverse group of international banks, including, ABN AMRO, Hypo-Vereins, UFJ (formerly Sanwa), and Wells Fargo.

Project Eleanor — A B2B e-payments system

Project Eleanor is an Identrus-led initiative to introduce secure, direct B2B payments. Project Eleanor provides Internet-based specifications to initiate B2B payments on traditional commercial bank systems.

I understand that this application got its unusual name because Identrus was originally codenamed "Project Roosevelt" (allegedly derived from the name of the hotel in mid-town Manhattan where the initial meetings took place) and this B2B payment solution is the companion to Roosevelt (now Identrus).

Project Eleanor combines various basic elements into six B2B e-payment instruments, namely, payment orders, payment obligations, certified payment obligations, conditional payment orders, conditional payment obligations, and certified conditional payment obligations.

Banks can deploy these instruments as e-payment products under their own brands to replace simple payments such as a check or a draft, through to more complex payment transactions, such as documentary collections and LCs.

Interoperability between different banks' product offerings is ensured by adherence to technical specifications based on XML and Identrus business operating rules (which are based on payment conventions and practices throughout the world).

Trading partners will have pre-established instructions with their banks for payment authorization, routing and settlement — this obviates the need to notify multiple trading partners whenever those banking details change.

Eleanor deals with payment initiation, as opposed to inter-bank messaging, clearing or settlement. It does not aim to replace existing paper or electronic clearing systems such as ACH, Fedwire, EBA, RTGS, or their equivalents within and between countries.

Eleanor ensures that a buyer's and seller's e-business systems can deal directly with each other throughout the payment initiation process, allowing both parties to automatically capture or exchange whatever data is required to facilitate automated end-to-end tracking, support and, most importantly, reconciliation. A basic payment obligation workflow provides a simple example:

- the buyer digitally signs a payment instruction and sends it to the seller;
- the seller adds its own information, including bank account data, and sends it to its bank;
- the seller's bank validates the seller's data, adds settlement details, and sends it to the buyer's bank; and
- the buyer's bank validates the buyer's data, including the employee's authority to make the payment, responds to the seller's bank, and executes the payment in due course.

Each party can capture and record whatever data it requires at each step in order to reconcile with invoices, etc. Buyers face the risks associated with ensuring good delivery and compliant order fulfillment. An Eleanor Conditional Payment Obligation can allow a buyer to enter into a transaction with full confidence that payment will only occur if agreements regarding quality, quantity, or timeliness of delivery are met. Likewise, the seller can confidently proceed to fill an order knowing that final payment will occur in due course. Any number of conditions can be placed on a Payment Obligation in the Eleanor system.

The buyer's bank acts as the repository for conditions and an independent "condition discharge party" (eg, customs agents, logistics companies, or quality inspection firms) can be used to monitor performance and notify completion.

Eleanor supports other combinations of payment types too. For example, there is a certified conditional payment obligation that combines the features of payment conditions that protect the buyer and a bank certification which protects the seller into one instrument, which can be used as a substitute for a traditional LC. Figure 11D illustrates the Eleanor conditional payment obligation. The advantages of the Eleanor system include:

- payments evolve seamlessly from the negotiation and ordering process instead of being a separate activity;
- complete payment information — what is being ordered, paid for, when and how — is linked to the electronic payment function itself;
- the bank processes required to execute the payment are transparent to the trading partner;
- the system offers an overarching legal architecture based on agreements that regulate the relationships between member banks and between users of the system inter se. This closed contract, legal architecture helps to mitigate risk, resolve disputes in an agreed format, and create financing tools; and
- Eleanor payment obligations are "bankable" and can be transferred as part of a receivables financing or discount facility.

One implementation hurdle with the Project Eleanor system is that it requires banks and their customers to install sophisticated cryptographic and messaging systems, in order to handle the intricacies and complexities of the highly secure and function-rich Eleanor protocol. In the first instance, Eleanor is more likely to appeal to larger financial institutions which can achieve high volumes in a variety of payment applications and/or have an eye for early adopter strategic advantage rather than short-term ROI.

The role of B2B exchanges in e-payments

B2B exchanges can play a leading part in introducing secure, direct B2B payments if they become Identrus certified and act as outsource providers of

Figure 11D: Eleanor Conditional Payment Obligation

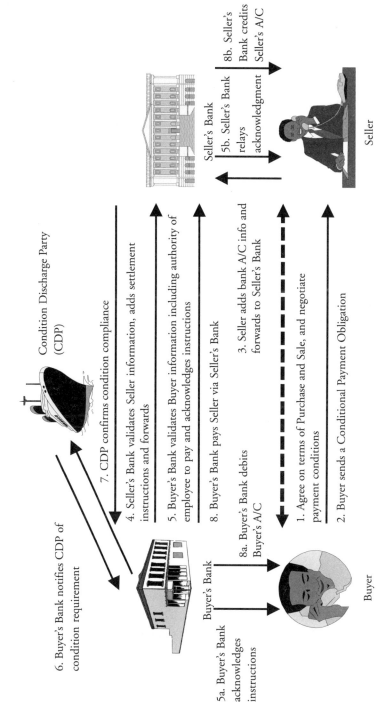

Source: Identrus LLC

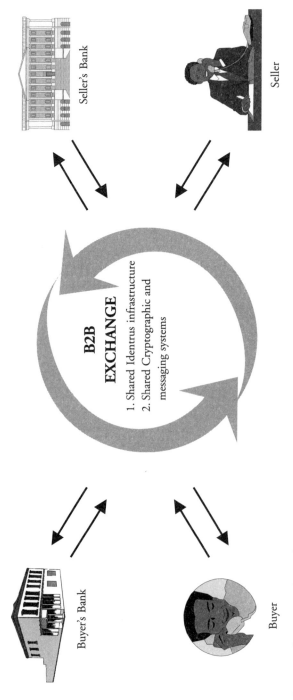

Figure 11E: B2B Exchanges' role in Eleanor e-Payments

Seller's Bank

Seller

B2B
EXCHANGE

1. Shared Identrus infrastructure
2. Shared Cryptographic and
   messaging systems

Buyer's Bank

Buyer

Source: Identrus LLC, Author

the necessary infrastructure to trading companies. The B2B exchange will then be the party that ensures that each buyer's and seller's e-business systems can deal directly with each other, and with the banks, throughout the payment initiation process. In other words, B2B exchanges can become the central hubs through which the Project Eleanor e-payments data flows.

Figure 11E illustrates a B2B Exchange's role in Project Eleanor implementation.

Delivery Versus Payment

One aspect of the high settlement risk associated with on-line exchanges is principal risk. Principal risk is the risk that the seller of a good or service could deliver the item but not receive payment or that the buyer of a good or service could make payment but not receive delivery of the item. Principal risk in clearance and settlement systems is generally recognized to be the largest potential source of systemic risk, that is, the risk that the inability of one institution to meet its obligations when due will cause other institutions to fail to meet their obligations when due, ultimately jeopardizing the stability of the whole market.

Delivery versus payment (DVP) occurs where final transfer of an asset or service is made if, and only if, final transfer of the cash payment (ie, "good funds") is made simultaneously. DVP is, therefore, highly desirable in B2B markets as it reduces or eliminates principal risk in settlement.

A key issue in establishing DVP is understanding when "final" payment is made. For this purpose "final" means that the payment is irrevocable. In the case of a payment made by check, there is no final payment until the issuing bank has cleared the check, and the funds have been credited to the seller's account. Even a bank draft (banker's check) does not represent final payment until it has been cashed — since the bank could go bust before the funds are credited to the seller's account. Clearly it is less likely that a bank will fail than it is that an individual's check will bounce, but the presentation of any form of check is not regarded as final and irrevocable payment.

Alternatively, the use of electronic payments is typically regarded as "good funds," since the wire, or other electronic instructions, are pre-checked against the payer's account before delivery to the recipient's bank.

B2B exchanges can ensure DVP by providing one of three services:

- an escrow facility;
- a central clearing account; or
- a central counter-party.

Escrow facilities

A simple escrow facility works as follows:

1. The buyer submits a payment (eg, by check, money order, wire transfer, or credit card on-line), the B2B exchange then verifies the payment and holds it in escrow.

2. Upon successful payment verification, the seller is authorized to ship the goods or services and submit tracking information, the B2B exchange provides a mechanism for the buyer to track the shipment and the exchange verifies that the buyer does in fact receive the shipment.

3. The buyer has a set number of days for inspection and the option to accept or reject the goods or services.

4. The B2B exchange verifies that the buyer has accepted the goods or services and then releases payment to the seller.

The transaction is then complete.

An escrow service will normally provide for an inspection period in which the buyer may examine the goods or services — and arrange for any authentication or appraisal processes that are necessary. The buyer must accept or reject the goods within this period and the B2B exchange will pay the seller at the end of the period if the goods or services have not been returned. If the buyer rejects the goods or services, the seller requires a brief time to examine the merchandise after it is returned. The B2B exchange can also offer a dispute resolution procedure to deal with any disputes that arise in the process. Escrow facilitators generally charge a fee for this service, which may be based on the value of the transaction.

A B2B exchange can outsource the operation of the escrow service to a third party provider such as Escrow.com. A B2B exchange can also offer a service that performs the quality inspection on the goods or services (or performs any other condition discharge service), on behalf of the buyer.

Central clearing account

A central clearing service requires each buyer to pay the funds into a central account prior to the final transfer of an asset or service. The central account is managed by the B2B exchange on behalf of the members. The B2B exchange then arranges payment to the seller simultaneously with, or immediately upon confirmation of, final delivery. As with an escrow service, the sellers are confident in making final delivery because they know that good funds are already held in the B2B exchange's clearing account.

In these scenarios, the B2B exchange gets to monitor the settlement process to ensure that fulfillment and cash payments are made — thus protecting and enhancing the integrity of the marketplace.

For example, The National Transport Exchange (www.nte.com) provides a cash clearing service. Shippers and carriers identify their available shipment or capacity needs, respectively, and their business requirements on the NTE Public Exchange. The NTE Public Exchange automatically matches compatible shippers with carriers. To ease financial settlement, NTE collects from the shipper and provides timely payment to the carrier.

Netting

If the B2B exchange provides a central clearing account, as we have seen above, it can also provide a "netting" service to reduce the actual number of payments that have to be made. Instead of requiring a trader to make each payment for each individual purchase and receive payment for each individual sale — the exchange can "net" that trader's cash settlement position down, for that specific trading period, to one single pay or receive amount.

Netting may be bilateral, where each trader's positions against another trader are netted down to one pay or receive, or multilateral. A central clearinghouse enables multilateral netting whereby the service nets the total amount each trader owes to all other counter-parties to produce a single net pay or receive amount between the clearinghouse and each counter-party.

By netting each user's cash settlement positions to one pay or receive, the central clearinghouse reduces the total number of payments that have to be made and reduces the amount of monitoring required. Each net payer has to pay into the central clearing account and then the clearinghouse pays out to the net receivers — with the central account clearing to zero after each settlement period. By reducing the number of payments, the clearinghouse can significantly reduce the costs of cash settlement.

Netting can also be applied to the fulfillment side of the trade. For example, in securities markets, a central clearinghouse can offset any trades each trader undertakes in the same securities with all the other counter-parties to produce a single net delivery or receipt in each security between the clearinghouse and each counter-party. For each cash receipt the central clearing service receives, it always has a corresponding payment obligation, and for each receipt of securities it obtains it always has a corresponding securities delivery obligation, so the net position of the exchange in both cash and securities should always be zero.

Netting can occur in respect of physical products too. For example, the London Metals Exchange (LME) provides a netting service. All LME contracts assume delivery of physical metal. To meet this need, large stocks of metal are held in warehouses approved, but not owned, by the LME at selected locations around the world. However, only a small percentage of LME contracts result in a delivery, the vast majority of contracts being hedged contracts that are offset (ie, bought or sold back) before falling due. As a result, the deliveries that do take place, either in or out of a warehouse, are deliveries of the net position, and reflect the actual physical market demand and supply.

In discussion with Thomas Krantz, the Secretary General of the World Federation of Exchanges (www.world-exchanges.org) he informed me that serious estimates made about central clearing facilities in securities markets show that market players might be able to reduce the volume of transactions that need to be settled by more than 75% because of netting. Whatever the exact number, the ability to net transactions would reduce volumes needing to be settled by a significant amount.

Netting can also reduce a firm's margin requirements (see "margining and cross collateralization" below), which can help increase the liquidity of the market by enabling a firm to trade higher volumes on its capital base than would otherwise be prudent.

Using a central counter-party

The key role of a central counter-party (CCP) is to reduce counter-party credit risk. The establishment of a CCP enables the market to move from bilateral trading — where the credit risk faced by each participant in a trade lies with its trade counter-party — to one where a CCP is interposed between the buyer and the seller.

By taking the contractual place of the buyer and the seller, the clearinghouse guarantees the trade. Legally this can be achieved by a process called "novation," whereby a trade made between Party A and Party B is replaced by two equal and opposite contracts, as soon as the trade has been matched and is cleared for settlement. The first contract is between Party A and the CCP and the second contract is between the CCP and Party B.

The establishment of a CCP between all buyers and sellers means that a market participant need only worry about the credit risk of the CCP itself, rather than having to monitor the creditworthiness of each counter-party with whom it deals.

The combination of a CCP and automated trading means that the identities of trading parties need not be revealed to each other, because the CCP becomes the counter-party to all trades. Therefore, market participants can retain their anonymity when trading on a B2B exchange with a CCP.

As mentioned above, the existence of a CCP is one way for an exchange to enable the implementation of true DVP, since the CCP can ensure that delivery of the goods or services is made simultaneously with final payment for those goods or services.

Clearing Systems and Counter-Party Credit Risk

First and second generation B2B exchanges relied on bilateral clearing. In these cases the two parties to the trade had to trust each other to make good on the trade. The B2B exchange's website acted only as the dating agency, which brought the parties together and offered no warranties or guarantees.

The risk that your counter-party turns out not to be creditworthy is often called "counter-party credit risk." Credit risk encompasses two major types of risk:

- **settlement risk** — which is the risk that a counter-party defaults on fulfillment where cash has been paid before delivery of the goods or services or vice versa; and
- **market risk** — which is the risk that the non-defaulting counter-party will incur a loss in replacing a trade not settled following a default.

Settlement risk arises if a trade is settled via a free-of-payment delivery mechanism, so that the cash is not delivered at the same time as the security. In such a situation, a company's exposure will equal the full value of the goods or services delivered or cash paid. DVP eliminates this risk by ensuring that final transfer of an asset or service is made if, and only if, final transfer of the payment is made simultaneously.

The second component of counter-party credit risk is the cost of buying in, or selling out, an asset in the case of a default — called market risk. This risk is faced irrespective of whether DVP or a free-of-payment settlement mechanism is used.

Some on-line markets have adopted "reputation rating" systems as a way of containing counter-party risk. In the B2C space, eBay has very successfully used this technique to reduce default rates. The system works by providing a central database where one side of a transaction can record their experience and enhance or reduce the reputation of the other party through the allocation of a rating. The system allows a trader to build up a public reputation as a trustworthy counter-party.

However, in some markets the parties do not wish to disclose their identities to the general market place. In such markets the exchange can allow users to pre-select a list of potential counter-parties with whom they are willing to do business and/or apply a credit risk limit to trades with specific counter-parties. This can severely restrict the liquidity of the market though, since parties are restricting their range of counter-parties.

In addition, if there is no CCP in a market, each market participant must monitor the creditworthiness of each of its counter-parties in order to manage and reduce its risk. This monitoring is a costly activity. Given that each trader in the market must monitor the financial ability of all its counter-parties, much of this activity is duplicative.

Credit risk becomes particularly important in the case of long-dated transactions that are not settled immediately, for example in the trading of forward contracts. In these cases, the credit risk extends over the whole period that the trader holds an open position. As forward delivery dates move out into the future, bilateral credit lines between the trading counter-parties are rapidly exhausted. In the case of derivatives, each trader's open positions must be monitored constantly. Regulated derivatives exchanges require that the open contracts are "marked-to-market" on a daily basis — ie, all market losses must be calculated on a daily basis. To contain credit risk, regulated markets require the traders to post additional margin to cover some or all of their losses if those losses increase over the life of the contract.

B2B exchanges can, therefore, either leave the credit risk issue for the market participants to sort out themselves — not a long-term strategy — or provide a centralized, multilateral clearing and settlement service that manages the credit risk issue on behalf of the market, and acts as a CCP.

To be successful in offering derivative securities a B2B exchange must introduce a central clearinghouse that manages risk and acts as a CCP (see Chapter 8).

CCPs reduce settlement risk

In an article entitled *What is multilateral clearing and who cares?*[1] published in the Chicago Fed Letter in 1994, James Moser, an economic advisor and research officer at the Federal Reserve Bank of Chicago, pointed out that centralizing this credit-risk monitoring activity within a CCP means that each market participant can be monitored at a lower total cost than would be incurred by all market participants if they had to monitor each others' creditworthiness bilaterally.

In any event, as Moser identified it is very difficult for any single trader to make a full assessment of the creditworthiness of all his other counter-parties. To do this, the trader would need to have a complete picture of all of the outstanding trades of each of his counter-parties. In practice, each company only has a complete picture of the trades between itself and its own counter-parties. This means that it can only estimate the extent to which it may be exposed to defaults affecting its immediate counter-parties. The presence of a CCP with knowledge of all the trades in the market undertaken by all the participants means that it will be able to build a much more complete picture of the creditworthiness of each market participant than can any single counter-party trying to do the same.

When there is a market crisis and there is no CCP, the creditworthiness of market participants immediately becomes the main issue. Market participants quickly draw up a hierarchy of credit-worthiness, and those institutions with higher credit ratings may stop dealing with those with lower credit ratings. Without the central guarantee of trades provided by the CCP a multi-tier market rapidly develops where market participants will only trade with those market participants that they believe have equal or higher creditworthiness than themselves. This reduces the efficiency of the market and rapidly reduces the liquidity of the market.

The Future Shape of B2B Exchanges

EnronOnline

The total collapse in November 2001 of Enron Corp.'s on-line marketplace, EnronOnline.com, is a classic example of what happens in a bilateral market when credit risk and the creditworthiness of counter-parties suddenly becomes an issue.

EnronOnline provided an Internet-based trading platform for about 1,800 contracts on products ranging from pulp to weather derivatives to electricity. The "notional" value of all contracts traded by Enron between November 1999 and November 2001 was over $1 trillion. Enron said in November 2001 that EnronOnline then handled about 60% of its trading business, or about $2.8 billion a day.

However, EnronOnline was not like a traditional exchange that brings together competing bid and ask offers from multiple parties. Rather, EnronOnline was a billboard for Enron to publicize its own bid and ask offers to the market. In other words, every third party that traded through EnronOnline was trading with Enron as its counter-party. There was no CCP in the middle of trades made on EnronOnline.

Enron began to unravel in October 2001, after it sliced more than half a billion dollars from its reported profits for the previous five years and reduced shareholder equity by $1.2 billion. Market worries about Enron first surfaced in the summer of 2001 when the SEC announced that it was investigating a number of partnerships with which Enron had major business deals and which appeared to be owned or controlled by the then CFO of Enron.

Volume in Enron's core North American natural gas and electricity trading operation suddenly plunged 20% as other energy-trading companies, unnerved by Enron's financial distress, steered business elsewhere. The rating agencies then announced a review of Enron's investment grade rating. Although Moody's and S&P's eventually maintained an investment grade rating for Enron, this was only after Enron's largest competitor Dynergy announced a friendly rescue takeover. The profit restatement caused Enron's share price to fall dramatically. From January to November 2001, the share price fell nearly 90% from a high of $82 a share to below $10 per share.

As its shares plunged, Enron faced a cash crunch because lenders and some trading partners lost confidence the company would have the cash to pay bills. Trading partners either demanded more collateral to trade, or restricted trading altogether, with the Houston-based company.

In other words, the market lost all confidence in Enron as the sole counter-party for trades made on EnronOnline.

EnronOnline stopped allowing trades altogether and Enron stopped posting bids and offers on-line around 28 November 2001. Dynergy pulled out of the proposed merger and Enron subsequently declared bankruptcy in December 2001. Enron ended up selling its trading business to UBS Warburg in January 2002. It was Enron's perceived credit-worthiness and trading acumen that drove the trading business up. And it was Enron's total loss of credit-worthiness that brought the trading business crashing down.

Since the demise of Enron, trading volumes in natural gas contracts on the New York Mercantile Exchange (NYMEX) have soared to record highs. NYMEX offers a central clearinghouse and CCP. And transaction volumes on the IntercontinentalExchange (ICE) grew 979% in the first quarter of 2002 over Q1 2001. ICE does not have a CCP yet, but it does have a counter-party credit filter that lets each user specify open or close credit limits with each other user; set tenor limits (ie, the number of days forward the user will trade with each user), and set daily dollar limits for trades with each other user.

CCPs reduce market risk

As a consequence of the guarantee it provides to market participants, a CCP is also exposed to market risk if one trader defaults prior to settlement. If a default occurs, a CCP's guarantee requires it to settle at the trade price, and this means that it is exposed to risk before settlement, as the market price may move. The CCP's exposure may be positive or negative, and will be the difference between the price of the relevant asset at the time of the original trade and the price at the time of the replacement trade. While market participants benefit from eliminating any replacement risk they face as a result of dealing with a CCP, these risks do not disappear. Rather they are centralized in the CCP and the cost of bearing this risk remains in the market as a whole.

Margining and cross collateralization

In a paper prepared for the Brookings/Wharton Conference, January–February 2002 entitled *The Future of Securities Exchanges*[2], Ruben Lee, a securities market expert and the Managing Director of the Oxford Finance Group, points out that a CCP will seek to minimize the risks it carries by requiring both sides of a trade to post margins prior to settlement. These margins reflect the replacement costs that the CCP expects to bear in order to perform the obligations of a defaulting party. Margin normally consists of an initial margin placed on a position prior to a trade and maintenance margin called for by the CCP. A

The Future Shape of B2B Exchanges

CCP seeks to limit market risk by marking-to-market on a daily basis the price change of outstanding positions in each product, and making a maintenance margin call if market risk has been increased (eg, if the replacement cost of the a trader's positions has gone up).

If a trader trades a range of products in multiple markets, each with a separate CCP, the trader may have to maintain margin in each CCP. Lee identifies that the total margin required for that trader's overall portfolio would be lower if the various markets he uses operate under a single CCP. This is because long positions in one product can be used as collateral in respect of positions in another market. The risk of a combined portfolio is, therefore, in most circumstances, less than the sum of the risks of the individual components of the portfolio. Lower margin requirements enable a firm to trade more than its capital could otherwise support — which increases the market's liquidity — or to utilize its capital more efficiently, as less of that capital is tied up in providing collateral for its trading activities. This process of collateral reduction is called cross-margining, or "cross collateralization."

Cross collateralization benefits those firms that trade in all the markets for which cross-margining via a single CCP is offered. Alternatively, separate clearinghouses can establish linkages that enable cross-margining between the different clearing facilities and thus provide the same cross collateralization benefits.

For example, BrokerTec Clearing Company LLC (BCC), the clearing affiliate for the BrokerTec Futures Exchange (BTEX), and Government Securities Clearing Corporation (GSCC), a subsidiary of the DTCC, established cross-margining between the two clearing organizations in April 2002.

The arrangement allows participating members of both entities to cross-margin their US Government securities buy-sell and repo activity against US Government securities futures contracts cleared by BCC. The BCC and GSCC arrangement allows participants to reduce their overall margin requirements, increase collateral liquidity and lower their operational costs.

Hank Mlynarski, President of BrokerTec's clearing company, stated "Cross-margining is an important component of the overall BrokerTec strategy. It will provide significant collateral savings to our member firms and its effectiveness in reducing systemic risk during times of market stress has been widely recognized."

Funding a central counter-party

In well-established markets, where the exchanges have been developed as mutual associations of brokers, the CCP has been funded by pooling the capital of the largest players and by developing a guarantee, or clearing, fund with contributions over time from the profits made by the members.

More recently, CCPs have sought liability insurance cover, over and above the levels of their internal guarantee fund. For example, the London Clearing House has bankers' guarantees provided by members and a Default Fund that currently stands at over £300 million in total. The Default Fund is supplemented by insurance cover of £100 million, provided by Lexington, a wholly-owned subsidiary of the AAA-rated AIG.

A brand new CCP to be established today for a B2B exchange will need to be funded by a combination of internal capital, contributions or reserves built up over time from the profits of the B2B exchange, together with lines of credit and catastrophe cover. In addition, the CCP can require clearing members to provide guarantees to cover their net cash settlement positions, instead of tying up capital by pooling the capital in the CCP.

For example, the Bermuda Stock Exchange (www.bsx.com) set up a central clearinghouse in 2001. Trading members are required to provide a guarantee that covers their daily net cash settlement position. In turn, the clearinghouse has a line of credit from a designated clearing bank to cover short-term liquidity requirements if a member fails to pay and its guarantee has to be called. Behind this line of credit, the clearinghouse has an insurance bond that pays out if one of the guarantors fails to pay.

Establishing a clearing fund

Requiring members to contribute to a clearing fund enables a B2B exchange to build up a reserve or cushion against a market failure. The size of the fund will also determine the level of catastrophe insurance that the exchange has to purchase. Most clearing funds require that all the non-defaulting clearing members have to top up the fund if it is ever called upon to cover losses caused by a defaulting member. Members cannot withdraw from membership until they have made the "top-up" to the clearing fund. This "survivors pay" model effectively mutualizes the risk of default. Since the survivors know that they will be required to pay the costs if any one of the members of a CCP defaults, each will seek to reduce the likelihood of such a default as much as possible.

This helps to keep the members focused on actively managing the risks in the system, but can also lead those members to create a "closed shop" to keep new members out. Provided that the B2B exchange remains open and neutral, it can resist the existing member's natural temptation to pull the drawbridge up and circle the wagons!

Many Successful Securities Markets Use a CCP

Up until the mid-1980s, the US had many competing clearing and settlement organizations. Prior to 1987, for example, all equity trades were settled by the delivery of endorsed certificates against payment by certified checks. There were hundreds of runners executing deliveries throughout lower Manhattan. Settlement was notoriously slow and from time to time the markets would have to close in order to allow everybody to catch up with their paperwork. Eventually, the "paper crunch" got so bad that the industry and the government got together to create one clearing organization — the National Securities Clearing Corporation — and one settlement depository — the Depository Trust Company. These organizations have subsequently merged to form the Depository Trust and Clearing Corporation (DTCC).

The DTCC, which is mutually owned by US banks and brokers, now handles the clearing and settlement of almost all US security trades. It acts as the CCP for all shares traded on the NYSE, AMEX and NASDAQ, and acts as a depository to record book-entry transfers of those securities. As the DTCC is the registered holder of the securities held through the depository there are fewer share certificates in the US and those certificates no longer physically change hands to settle on exchange trades. Instead, since the formation of the DTCC, the settlement of all trades made on US stock exchanges is done by book-entry at DTCC against wire transfer. As stated above, this central infrastructure has assisted in making the US market the most liquid capital market in the world. The US cost base, of five cents for an average equity trade, is relatively low.

By way of contrast, Europe now has four main central counter-parties. The London Stock Exchange uses the London Clearing House (LCH), which works closely with Crest (the UK's settlement organization). France, Belgium and Amsterdam (the three members of Euronext) use Clearnet, a joint venture between Euroclear (a Pan-European settlement house) and the French settlement agency, Sicovam. The Deutsche Börse has its own clearing organization and now owns Clearstream, which is a Pan-European settlement organization. And finally, European Central Counterparty Limited (EuroCCP) has been created to deliver a seamless, low-cost clearing and settlement solution to support NASDAQ Europe's pan-European market and the other European stock exchanges. Euroclear and CrestCo. (which operates Crest) have recently agreed to merge to form Europe's largest settlement organization, but that still leaves four separate clearing houses.

Some people argue that securities clearing and settlement in Europe would be more efficient if there was just one, Europe-wide CCP.

LCH also acts as the clearing house for all trades made on the LME which, as we saw above, trades futures and options contracts on aluminum, copper, zinc, tin, primary nickel, and lead. It also trades traded-average price contracts for aluminum, copper, lead, primary nickel, tin, and zinc. The LME introduced futures and options contracts based on an index of its six primary metals in April 2000. The LCH assumes a contractual role in all matched trades, becoming the buyer to the seller and vice versa. Therefore, clearing members are protected from the risk of business failure by other clearing members.

Who Should Own the Clearing and Settlement Mechanism?

As illustrated in Figure 11A toward the beginning of this chapter, the three functions of trading, clearing, and settlement in securities markets have historically been viewed as different levels in the vertical structure of the markets. Where an exchange owns its own clearing and settlement system it can be described as a vertical "silo." A controversial question that has recently arisen in the securities industry is whether exchanges (ie, the providers of trading systems) should also own the clearing and settlement system.

Ruben Lee summarises the advantages of vertical silos in his insightful paper *The Future of Securities Exchanges*[2], as follows. Vertical silos enable STP (straight through processing) since the trading system is directly linked with the clearing and settlement system, with trades being electronically matched and passed straight through to the clearing system. STP serves to minimize operational risks by reducing the extent to which trades are processed manually. As it is difficult to trade the same products on different exchanges, unless there are good mutual offset arrangements between the competing exchanges' clearing and settlement systems, users are naturally attracted to trade on one exchange — the one with the most efficient STP systems.

Vertical integration also enables the exchange to capture the full advantages of netting and cross collateralization set out above. There are many economies of scale between the different activities undertaken by the exchange and the clearing and settlement system. Since there are efficiencies in providing these services jointly, separating out the individual parts is difficult.

The Future Shape of B2B Exchanges

Vertical integration between an exchange and a settlement system also provides an additional and valuable revenue source for the exchange. Recent experience of competition between stock exchanges in Europe has highlighted the fact that electronic trading systems are now widely available and it is difficult for any one exchange to charge high transaction levies without losing trading to other competitors. On the other hand, the settlement process still commands high fees per trade, or for custody of securities. In some cases, revenues from the settlement system may not be directly tied with those arising from trading on that exchange (ie, the exchange can offer its clearing and settlement function to other trading platforms). This may allow the combined revenue streams to be less volatile.

Market players are also less likely to switch from an exchange that provides a clearing and settlement system — due to the beneficial effects described above. In a vertical silo, the exchange that owns or controls the clearing and settlement system is stronger than any competing exchange that just provides trading and information dissemination.

If the provision of the two elements of clearing and settlement are separate from the trading function in a market, the exchanges will face horizontal competition. This is because the trading exchanges will all be competing on the provision of trading services without any restrictions on access to the clearing and settlement system by competing exchanges. Since good trading system technology has now become a commodity product, which is readily available from a number of vendors, the exchange's trading services become nothing more than a commodity and the intense competition between trading systems rapidly reduces revenues and erodes margins.

For example, the Deutsche Börse in Germany trades equity, debt and derivative products and has merged its own clearing and settlement system with Clearstream (and is purchasing the remaining 50% of Clearstream that it did not own). Deutsche Börse is now the master of its own destiny. On the other hand, the London Stock Exchange (LSE) lost control of its own settlement system in the 1980s after it tried to introduce an expensive new system called Taurus that was rejected by the market in a major fiasco. Crest, the successor settlement system in the UK, is now owned by the major market players (banks and securities brokers). Since the LSE is now only a trading system for equities and debt (it recently lost out in a bid to acquire the London International Financial Futures Exchange to add derivatives to its product range), it is extremely vulnerable, and likely to be taken over by, or have to merge with, another European stock exchange in order to survive.

Market efficiency

On the other hand, multiple CCPs can create inefficiencies and raise costs for users. This is particularly true where the individual CCPs have been established with a national focus and the market then expands to become international — as is happening with the securities markets in Europe.

For example, it has been argued that it would be better to have a single public body to act as a Europe-wide CCP and deal with trade clearing for all European securities markets, even if it is linked to more than one settlement organization. The argument goes that this would significantly lower the clearing and settlement costs in Europe and help the Pan-European capital market to compete better with the US. The single CCP would achieve major benefits in netting and allowing users to cross collateralize, for all trades across Europe. *The Economist*, which promotes this idea, has christened this the "hourglass" model. The market structure would look like an hourglass with competing trading platforms at the top, a single CCP in the middle to maximize the scope for netting and cross collateralization, and maybe two or three settlement bodies underneath.

It is not clear who would own this central CCP. Such an entity would have the characteristics of a public utility and would be a complete monopoly. It would probably have to be owned by the industry — as a mutual association — and would have to be regulated as a monopoly.

Competition issues

In addition to being of concern to exchange operators and market participants, the question of who should own a CCP or settlement system has also drawn the attention of some regulators of competition policy. It is believed by some that where an exchange does operate both the trading system and the CCP, some of the exchange's behavior is likely to be anti-competitive.

By way of illustration, in his paper on *The Future of Securities Exchanges*[2], Ruben Lee points out that:

"*There are many ways in which a securities exchange may seek to exploit the monopoly power of a CCP, if it owns one. It may seek to cross-subsidize its trading system by using the profits it obtains from its CCP. The possibility of doing this may be increased by the difficulty of distinguishing the costs of clearing from the costs of trading in a vertical integrated organization. The ability of trading systems without access to such cross-subsidies to compete with an exchange supported by revenues from a CCP may be limited.*"

The Future Shape of B2B Exchanges

An exchange may also restrict access to its CCP to other competing trading systems. In order for netting to be viable it is necessary that positions can be off-set against each other in a clearing-house, or be fungible with each other. Without such fungibility, no netting is possible. The extent to which market participants will be able to net any positions they take on different trading systems, is therefore dependent on whether these trading systems have access to the relevant CCP. If, for example, one exchange owns the CCP on which most clearing is done, and restricts access to this CCP by another competing exchange, market participants will not be able to net any trades they execute on the second exchange through the first exchange's CCP. The ability of the second exchange to compete with the first exchange will therefore be reduced."

On the other hand, vertical integration of trading, clearing, and settlement does not necessarily reduce competition. It simply means that exchanges must compete by offering market participants different full service offerings (comprising trading, clearing, and settlement) in a vertically integrated package.

Even where one, vertically integrated, exchange comes to dominate a B2B market, monopolistic provision of the clearing and settlement service is not automatically undesirable. In some circumstances, it is more efficient, and cheaper, for a service to be provided by a single natural monopoly. The provision of clearing and settlement system services has elements of a "natural" monopoly and a single system may dominate simply because it is the most efficient way of supplying such services. Indeed, the network effects associated with netting and the calculation of the collateral that market participants are required to deposit is a strong reason why the activities of a clearing and settlement system may be provided more efficiently by a single supplier for each asset class.

Successful B2B Exchanges Should Own their Own Clearing and Settlement System

As we have seen above, a wide range of benefits can flow from vertical integration in the areas of trading, clearing, and settlement.

By ensuring that it has an efficient clearing and settlement solution a B2B exchange will promote confidence in its marketplace and reduce the transaction costs of its marketplace — thereby helping to generate critical liquidity.

A B2B exchange that provides, and owns, its own CCP will also benefit from the network effects of netting and cross collateralization. The more traders that use a particular CCP, the greater the benefits of netting, and the more likely that other market participants will join the exchange that owns that CCP. Similarly, the more assets that are cleared through a particular CCP, the greater the scope for cross collateralization, and the more likely that other market participants will join the exchange that owns that CCP.

The creation and operation by an exchange of an efficient clearing and settlement system will thus enable that exchange to obtain a sustainable competitive advantage in its business environment.

As B2B exchanges are creating new market places that are truly global from the start, the dominant exchanges have the unique opportunity to establish one CCP and achieve all the benefits of vertical integration, netting, and cross collateralization within their industry marketspace.

Owning the clearing and settlement system also ensures that a B2B exchange's relationship with its customers extends over the whole life cycle of a trade — therefore enhancing the potential to sell other services (eg, insurance or credit enhancement products) to the users.

However, the experience offered by securities markets, and the calls for the reform of on-line trading platforms in the US following the failure of Enron, suggest that those successful B2B exchanges which are vertically integrated will ultimately face regulation in the same way that stock exchanges and securities clearinghouses are now regulated in the US and the EU.

End Notes:

1. *What is Multilateral Clearing and Who Cares?*, James T. Moser, Chicago Fed Letter, November 1994.

2. *The Future of Securities Exchanges*, Ruben Lee, a paper prepared for the Brookings/Wharton Conference, January–February 2002.

The Future Shape of B2B Exchanges

Part IV:

The Future Shape of B2B Exchanges

The Future Shape of B2B Exchanges

Chapter 12

Moving Offshore: The Natural Home for Global e-Business
"It is no longer physical geography that determines the winners."

A B2B exchange that supports cross border trading can effectively now choose where it wishes to be located. It can be set up and managed virtually anywhere and the e-marketplace itself can be operated in a separate jurisdiction or in multiple jurisdictions.

This level of freedom derives from the benefits of the knowledge economy and the specific nature of B2B exchanges.

Choosing a Location in the Industrial Age

In the industrial age the main factors of production were land and capital. Accordingly, a business would choose its location based on the following major factors:

- physical location:
  - proximity to the necessary raw materials;
  - proximity to the market; and
  - access to a sufficiently large and cheap labor pool;
- infrastructure and land requirements;
- access to capital;
- legal requirements: laws of contract, intellectual property, etc.;
- regulation — either a lack of restrictive regulation or a domicile with beneficial regulations;

- efficient dispute resolution mechanisms; and
- tax considerations.

Physical location

Businesses that manufacture, sell, or provide physical products and services have always been tied to an optimum physical location. This means that the business must be located close to its supply of raw materials or close to the market for its products or services, because of the time and cost involved in transporting these physical objects. Sometimes the business had to be located close to both. Many industrial age businesses also required a large and relatively cheap labor pool.

Infrastructure

Metal bashing and other manufacturing operations usually require large amounts of land and power, water, etc. Distribution businesses require a well-developed transportation and communications infrastructure. Hardware manufacturers require access to the best information technologies and research available. These infrastructure demands may well dictate the most suitable location for an industrial age company.

Access to capital

In the past, the major pools of capital were onshore in the most developed industrial countries that were rich in land and labor. Since people were reluctant to invest outside their home country, the business normally had to be located in that developed industrial country in order to attract capital. Today, capital searches the globe for the best returns, looking for innovation. This has led to the globalization of capital. Capital continually circulates in search of maximum investment opportunities. Information technology has accelerated this process and made it more successful.

Today, cross border capital flows are commonplace and great ideas can attract capital investment from anywhere in the world.

Legal requirements

For any business to thrive it must be assured of certain basic property rights, such as the right to private ownership of property, the ability to form and enforce legally binding contracts, and the ability to protect intellectual property rights.

These are the basis upon which western democratic nations have preserved a free market economy and prospered economically. In a nation state, these basic laws are supported by the full faith and force of the government — literally. As a last resort, the nation state claims a monopoly on violence and it uses force to require compliance with its laws.

The Internet of course operates irrespective of traditional constraints on distance or time, boundaries or law. This new "cyberspace" exists where geographical locations and borders are irrelevant, making it difficult to apply conventional law. When a supplier in London sells a product to a company in New York and the transaction is settled through a bank in a third country, with all of the communications in cyberspace, where does that transaction occur? Issues such as personal jurisdiction, choice of law, and venue are all in flux for international courts adjudicating on e-business issues. A body of law is gradually being built up in the US and elsewhere that is coalescing into a view of where transactions have the nearest "substantive connection." But, since the Internet is an international phenomenon and not merely a US one, the political issue has been how to co-ordinate the legislative and judicial approaches of many nations into a seamless regime. To this end, the UN, through its commercial arm UNCITRAL, has produced a model code for domestic governments to adopt into law. Other organizations such as the World Intellectual Property Organization have also promulgated model codes for their particular areas of law.

This issue is explored in great depth in relation to B2B exchanges by Christina Ramberg in a book entitled *Internet Marketplaces: The Law of Auctions and Exchanges Online*, published by the Oxford University Press in mid-2002. As Ramberg states:

"It is fascinating how little support from a national state an electronic marketplace needs. An Internet marketplace can function rather well without a structure based on a latent threat of violence. An Internet marketplace has at its disposal a more sophisticated — but yet more powerful — sanction than violence; access denial."

In other words, a B2B exchange operates on the basis of members voluntarily signing up and agreeing to be bound by a globally uniform, contractual relationship between the members and the exchange (and between each of the members of the exchange). This closed contractual system includes provisions specifically intended to cover contract formation, dispute resolution, etc. (ie, those issues which companies previously looked to a nation state to establish on their behalf).

The Future Shape of B2B Exchanges

Regulation

Choosing a domicile for an industrial age business may require a review of any regulations that are too restrictive. For example, consumer protection laws or labor laws may be too onerous to ensure profitability.

On the other hand, some jurisdictions offer regulations that support and nurture particular types of business. For example, the regulation of securities markets in the US has supported and nurtured the NYSE and NASDAQ by creating artificially high barriers to entry for potential competitors. And, following the 1929 stock market crash, those regulations have helped restore confidence and build greater trust in the securities markets allowing them to grow.

Dispute resolution mechanisms

In order to be attractive to business, a jurisdiction must offer efficient dispute resolution mechanisms. In the past, this has generally meant a legal system that includes sophisticated commercial courts with highly trained judges who observe precedent and provide consistent decisions.

More recently this has meant a well-established arbitration system, which conforms with the New York Convention on international arbitration.

Tax considerations

Businesses naturally seek the jurisdiction or jurisdictions that provide them with the lowest overall effective tax rate — so that they can maximize the return for shareholders.

Choosing a Location in the Knowledge Economy

"For countries in the vanguard of the world economy, the balance between knowledge and resources has shifted so far towards the former that knowledge has become perhaps the most important factor determining the standard of living — more than land, than tools, than labor. Today's most technologically advanced economies are truly knowledge-based."

Source: World Development Report, 1998/99 [1]

Knowledge is now recognized as a key factor in production. Economic growth is now driven by the accumulation and use of knowledge. In short, the knowledge economy is one in which the generation and exploitation of knowledge plays the predominant part in the creation of wealth.

In other words, it is no longer physical geography that determines the winners.

Knowledge-driven innovation and intellectual capital now determine an economy's position in the global hierarchy. The more innovative and intelligent a business location is, the higher its rank in the ladder of global investment. Small offshore countries like Bermuda, Ireland, and New Zealand are in a far stronger position to take advantage of the information revolution than they were to exploit the industrial revolution.

For example, Ireland has transformed itself in one decade from an ailing, virtually bankrupt economy into one of the fastest growing, dynamic economies in the developed world. Ireland has been a model of fiscal restraint, tax reform to lower tax rates, income moderation, and labor market flexibility. Between 1990 and 2001 Ireland's economy grew at an annual average rate of just under 7%, compared with annual growth of less than 2% in the EU overall. Ireland has attracted more foreign direct investment than either Japan or Italy in recent years, based largely on its attractive 10% corporate tax rate for manufacturing and financial services.

Unbundling the Value Chain

In *Blown to Bits* (Harvard Business School Press), Philip Evans and Thomas S. Wurster pointed out that the Internet can blow away practically any business, and they write that the "glue that holds today's value chains and supply chains together" is melting. The Internet and web-based services are indeed creating the opportunity for companies to "unbundle the value chain" and place some high value functions in their location of choice.

For example, large multinational enterprises are now positioning their group procurement operations, their customer relationship management applications, their supply chain management solutions and their intangible assets in offshore centers. As we have seen in Chapter 9, the low cost, but highly secure networks that can now be established on the Internet enable all of theses operations to be linked in real-time. The new, web-based global value networks that result are illustrated in Figure 12A over the page.

Figure 12A: Web-based Global Value Network

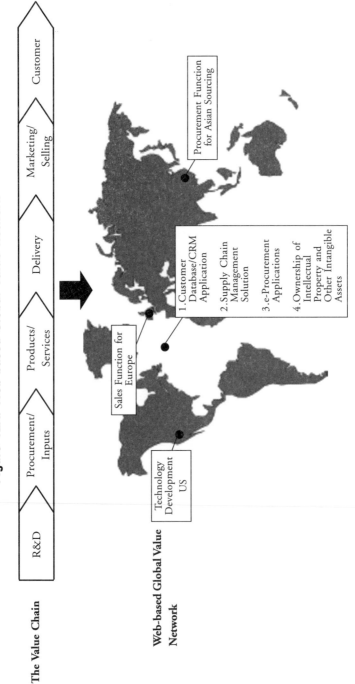

Source: Author

The main reason why companies are choosing to locate certain functions in offshore domiciles is to secure competitive advantage through:

- neutral taxation of cross border income flows;
- more flexible regulation for global operations; and
- increased privacy of data and trade secrets.

B2B Exchanges Fly Free

Most B2B exchanges can be and should be incorporated offshore.

B2B exchanges are free from nearly all of the traditional constraints on physical location because they are:

- fully electronic members of the knowledge economy;
- restricted to business-to-business;
- virtual communities of members that operate closed contractual systems; and
- exclusive information sources.

This means that B2B exchanges, like companies, are able to locate some or all of their high value functions in offshore domiciles.

Fully electronic

B2B exchanges are by definition, web-based, fully electronic organizations that can be physically located anywhere where the computers can be securely operated and the key management personnel are willing to live.

Business-to-business

B2B exchanges are not restricted by consumer-focused legislation around the world. Instead, by definition, they involve businesses doing business with other businesses, and this activity is not regulated in the same way. Businesses are generally treated as being "grown-up" and well able to take care of themselves.

Virtual communities of members

B2B exchanges are closed communities of members who have to meet basic requirements to join, and then have to accept the terms and conditions of the exchange as part of the membership process.

This means that B2B exchanges can create their own internal regulations as between the exchange and the members and as between the members *inter se.*

The Future Shape of B2B Exchanges

The result is that a B2B exchange can be largely self-regulating, away from and free of the need for government support and power.

Like VISA and MasterCard, a B2B exchange operates a globally uniform, closed contractual system under which the rules regulate how contracts are formulated, how trades are settled and paid for, and how disputes are dealt with.

In this environment the exchange and the contracting parties can choose which jurisdiction's laws will be the applicable law in respect of their legal agreements.

The membership agreement and the terms and conditions of the exchange must clearly state the applicable law for the relationship between a member and the exchange, on the one hand, and the relationship between members in respect of trades, settlement and dispute resolution, on the other hand. In the on-line environment it is particularly important that the terms and conditions of the exchange are crystal clear on such issues as when the trade is actually made on the exchange and when — if ever — a member can back out of a trade (eg, because they made a mistake in the bid).

Exclusive information sources

B2B exchanges do not have to rely on the threat of state sanctioned violence to enforce their rules. As exclusive trading places they can refuse entry to those who may not be willing to comply with the exchange's requirements and they can expel any member that does not comply with the rules. In addition, exchanges can fine, censure, or suspend members. This reinforces the self-regulating nature of the exchange, and does away with the need for any particular nation state's monopoly on the power to enforce compliance.

In addition, B2B exchanges can adopt international arbitration as the method of settling disputes between members, so that, again, the exchange is not dependent on the courts of any one country.

What is an "Offshore" Jurisdiction?

So called "offshore" jurisdictions are characterized by neutral (ie, low or zero) taxes on international, cross border business, liberal company laws for international business corporations, strong banking secrecy, and light but effective regulation. However, just about any jurisdiction that offers a materially lighter burden in respect of either fiscal or regulatory matters can be construed as an "offshore" haven in the eyes of a more onerous regime. For example, the US has very heavy regulation of finance, securities, insurance, and many other areas. Going offshore means establishing a business in a manner that escapes the heavy-handed regulations of the US, or any other "high maintenance," government.

Generally, these features have only been found in smaller jurisdictions that do not have large domestic populations demanding significant social services — which generally require high domestic tax rates to fund — and which have been insignificant, or on the margins of, global markets. Accordingly, many offshore jurisdictions are small islands in the Pacific, Caribbean or Atlantic oceans. However, some larger landmasses — and even some land-locked ones — have developed into quasi-offshore centers. Examples of island states are Bermuda, the Bahamas, the Cayman Islands, and the Cook Islands. Examples of larger or land-locked jurisdictions include Switzerland, Liechtenstein, and Ireland.

Many of these offshore jurisdictions have tended to be relatively underdeveloped in the industrial age (due to their limited natural resources) and have been regarded by many as third-world jurisdictions — characterized by palm trees, beaches, and shanty town housing.

In recent years these distinctions have been breaking down as many traditional "onshore" centers have been moving aggressively to lower their overall tax rates in order to retain or attract more business. Some people refer to the US and the UK as "offshore" tax havens these days because both jurisdictions have aggressively moved to provide tax incentives for specific types of business that might otherwise move to lower tax jurisdictions.

On the other hand, some truly offshore centers have begun to abandon banking secrecy and to impose more regulations and greater supervision, in order to become tightly integrated into the global financial economy. And they have become significant international financial centers in their own right.

The trick is finding an offshore center that combines light regulation of international business and a neutral tax regime with a sophisticated, first world level of services — so that you can escape the heavy handed onshore environment but still maintain the same presence and rich relationship with the market and with customers.

The main offshore jurisdictions to consider are Anguilla, Andorra, Antigua, Aruba, Bahamas, Bahrain, Barbados, Belize, British Virgin Islands, Cook Islands, Dominica, Gibraltar, Grenada, Guernsey/Sark/Alderney, Ireland, Isle of

The Future Shape of B2B Exchanges

Man, Jersey, Liberia, Liechtenstein, Maldives, Marshall Islands, Monaco, Montserrat, Nauru, Netherlands Antilles, Niue, Panama, St Kitts and Nevis, St Lucia, St Vincent, Seychelles, Switzerland, Tonga, Turks and Caicos, US Virgin Islands, Vanuatu, and Western Samoa.

E-security Offshore

With all e-business the standards for operation from a practical, legal and technological perspective need to be set so that all trading partners can trust that:

- their transactions are only with the intended party;
- the transactions will be protected in transit over the Internet;
- on-line transactions are legally binding; and
- they will have financial recourse should something go wrong.

Without that level of trust there may be no deal on-line.

B2B transactions are heavily document based. If electronic records, which can easily be altered or copied, are to replace signed paper documents, the trading parties need total assurance that the electronic records are authentic. When data is stored electronically, the parties need to be sure that it is secure but also accessible by authorized persons.

E-security is therefore critical to creating enforceable and trustworthy e-business transactions. E-security is particularly important if the B2B exchange is positioned in an offshore center and is servicing users from all over the world.

Digital certificates

Internationally accepted, standard public key infrastructure (PKI) technologies now provide for authenticating secure on-line transactions using digital certificates.

Advanced e-security, using both SSL and user digital certificates, enables the following:

- **Identity:** Both B2B exchanges and their users need to be certain of who is at the other end of a sensitive communication or transaction. Without clear proof of identity, both sides risk disclosure of information to unauthorized individuals. Digital certificates are used as "electronic passports" that prove identity over electronic networks. Users can securely identify themselves without sending secret information (such as passwords) over the network. Digital certificates can facilitate stranger-to-stranger commerce on a B2B exchange.

- **Access control:** As B2B exchanges introduce advanced applications and networking solutions, they need to grant access to groups of employees, users, and business partners — all with varying privileges and responsibilities. Shared secret systems, such as passwords, are quickly swamped by the number of users and their changing privileges. B2B exchanges can use digital certificates to manage the access and privileges of varied user groups, reducing the risks of inappropriate disclosure.

- **Accountability:** Digital signatures and digital receipts create a strong auditable record of a transaction, so that neither party can repudiate it. The recipient of a digital signature can easily determine if data has been tampered with or altered since it was signed.

- **Privacy:** Confidence in on-line privacy is critical for both B2B exchanges and users to engage in high value transactions or the sharing of sensitive information. Encryption using digital certificates can keep important data secure both in transit and in storage.

- **Jurisdictional certainty:** The trust behind digital certificates comes from two sources: the strength of the encryption and the framework of legal agreements that assigns roles and responsibilities in the operations of the certificate issuing authority. Most certificate agreements — and thereby any disputes arising from their use — are linked to the jurisdiction of the certificate issuing authority.

As described in Chapter 11, the Identrus-backed B2B e-payment solution called Project Eleanor is based on the same security principles and digital certificates. The technologies that comprise the Identrus solution include:

- PKI-based crypto-secured digital identities; and
- real-time validation of those digital certificates.

Bermuda — the Offshore B2B Island

Bermuda is already a major offshore financial center. I believe that Bermuda is also the world's most attractive offshore jurisdiction for e-business. This position has been earned from its track record as a leading offshore financial center for wholesale reinsurance and offshore mutual funds.

The Future Shape of B2B Exchanges

Some offshore jurisdictions focus on providing offshore services to private individuals (eg, offshore bank accounts and private trusts). Bermuda specializes in providing offshore services to international businesses. As such, I call Bermuda — the offshore B2B Island.

Bermuda has established leadership in e-business through:

- e-business specific laws;
- e-business specific infrastructure;
- tax neutrality;
- efficient dispute resolution mechanisms; and
- a premier reputation.

Serious financial center

Bermuda is now a tightly integrated part of the global financial economy based on the highly developed wholesale reinsurance market that is based there. Bermuda is already home to over 1,600 insurance companies with over $100 billion in assets and over $25 billion in annual premiums received. These Bermuda-based reinsurers now provide over 25% of the underwriting capacity of Lloyd's of London. The tragic events of 11 September 2001 have ironically served to emphasize the maturity and importance of the Bermuda reinsurance market. Several Bermuda-based companies had reinsured the World Trade Center and have been able to make full payment on claims in excess of $500 million. Ace and XL Capital have both settled with the owners of the World Trade Center and paid up, whereas other European and US insurers are litigating the claim. Since the terrorist attacks, over $15 billion in fresh capital has been injected into 12 brand new property and casualty insurers set up in Bermuda to offer cover in the wake of the attacks.

Following the attacks, many insurers in the US simply stopped writing terrorist cover. The Bermuda market's rapid response to those tragic events provided stability during an unprecedented void in onshore capacity and has proved to be a major part of the solution to the crisis that was caused in world insurance markets. Bermuda-based insurance companies provide cover for a wide range of unusual risks such as satellite launches, film financing deals, and crop harvests in third-world countries. The US and the rest of the world, therefore, need Bermuda's offshore insurance market.

Bermuda is also a major offshore financial centre for Asia. More than half of all the public companies listed on the Hong Kong Stock Exchange are incorporated in Bermuda. Again, Bermuda played a crucial role at an extremely difficult time by allowing Hong Kong companies to remain in Hong Kong during the instability of the handover to the People's Republic of China in 1997. Re-domiciling to Bermuda ensured that those companies' non-Hong Kong assets would remain outside China after the handover, and that added insurance policy enabled those companies to stay in Hong Kong — thus facilitating a smooth and successful handover of sovereignty from Britain to China.

Jurisdictional neutrality

Bermuda is often chosen as the jurisdiction to incorporate multi-national joint venture deals, because it is commercially and culturally neutral for all parties.

For example, when some of the state-owned entities in the People's Republic of China wanted to raise capital on the New York Stock Exchange in the mid-1990s (the so called "Red Chips"), they chose to incorporate in Bermuda, because it was acceptable to both the US investors and the powers that be in Beijing. Bermuda is also the natural home for global firms such as the global consulting groups Accenture and Monday (formerly PricewaterhouseCoopers' consulting arm).

E-business legislation

Bermuda's Electronic Transactions Act 1999 (ETA) positions Bermuda as one of the world's leaders in the codification of Internet law. With the enactment of the ETA, Bermuda became one of a handful of leading nations in the codification of the law of the Internet. However, while following international norms where applicable, the Bermuda approach has been to refine the UNCITRAL "model law" so as to enable a flexible, technologically neutral regime that is specifically designed for international business. In particular, the ETA ensures that all contracts formed on-line are equally valid and as enforceable as any written contract.

Like the US E-sign law, Bermuda's ETA states that digital signatures hold the same legal standing as wet ink (ie, handwritten) signatures. This creates new opportunities to move document-based processes (such as B2B exchanges) on-line, to reduce transaction processing costs and to increase the speed of doing transactions.

Tax neutrality

Like most offshore financial centers, Bermuda does not levy income or capital taxes. By way of assurance to foreign-owned companies incorporated on the Island, a certificate is issued by the Minister of Finance confirming that no such taxes will apply to the company until at least 2016. Regular extensions of the time limit are made. There are no on-line transaction taxes in Bermuda, nor is there any intention to seek tax revenues from Internet traffic through Bermuda.

A growing number of international companies are incorporating in Bermuda to lower their total, worldwide effective tax rates. Insurance companies led the way, but now manufacturers and other companies are following. For example, Leucadia National, Foster Wheeler, Ingersoll-Rand, Nabors Industries, a Texas company that is America's largest oil well services company, Cooper Industries, and Weatherford International have either moved recently or are moving to Bermuda. Other international companies that are already incorporated in Bermuda include: Accenture; Global Crossing; Teledesic; Tyco International; and Elan Corporation.

Excellent e-business infrastructure

Bandwidth

Bermuda received one of the first underwater telecom cables in the 1890s and now boasts a highly-developed communications infrastructure, with extensive bandwidth available through fiber optic and satellite networks operated by multiple vendors. Cable & Wireless and TeleBermuda between them have four diverse fiber optic routes, with satellite back-up, and are fully redundant in the event of primary failure.

Situated at the North Atlantic junction of the Global Digital Highway with direct fiber optic links between the US and UK, together with a further fiber optic link to the Caribbean and South America, Bermuda enjoys a key international location.

Hosting facilities

Bermuda provides high quality hosting facilities with maximum security and full redundancy.

Tier 1 Facilities

The SecureCentre www.eventurecentre.com[2]	Located in the Zurich Centre. The SecureCentre is a Lampertz IT Security Room and is the only complete IT facility in Bermuda to carry a guaranteed level of certified BS-EN 1047 performance, backed by ISO9000/1/2 liability insurance.

Cable & Wireless' Teleport facility
www.cwbda.bm

> The Teleport facility is Cable & Wireless'
> main telecommunications centre in
> Bermuda. The campus itself is located
> at one of the highest points on the island,
> has full security and is capable of
> withstanding the very worst weather
> conditions. In 2001, this facility was
> awarded a SunTone certificate by Sun
> Microsystems.

<u>Tier 2 Facilities</u>

TeleBermuda
www.telebermuda.com

> Situated by the airport in a former US forces
> secure facility.

Fort Knox
www.fortknox.bm

> Situated by the airport in a former US forces
> secure facility.

Liberal incorporation policies

In addition to a sophisticated Companies Act (the Companies Act 1981), which
enables the incorporation of foreign-owned international companies, Bermuda
is unique in being able to offer the ability for a company to petition the Bermuda
Parliament for the enactment of special legislation in favor of the company.
Such private legislation is frequently instrumental in effecting innovative
structures a client may propose, but which would otherwise not be permitted
under either the Companies Act, or at common law. Therefore, most prominent
e-business entities have been structured as "designer" companies created for
the purpose, with a private act obtained to give unique characteristics to the
corporate powers of the company concerned.

In addition, the Segregated Accounts Act 2000 enables a company to
effectively segregate assets and liabilities within segregated cells, but still
protect general creditors and the public.

The Future Shape of B2B Exchanges

The obvious benefits of segregated accounts, as they relate to a B2B exchange, are the substantial economies of scale that can be achieved by establishing legally segregated e-marketplaces and trading accounts within one low-maintenance corporate shell.

E-security infrastructure

Bermuda is host to an advanced, offshore, commercial digital certificate issuing authority (CA), called QuoVadis Limited[2] (www.quovadis.bm).

QuoVadis (QV) issues digital identities and helps B2B exchanges create networks of trust based on mutual authentication using both SSL certificates (which identify a company or device) and client certificates (which identify users).

The QV solution is based on internationally accepted, standard PKI technologies for authenticating secure transactions using digital certificates. But it is more than a collection of technical solutions. QV's certificate policies, which are subject to Bermuda law, together with its offshore status create a complete infrastructure to help companies operate effectively and safely on the Internet, across economic and political boundaries, with familiar business partners and with new ones.

QV's root certificate is securely hosted in Bermuda. This means that transactions which rely on a QV certification are always concluded in Bermuda and no personal user data is stored onshore (eg, in the US as for Verisign). Bermuda's ETA was one of the first international laws dealing with electronic contracts and digital signatures. Bermuda's law allows recognized certificate authorities — such as QV — to issue accredited (known elsewhere as qualified) certificates, and does not require private key escrow. QV is the first authorized certification services provider under the Act.

QV has chosen not to "chain" to a larger onshore CA (eg, Verisign) in order to protect its unique offshore status. This means that the QV root certificate, and all the archived keys generated by the QV CA, remain in Bermuda.

Offshore status of transactions

Offshore organizations and their clients are extremely sensitive to jurisdiction, and wish to affiliate their on-line operations more closely with their preferred offshore environment. Use of an offshore CA is one way to protect the offshore status of the company, its clients, and its transactions.

CAs can, therefore, occupy a critical place in international e-business transactions. Their role is largely invisible in the course of the actual transaction, but there are a number of circumstances where tangible benefits accrue as a result of the use of a CA located offshore.

The location of the CA service used for securing on-line transactions will have a direct and important influence on an onshore court's decision concerning:

- where the on-line transaction occurred;
- the governing law of the on-line transaction;
- whether or not the CA's offshore domicile is the most convenient forum for the resolution of disputes concerning the on-line transaction; and
- whether or not an onshore court should have jurisdiction over the on-line transaction.

While the location of the CA will usually not be the only deciding factor in the choice of a CA or other on-line transaction service supplier, I believe that significant competitive legal advantages exist for offshore B2B exchanges that select an offshore-based CA like QV.

In a confused Internet world where jurisdiction is often not certain, the use of an offshore CA service by a B2B exchange along with the other attributes of offshore on-line transactions is an important factor in the reduction of that confusion.

Onshore vs. Offshore Tax Regimes

In a 2000 survey entitled *Globalisation and Tax, The Economist* asked if tax competition between countries is a good or a bad thing and the following extract from the survey includes a quote from me:

"'Bill Gates would be fabulously more wealthy if he had started Microsoft in Bermuda,' says William Woods, chief executive of the Bermuda Stock Exchange. 'He may have known a lot about computer programming when he started the company, but his ignorance about tax cost him a fortune.' Mr. Gates has not done badly even so, but he knows better now. Teledesic, a company co-founded by the Seattle-based billionaire that plans to offer broad-band Internet access by satellite, is incorporated in Bermuda."

Source: *The Economist*, 27 January 2000

The Future Shape of B2B Exchanges

Nearly all major countries have been forced to pursue major tax reforms over the last few years in order to ensure that their economies remain attractive for investment. Within the 30-nation Organisation for Economic Co-operation and Development (OECD), the average top personal income tax rate has fallen 20% since 1980 and the average top corporate tax rate has fallen 6% since 1996. Corporation taxes in most onshore jurisdictions now range from below 20% to over 50%.

However, the US has not reduced its corporate tax rate for many years. As a direct result, the US now has the fourth highest corporate income tax rate in the OECD.

The combined US federal and average state rate of 40% is almost 9% higher than the average OECD top corporate rate of 31.4%. In addition, the current corporate tax regime in the US is both unusual and, in a global on-line, knowledge-led economy, highly uncompetitive. It states that a US corporation is subject to US corporation tax on its **worldwide** income. In other words, domestic residents are taxed on income regardless of where it is earned. Therefore, a US corporation with foreign operations is subject to US tax on the income from those foreign operations in addition to the tax imposed by the country where the operations are located.

However, this extra-territorial regime has been significantly mitigated for US companies in the past by three main provisions:

- foreign sales corporations (FSCs);
- the tax and accounting treatment of share options in the US; and
- the existence of double tax treaties.

FSCs

The FSC program was introduced as an incentive to increase exports by US manufacturers. The Tax Reform Act of 1984 provided for a reduction in US income taxes on net foreign profit realized from exports. Due to GATT limitations, the export promotion program could only be implemented through a related corporation formed in a foreign county. Hence, the birth of FSCs, incorporated outside the US in jurisdictions like Bermuda and the Cayman Islands. In July 1998, the EU petitioned the WTO claiming that the FSC tax provisions constitute a prohibited export subsidy since the FSC provisions granted tax breaks that were exclusive to US exporters. The WTO dispute settlement panel agreed and, in January 2000, issued a final dispute settlement report concluding that the FSC provisions were in violation of the WTO's rules on subsidies.

In November 2000, President Clinton signed the FSC Repeal and Extraterritorial Income Exclusion Act of 2000. The new legislation replaced the FSC provisions with incentives similar in scope and effect. The changes to the FSC provisions were intended to bring the US into compliance with WTO requirements.

However, the WTO appeals panel decided in January 2002 that the new provisions are still in violation of the WTO's rules on subsidies. The WTO argued that the changes were not made within the prescribed time and did not sufficiently address the issue of the tax breaks because the US government was still forgoing tax on income that it would otherwise be due and which is not taxed elsewhere, and because it relates only to goods being sent abroad. Unless the US changes its laws, the EU could ask for the authority to impose retaliatory tariffs on US imports that could amount to more than $4 billion annually.

The US must therefore remove this export subsidy and the Bush Administration is now considering revising the tax code to limit US corporation tax only to US source income and any income remitted into the US.

When this tax shelter for export income is removed, international sales organizations like Boeing, Microsoft, Cisco, and Intel will have a major incentive to move their headquarters offshore — in order to ensure that foreign income is not taxed in the US — unless the US amends its tax code to restrict US corporation tax to US source income only.

The cost of issuing share options

Under current US accounting and tax rules a company can exclude the cost of employee options from its earnings numbers and at the same time deduct the cost of options (based on the difference between the cost of those options at the exercise price and at the market price) from its tax return. In other words, a company can count options as a cost when they calculate their profits for the IRS, but ignore that cost when they calculate profits for their shareholders.

In fiscal 2001, Microsoft, Inc. paid $1.3 billion in corporate income tax on revenues before tax of over $11 billion because it could deduct more than $2.1 billion from its reported earnings on its tax return, using this device. At Cisco, the total deduction from reported earnings for fiscal 2001 came to $1.4 billion.

In 1993, the Financial Accounting Standards Board (FASB), the US accounting standards body, tried to reverse this position — but deducting the cost of options from reported earnings was only made voluntary after intense corporate lobbying of Congress. Following the Enron scandal, all such accounting wrinkles are under closer scrutiny. Draft legislation has been prepared in the US that provides that only companies that include the cost of options in their reported earnings numbers would, under the terms of the bill, still get to claim a tax deduction for the full cost of the option. Companies that do not include the cost of options in their reported earnings would not be entitled to any tax deduction. And all deductions would be limited to the original theoretical value of the option based on the exercise price — not the market price.

Again, if this Bill, or another similar provision is passed, international organizations with global sales (like Microsoft, Cisco, and Intel) will have a further, major incentive to move their headquarters offshore, to reduce their US corporation tax bill.

Effect of double tax treaties

Under various double tax treaties, the IRS generally gives a US corporation a full credit for any taxes paid on foreign source income in the foreign country when that income is remitted to the US.

In addition, some double tax treaties with some non-US jurisdictions allow a US company to deduct certain payments on their American tax return. These tax-deductible expenses include interest payments made to a non-US parent company, royalties paid to the parent company for use of the group's corporate logo and other intellectual property and fees for management advice rendered from the overseas parent company. In the case of a non-US corporation, its US subsidiaries are able to benefit from deductions allowed under relevant tax treaties.

However, complex rules apply to limit the availability of foreign tax credits by requiring the categorization of income into baskets to which the foreign tax credit rules are applied separately, and by requiring the reduction of income for which foreign tax credits may be claimed to reflect a broad allocation of US-incurred expenses. The US administration has stated that it will be re-negotiating many of its existing tax treaties. For example, the US Treasury Department has recently stated:

"Our tax treaties should be evaluated to identify any inappropriate reductions in US withholding tax that provide earnings stripping opportunities."

To the extent that the US waters down the provisions of existing treaties it will be adding further incentives for large US companies to move offshore.

Moving Offshore to Remain Competitive

Due to the peculiar nature of the US corporate tax code, a US company with global sales can reduce its worldwide tax bill by moving its headquarters outside of the US — in order to ensure that non-US source income is not subject to US corporation tax. Once the company is no longer a US corporation, its remaining US subsidiaries may also be able to benefit from deductions allowed under relevant tax treaties for amounts paid to the new offshore parent (eg, deductions for interest payments made by the US subsidiary to the parent on inter-company loans). However, the taxes saved in this manner are usually lower than the savings made by ensuring that non-US source income is not taxed in the US.

The overall tax savings obtained through an inversion are most dramatic in the case of a foreign parent corporation located in a tax-neutral jurisdiction (ie, an offshore center with low or no corporation tax). If the new foreign parent is located in a jurisdiction that does not impose corporate income tax, any income that can be shifted from the US is subject to no corporate-level tax at all. The same result can be achieved if the corporate group is structured from its inception with the parent located in a tax-neutral country (eg, as with Accenture).

US based entities are, therefore, able to lower their total, worldwide effective tax rates by incorporating a new holding company in an offshore jurisdiction.

For example, The Stanley Works (NYSE:SWK), for 159 years a Connecticut maker of tools and hardware recently proposed to move to Bermuda. The company announced that by doing so it would cut its tax bill by $30 million a year, to about $80 million. Tyco International, a diversified manufacturer with headquarters in Exeter, New Hampshire US, has been headquartered in Bermuda for many years and claims that being a Bermuda corporation saved it more than $400 million in taxes in the year 2001 alone. In 2000, Seagate Technologies re-domiciled in the Cayman Islands. Both Accenture and PricewaterhouseCoopers' consulting practice have incorporated their global holding companies offshore, in Bermuda. As mentioned above, Leucadia National, Foster Wheeler, Ingersoll-Rand, Nabors Industries, Weatherford International, and Cooper Industries have already moved or are in the process of moving to Bermuda, primarily for the same reason.

In the wake of 9/11/2001, some commentators have questioned whether it is unpatriotic for a US corporation to re-domicile in an offshore jurisdiction. Some politicians have described the tax benefits of re-domiciling offshore as a "tax loophole." Draft legislation has been proposed in Congress that seeks to continue to apply US corporation tax to a corporation's worldwide income, even if it re-domiciles offshore, if its main business is still in the US. Such a proposal is clearly absurd.

First, this is not a "loophole." All US source income remains subject to US corporation tax, irrespective of whether a company is domiciled in the US or offshore from the US.

Second, the reality is that a for-profit corporate entity is owned by its shareholders and the directors owe a fiduciary duty to those shareholders to maximize the return on the shareholders' investment — not to put loyalty to the country in which the company is incorporated ahead of the interests of the shareholders (who may or not be citizens of that same country). It therefore behooves the directors of a public company to continually find ways to lower the corporation's total, worldwide effective tax rate.

In addition, as we saw above, the US tax code is out of step with the rest of the world and with the metrics of the knowledge-led economy, and the Bush Administration is currently reviewing how to make the US more competitive in a global environment. It is an economic fact that few countries try to impose domestic corporate tax on a corporation's world-wide earnings. As we have seen, the Internet and web-based services are creating the opportunity for companies to place high value functions in their location of choice. In a global knowledge economy no country can sustain an uncompetitive corporate tax policy for long.

Penalizing companies that move offshore will only make a bad US tax law worse. It will also encourage US entrepreneurs to incorporate their start-up companies outside of the US.

The foreign entity is just as able to operate in the US market from the start and will avoid the process of re-domiciling at a later date, in order to shelter its non-US income from US corporation tax.

The only economically sensible and fair solution is for the US to adopt the international standard of territorial tax laws and only seek to tax US corporations in respect of income which is sourced in the US.

Structures and Tax Treatment of E-business Offshore

Some large enterprises already have group e-procurement entities set up offshore. For example, International Steel Industries Inc. has a group procurement and marketing arm in Bermuda called Galvex Trade Limited (www.galvex.com).

The structure of an offshore e-procurement operation is illustrated in Figure 12B over the page.

If the offshore entity is structured properly, the profits generated in the offshore procurement company can accrue free of income, profits, and capital gains taxes.

The offshore company is established as an international intermediary between importers and their suppliers or between exporters and their customers. The offshore company may either:

- buy products, on behalf of the importer, at the negotiated price level and then sell or re-invoice these same products to the importer at a higher price (ie, with a mark up), thereby accumulating profits offshore where there is no tax liability and significantly reducing profits in the onshore country of destination where there is tax liability; or
- buy products at discount prices from the exporter, thereby creating a very small profit in the onshore exporting country where there is a tax liability and sell, or re-invoice, these same products at market value prices to overseas buyers, thereby accumulating profits offshore where there is no tax liability.

In other words, the offshore vehicle converts what was previously US source income into foreign sourced income.

In the distant past, the general rule regarding the taxation of foreign company income owned by a shareholder based onshore was that the shareholder did not pay income tax on the company's income until that income was distributed to the shareholder as a dividend. This is referred to as the "deferral rule." To restrict the use of such offshore structures, many countries have introduced "anti-deferral" rules to impose immediate taxation on offshore income (called Subpart F Income in the US). In 1962, the US was the first country to introduce anti-deferral rules in the form of controlled foreign company (CFC) legislation. US CFC legislation was introduced specifically in response to a massive outflow of capital from the US to foreign countries in the years

Figure 12B: Offshore e-Procurement Operation

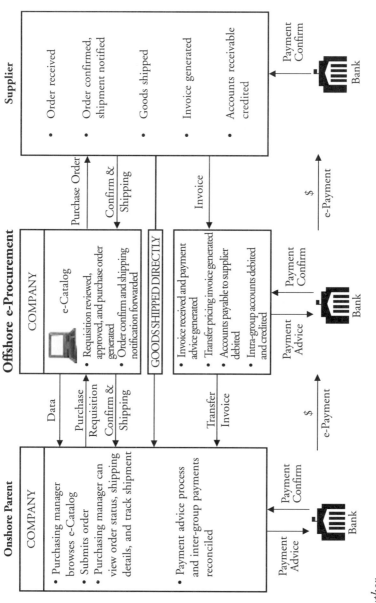

Source: *Author*

following World War II. Since 1962, numerous other nations have introduced CFC legislation including, for example, Canada (1976), Japan (1978), France (1980), the United Kingdom (1984), and Australia (1990).

Under the CFC rules, the onshore shareholders of CFCs are generally taxed on their pro rata share of certain types of undistributed profits of the CFC. The CFC rules can, therefore, cause a cash-flow problem for onshore shareholders who are taxed on income that has not been distributed to them by the foreign company — which can be an extremely negative tax position.

Under the US rules, a CFC is a foreign company the stock of which is, by vote or value, more than 50% owned by US shareholders. A "US shareholder" for this purpose is any US person who owns at least 10% of the foreign corporation's voting stock. In determining the 10% threshold of ownership necessary to constitute a "US shareholder," actual, indirect, and constructive ownership are taken into account. A US shareholder of a CFC is currently taxed on Subpart F Income whether or not this income has been distributed.

Given the number and complexity of the reporting and tax rules relating to Subpart F Income, it is usually advisable to avoid having the foreign company fall within the definition of a CFC.

B2B exchanges can avoid these anti-deferral tax rules if they are sufficiently widely owned. Where a B2B exchange is owned by a wide enough group of owners, they can all avoid the anti-deferral tax rules, even if several US corporations own it. This works particularly well for industry consortia exchanges that can aggregate the e-procurement requirements of all the members in one offshore vehicle.

End Note:

1. *World Development Report: Knowledge for Development,* World Bank, 1998/99.

2. Please note that the author is currently employed by the eVenture Centre as an "Entrepreneur in Residence" and the eVenture Centre is the major shareholder in QuoVadis.

The Future Shape of B2B Exchanges

Chapter 13

The Seven Secrets of Success for B2B Exchanges: Revisited

"The benefits of specialization mean that there will be only one major winner in each vertical sector...we have certainly seen major consolidation of B2B exchanges in most industries."

The heart of the first book was a section called *The Seven Secrets of Success for B2B Exchanges*, in which we sought to identify the key issues for anyone responsible for developing a B2B exchange at that time.

As they say hindsight is 20/20 vision. So, with the benefit of hindsight and two more years of practical experience, it is now a timely opportunity to revisit those secrets.

As the first chapter of this book has illustrated, those two years have seen a rapid proliferation of B2B exchanges followed by the bursting of the high-tech bubble in the US and the start of globally synchronized recession. This has led to a rapid drop off in corporate investment, a sudden drought in further venture capital and the consequent demise of hundreds of B2B exchanges.

So, how do the Seven Secrets stand up in this radically different and new environment? Let us revisit them here in summarized form with my updated analysis.

The Future Shape of B2B Exchanges

Secret # 1:
Stay Focused — Specialize on a Vertical

The most important secret of success in the initial phases of developing a B2B exchange is to target a specific industry in which you have strong expertise, and then specialize on a vertical within that industry. Specialization enables you to dominate your chosen space quickly, which creates mind share and liquidity, and then helps you to scale up quickly. Specialization means that the business model can be tailored to match the target market's distinct characteristics.

Once domination of the chosen vertical has been achieved, it is possible to start to widen the scope of the exchange into verticals within a chosen industry, but this luxury can only be achieved if there is proven liquidity and the ability to dominate has been clearly demonstrated.

In May 2000, after the first book was published, Geoffrey Moore, best selling author of *Crossing the Chasm* and *Living on the Faultline*, wrote an article on B2B exchanges in *The Industry Standard* entitled "Approaching the Chasm" in which he emphasized the need to stay focused. He stated "*Part of the problem is that at the outset, creating liquidity rewards narrowness of focus, whereas early market investors were bidding up breadth of focus. As long as the markets reward breadth, exchanges will spend their energies adding new markets, rather than deepening penetration of existing ones. Now, with the stock market's pullback, we will see investors reject more superficial expansion, leading to more targeted chasm-crossing efforts.*

Let's be clear, however. Focusing deeply on niche markets to create liquidity in and of itself does not generate anything like the returns business-to-business exchanges have promised their investors. At the end of the day, companies must deliver both depth and breadth."

E-business companies that lose their focus quickly lose their way. Priceline.com (www.priceline.com) is a classic example of an e-business company that lost its way through lack of focus, but managed to survive by regaining that focus before it was too late. Founded in 1998 by Jay Walker, Priceline.com started by specializing in on-line travel services. It pioneered the use of reverse auctions on-line to enable consumers to request competing bids from companies in respect of airline seats and hotel beds. The idea proved highly successful with airlines and hotel chains using the service as a very low cost way to move excess capacity.

Despite weak interest from suppliers, Priceline then chose to plunge into the gas (petrol) and grocery businesses, creating an offshoot called WebHouse Club that burned through nearly $400 million of investor money in less than a year. Meanwhile, Priceline's own losses mounted as the company prepared to market insurance, credit cards, and B2B web services. In October 2000, Priceline.com closed down WebHouse Club, the shareholders then ousted Jay Walker and Priceline.com refocused on its core market of travel.

EnronOnline was a very successful trading platform where Enron made a market in various energy contracts. Enron expanded its markets too quickly beyond its core competency of energy trading. For example, Enron moved into trading telecommunications bandwidth. It cost Enron over $600 million to build a network to ensure that it could deliver bandwidth, on a scale that never materialized. With margins shrinking, Enron tried to stretch the brand into new areas. Enron grew to offer contracts in about 1,800 business lines ranging from credit insurance to metals trading. In practice, this meant taking ever bigger bets, and eventually Enron collapsed and EnronOnline was sold to UBS Warburg.

As we have seen, Verticalnet started as a B2B exchange for the electronics industry. It then expanded its ambitions in 1999 to be an operator of industry-specific websites designed as on-line B2B communities for 59 industry specific marketplaces. In 1999, we called this model a horizontal exchange because the company sought to offer similar applications and support all the buyers and sellers across multiple diverse industries (or verticals). Back then we predicted that horizontal exchanges like Verticalnet's 59 e-marketplaces would not survive.

In February 2002, Verticalnet announced that it was selling off its suite of 59 e-marketplaces to focus on selling complex software solutions to large enterprises.

Vertical specialization

Industry sectors can be divided into "vertical" market spaces, which can be defined by geography, regulations, or product characteristics. These divisions act like fissures in the on-line world and can allow different B2B exchanges to service each of the separate verticals. The point here is that a laser-like focus on a specific vertical category can yield a tremendously profitable space for a unique B2B exchange.

The Future Shape of B2B Exchanges

Other success factors important to vertical specialization include:

- *choosing a monster market* — it obviously makes more sense to focus on markets with high value/potential, where there is frequent trading and where the most profits can be made; and
- *vertical knowledge* — this is critical for an exchange, to build credibility within a vertical quickly and to ensure that the exchange is tailored to suit that particular market.

Many of the dot-com founders discovered that, although they may have worked in an industry, they did not have the breadth of industry contacts or depth of vertical knowledge to be able to bring all the major players together. However, many of the industry-led consortia did collectively have the deep industry knowledge required.

The rainforest effect

In the ecosystem of a rainforest, there is intense competition to reach the sunlight above the canopy of trees. In the same way, B2B exchanges must focus on a vertical, scale up quickly, and grow as fast as they can. Once "through the canopy," and dominance is achieved, it is possible to spread out and introduce new products, attack other verticals, and add extra services.

A good example of this effect is the way in which ChemConnect has been able to expand from chemicals to plastics and now natural gas, after it first became dominant in chemicals. ChemConnect the leading B2B exchange in the chemicals verticals expanded into plastics and then merged with the rival CheMatch market in February 2002. CheMatch traded chemicals, polymers, feed stocks, and fuel products and is now integrated with ChemConnect. In March 2002, ChemConnect expanded further by acquiring a natural gas liquids marketplace from Altra Technologies.

Similarly, in financial services, TradeWeb is now expanding its business into corporate bonds after building a strong position in US Treasuries. In March 2002, TradeWeb LLC announced that its cumulative trading volume had surpassed the $10 trillion mark since trading began in 1998. TradeWeb's volumes are now about $2 trillion per quarter. TradeWeb's current product offerings include US Treasuries, US agency debt, euro-denominated sovereign debt, agency mortgage-backed securities, and commercial paper. New products scheduled for introduction on the TradeWeb platform in 2002 include corporate bonds, agency discount notes, euro-denominated supranational issues, and euro commercial paper.

Also in financial services, BrokerTec and eSpeed are expanding their trading application from US Treasuries and corporate bonds to municipal bonds and asset-backed securities. BrokerTec started out in June of 2000 trading just US Treasuries and Euro sovereign bonds. In November 2001, BrokerTec expanded its mission to modernize and innovate in the fixed income marketplace by launching BrokerTec Futures Exchange (BTEX). BrokerTec aims to replicate the advantages of its cash and repo markets — low cost, liquidity, transparency and straight through processing — in the futures market for fixed income products. Since the launch, BTEX has fostered steady growth and liquidity in US Treasury futures, including: US Treasury Bonds (30 year), US Treasury Notes (10 year), and US Treasury Notes (5 year).

Secret # 2:
Play to Win — The Need to Dominate

The benefits of specialization mean that there will be only one major winner in each vertical sector. This means that a successful exchange must try to be one of the "first to market" in its chosen vertical. Therefore, in true Internet fashion, the founders of a new B2B exchange must "plant their flag, declare victory, and then run like hell."

This is certainly proving to be the case, with major consolidation of B2B exchanges going on in most industries today. Unfortunately, "first mover" advantage, which the independent dot-coms generally had, proved to be less important in B2B than "first improver" advantage — which many industry consortia delivered.

Viral growth

For B2B exchanges, the site with the most or the best buyers will attract the most or best suppliers, which will generate transaction liquidity — and that, in turn, will attract more buyers. Once this "virtuous circle" has been set in motion, it acts like a vortex that sucks in more players into the exchange and becomes self-sustaining. This virtuous vortex also helps to repel potential competitors, because players who join one successful exchange will be reluctant to move to another exchange.

Liquidity, liquidity, liquidity

Achieving dominance means having the greatest liquidity — that is, having the most trades executed on your exchange. At the same time, building volume of trades is more important than the number of users at the start. This means that exchanges must target key players who are likely to trade the most and get them to join early. Intermediaries that are willing to "make a market" are particularly important as they help to create liquidity by continuously offering to buy or sell.

Critical mass

Liquidity is enhanced if you can build a critical mass of users as quickly as possible. In order to achieve sign-up, most exchanges have had to waive the standard subscription fees in the early stages (eg, CATEX has now waived all transaction-based fees). Waiving fees at the start can put a lot of pressure on an exchange's finances — so the exchange needs to be very well capitalized and funded at the start. However, market share is worth more than profits in the early stages of the launch of a B2B exchange.

Domination vs. anti-dilution

Winning as a B2B exchange is about dominating your vertical; it is not about coming in second or third place while trying to avoid dilution of your existing market share. Therefore, for those exchanges that are running in second or third place, there is no point in trying to compete against each other, they must merge and seek overall domination.

Case study 1: ChemConnect

ChemConnect the leading B2B exchange in the chemicals and plastics verticals announced it would buy rival CheMatch in a stock swap, in February 2002. The two companies have been growing steadily since their creation more than two years ago. In 2001, ChemConnect reported $3 billion in transactions, while CheMatch posted $1 billion. Although ChemConnect was emerging as the market leader, there was intense competition between the two exchanges. Meanwhile, smaller rivals such as Plasticsnet.com have been forced to close down. The merger has been welcomed by the industry and the combined revenues of the company, as well as the cost-savings associated with the merger, look like they will guarantee the exchange's success.

The combined exchange is now on the way to being totally dominant in the chemicals and plastics sector.

Case Study 2: MetalSite versus e-STEEL

MetalSite, an early leader as the first B2B exchange in steel, ceased operations on 15 June 2001, when it could no longer secure sufficient operating capital. The original founders and equity investors in MetalSite included Weirton, LTV, Steel Dynamics Inc., Bethlehem (now in Chapter 11 bankruptcy), and Ryerson Tull.

The Seven Secrets of Success for B2B Exchanges: Revisited

In August 2001, Management Science Associates (MSA) announced that it had bought the assets of MetalSite Inc., and would relaunch MetalSite and ScrapSite (for scrap metal). In July 2002, MetalSite announced that it had acquired the Global Steel Exchange.

MetalSite should perhaps have merged with e-STEEL in 2001 to achieve total domination. Now MetalSite has been closed down and re-launched while e-STEEL has been renamed as NewView Technologies and is focusing more on software licensing. However, NewView continues to operate the e-STEEL Exchange, a leading e-marketplace for the global steel industry.

Branding

Building a strong brand name is very helpful in achieving domination. Therefore, it's important to get the name right at the start. Use caution, however, in selecting a name that is too product-specific. While this may initially help to build brand recognition in your chosen vertical, it could later become constraining as you expand into other complementary verticals and outgrow the name.

For example, the name Plasticsnet.com limited that exchange to plastics only and now the exchange is dot-gone. Chemdex changed its name to Ventro when it tried to expand in to other products. CATEX remains saddled with a name that suggests it only handles catastrophe risk insurance.

On 13 November 2001, e-STEEL announced that it has changed its name to NewView Technologies Inc. to more accurately reflect its expanded product offerings and strategic direction. The firm had just completed the migration of its technology platform and business plan to a licensed software model. Its inter-enterprise software supports a broad portfolio of network business processes essential to managing complex direct material supply chains.

The change in name reflected the evolution of the company from a B2B exchange for the steel industry to an inter-enterprise business process software innovator for multiple industries.

Prepare for the long haul

Finally, achieving domination will not happen overnight. Indeed, if your exchange represents a major paradigm shift for the industry, then be prepared for a long haul in getting "buy in" and widespread usage.

The Future Shape of B2B Exchanges

The last two years have certainly proven that the move to on-line trading between companies and the whole revolution in supply chain management that B2B exchanges have enabled IS a major paradigm shift for most industries and it DOES take a long time to effect.

Preparing for the long haul means being properly capitalized and funded from the start and working with the major players in the industry to get liquidity quickly and it means adopting a "hybrid" model (see Chapter 7) that allows the industry to evolve into on-line trading.

Secret # 3:
Maintain Commercial Neutrality

Because an exchange provides a centralized market space for multiple competing members, and both buyers and sellers, it must stay neutral in order to be credible and build trust. This need for neutrality must permeate the whole exchange, the way it is designed, the way it operates, and the way in which it secures users' confidential information. The exchange's trading rules must not favor any single participant.

This means that the exchange must be perceived as a neutral third party by all other parties, as well as actually act as a neutral body; and it must be designed to benefit all the players in the industry it serves. This may not be easy because as the exchange starts to succeed and grow, key strategic partners or specific user groups will seek to control you.

However, many founders of B2B exchanges took the view that "neutrality" is like "virginity": you either have it or don't.

This view is dead wrong and may have cost many exchanges the opportunity to reach critical mass and to build sufficient liquidity to survive.

As we emphasized in Secret # 2, a successful exchange must be able to build liquidity quickly and expand to meet the demand in "Internet time." By far the easiest way of achieving this, as proven by the successful B2B exchanges, is to work with strategic partners from the very beginning.

Working with these partners does not poison the exchange, as long as it remains commercially neutral. This means that no one user group (eg, buyers, sellers, or existing brokers) should be seen to control the market.

How do you achieve this delicate balance? Here's one way — proportional representation.

As a successful B2B exchange develops and starts to dominate a particular industry, it will become increasingly more important for that exchange to represent all users of that market space. One way to achieve this is to partition the ownership between constituencies — sellers, intermediaries, and the general public. In this way, you can be sure that all stakeholders are properly represented in ownership and on the board of the company.

Moreover, the only fair form of corporate governance is a "one share, one vote" system. In such a system, a particular shareholder's influence is directly proportional to the amount of capital that they have provided.

In Chapter 5 we saw how AviationX, an independent exchange, was constrained by consortia exchanges formed by the largest players in aviation. We have also seen how the independent e-STEEL focused on neutrality versus MetalSite, which was set up by, and seen as dominated by, the steel producers.

We have also seen several industry consortia, such as Covisint and Exostar, using 2001 to restructure themselves into independently managed entities, in order to present a neutral face to all the industry players — a hybrid of the two business models.

Flexibility to "morph" the business plan

B2B exchanges must be incredibly light on their feet, and be able to innovate quickly. This means that the business plan must be fluid and rewritten every few months in order to stay ahead.

For example, many exchanges have turned to software licensing to generate revenue as they work to build transaction volume. Even Covisint, backed by the largest auto manufacturers, has morphed its business plan to include setting up private networks for users such as Ford Motors, in order to build volumes.

Maintain confidentiality of users' data

Successful B2B exchanges are building up an extremely valuable database of information about their chosen vertical market space. Over time, this data will become a major component of the exchange's value proposition — adding richness and color to the on-line trading experience.

However, it may be necessary to have an independent auditor review the systems and business practices of the exchange on a regular basis in order to provide potential members with an independent confirmation that their data will be kept secure.

The advisory board and user committees

A B2B exchange must ensure that all of its user groups are represented in the decision-making process. The easiest way to achieve this is to institute an advisory board and to set up committees comprising the different user groups. The advisory board should provide a forum for the key players in the industry to have adequate input on policy without them having to have a controlling interest or to control the board of directors. A compliance function within the exchange should report directly to the advisory board.

Secret # 4:
Ensure Transparency and Integrity

Because an exchange provides a centralized market space for multiple competing members it must be an open and fair market in order to be credible and gain the users' trust. A fair market is one that is transparent and built on integrity.

Some members may resist this if they believe that they can profit more from inefficiencies in the market (eg, a lack of pricing transparency). Successful exchanges set and enforce market rules that do not favor any one user or group of users.

Industry consortia need to be particularly cognizant of this point, to avoid potential anti-trust issues.

Most traditional stock exchanges were set up by stockbrokers and are still exclusively owned by the brokers, eg, the NYSE. This type of exchange operates rather like a "mutual society" or private club.

Over the last five years there has been a steady stream of securities exchange that have "de-mutualized" to become "for profit" entities and some have even gone so far as to list on their own market (eg, the Australian Stock Exchange, Deutsche Börse, the London Stock Exchange, and the Stockholm Stock Exchange).

By way of contrast, B2B exchanges are all being set up from the start as "for profit," neutral market spaces. This follows from their objective of bringing as many buyers and sellers together as possible, in order to create dynamic pricing, and to lower the cost of procuring supplies for buyers and expand the range of potential buyers for the suppliers. Whether they are set up as dot-coms or industry consortia, in all cases they are seeking to be neutral and independent markets with open access to all players in that industry.

Need to be a self-regulatory organization

The exchange can only ensure it is open and fair if it is prepared to regulate the users of the exchange's centralized market facility. The form of regulation most appropriate for an Internet-based exchange is self-regulation. A B2B exchange should be a self-regulatory organization (SRO); an SRO imposes regulations on its own members and then enforces those regulations.

Self-regulation is really enlightened self interest, since it is always in the best interests of the exchange to maintain an open and fair market place.

Transparency

Transparency is a critical element of fairness and should be enforced by the exchange. At a minimum, all transactions made on the exchange should be reported promptly to the exchange with full details on price and volumes. With fully-automated execution these details are immediately captured by the exchange's systems, but with post and browse and some auction-based exchanges the information must be given to the exchange by the parties to the trade.

The exchange should have rules and regulations that encourage transparency. Pricing transparency creates a more efficient market, which often leads to lower prices and greater liquidity.

Full disclosure is the "mantra" of a fair and open exchange.

Transparency also applies to the products traded through the exchange's systems. Sellers must disclose full information about the items that they are selling in order to enable the buyers to make a reasoned assessment of the true value of the products. The exchange should, therefore, enable sellers to put full product specifications and details on the website.

Integrity

The centralized pricing system is the most important function of an exchange and the exchange must seek to ensure the integrity of that pricing mechanism. The key elements of a fair system are:

- equal access;
- rules which determine order priority;

- equivalent orders are treated on a first in, first out basis;
- effective procedures to ensure that each seller's products are posted correctly and that each buyer's bids and orders are transmitted accurately; and
- trades are consistently executed in accordance with the published rules of the exchange.

B2B exchanges that are truly open have objective criteria to determine who may have access to the centralized, electronic marketplace, and provide equal access. Equal access means that every trading member has equal access to the exchange's trading system, irrespective of size or duration of membership. Price priority means that a new order which sets the best price (ie, the lowest ask or the highest bid price) must take priority over other orders with a less attractive price — unless there are clear rules about orders for larger size having priority over smaller orders.

The rules of a successful B2B exchange will require members to honor the integrity of the exchange's pricing mechanism. This means that members must agree not to do anything that will hinder or disrupt the fair and orderly functioning of the market.

Finally, members should be under a general obligation not to mislead or deceive customers in advertising goods or services through the exchange or by completing transactions through the exchange's systems.

The exchange's gatekeeper role

In order to maintain credibility and trust, an exchange must regulate access to its centralized market space. In implementing this concept, the exchange must decide what standards and qualifications it will impose for joining the exchange and for continued membership. In all cases, the firm and the relevant employees of the firm should be fit and proper persons without any record of dishonest or fraudulent trading activities.

Standardization

One of the value propositions of an exchange as opposed to an unregulated telephone market lies in the standardization of the product, standardization of the legal environment, standardization of the trading and settlement terms, and standardization of the documentation.

A successful B2B exchange itself draws up the rules (or encourages members to adopt existing industry standards) that regulate the quality of the products offered on the exchange, the lot sizes in which they are offered, the way in which they are priced, the acceptable pricing increments (called the tick size), and the standard terms for trading and settlement.

In B2B, as we have seen, exchanges are playing a critical role in setting the technology standards that allow all the players in a particular industry to integrate their electronic systems (see Chapter 9).

Complaints and dispute resolution

The members of the exchange, as members of a closed contractual community, should be required to honor the just and equitable principles of conduct set out in the exchange's rules and commonly practiced in the market space where they are conducting business. This should include a requirement to honor the trading obligations to one another that arise from trading on the exchange.

Successful B2B exchanges provide a mechanism, which may be formal or informal, for a prompt and orderly resolution of complaints and disputes between trading members.

Systems integrity

The exchange must ensure that all of its systems are robust to avoid systemic failures. As users become dependent on the exchange for pricing, trading and data it becomes more and more essential to provide fully redundant, highly secure systems. In the B2C space the bad publicity experienced by eBay following several well-publicized outages of its core systems demonstrates graphically the dangers of system failures for a B2B exchange.

Security of data on the exchange's systems must be high (eg, through the use of serious levels of encryption) to build up the trust of members. Members must be satisfied that their confidential data is secure within the exchange and that there can be no unauthorized use of that information.

B2B exchanges must adopt sound self-regulatory practices to avoid calls for government legislation to regulate and license their activities as national markets once they become dominant in their industry.

The Future Shape of B2B Exchanges

Secret # 5:
Add Value by Building a Virtual Community

Although the primary function of an exchange is to provide a centralized pricing mechanism and market space, successful B2B exchanges grow beyond this and develop into fully-fledged exchange communities. This means that they provide the services that allow people in the same vertical to network effectively and to access all the business information they require in one place.

Successful B2B exchanges, therefore, become powerful collaborative communities.

The six Cs of on-line services

In the first book we wrote that B2B exchanges must build the six "Cs" of on-line communities in order to create a valuable trading community:

- commerce — the centralized market space;
- content — trading data, pricing, product information, industry specific news, etc.;
- context — specialization on a vertical;
- community — added-value services that attract and hold new users;
- communications — the ability for members to meet each other and communicate with each other on-line; and
- connectivity — use of open, web-based applications so that members can use the Internet to connect to the exchange.

The importance of technology standards for B2B exchanges to enable integration within an industry is demonstrated in Chapters 9 and 10.

Enhancing B2B exchange community services

Many B2B exchanges never made it past the first phase of providing an information portal and an on-line catalog (e-catalog) for an industry sector. Some second generation exchanges, especially industry consortia, managed to get as far as providing auction functionality, automated request for proposal (RFP)/request for quote (RFQ) systems and — in a few cases — continuous trading. In some cases, the failure to generate transaction volume through their systems drove many B2B exchanges to refocus their efforts on providing software applications to companies on a service bureau basis — as "application services providers."

The Seven Secrets of Success for B2B Exchanges: Revisited

Building the community means extending the value proposition for users to include, private networks, fully integrated clearing and settlement functionality, supply chain management, derivatives trading and, ultimately, web-based services.

Providing supply chain management and clearing and settlement functionality applications is not an "either-or" choice for public B2B exchanges. Successful exchanges must provide it all.

The securities markets offer plenty of examples of how successful exchanges must provide more than just a trading floor — physical or virtual. The NYSE, for example, which has been around for more than 200 years, is not just a trading floor. The NYSE part owns the US clearing and settlement organization called DTCC. It also owns two-thirds of the Securities Industry Automation Corporation (SIAC). The remaining one-third is owned by the American Stock Exchange LLC (AMEX). SIAC is a major technology provider for not only those two US stock exchanges, but also the back-office systems used by the brokers who use those exchanges. SIAC provides communications, clearing, and data processing operations and systems development functions to both exchanges. In addition, SIAC provides telecommunication and outsourcing services. The NYSE is currently negotiating with the AMEX to purchase the whole of the AMEX, or at least its one-third interest in SIAC. SIAC's Shared Data Center is linked to the securities industry by more than 1,000 communication lines over which an average of 70 billion bytes of data are transmitted daily.

In addition, the NYSE sells its data through the consolidated tape organization. Out of the gross revenue of the NYSE and its wholly-owned subsidiaries in 2000 of $815.3 million, $140 million came from market data fees.

In Europe, the Deutsche Börse — now a $4 billion company — is similarly diverse. It owns an equity and debt securities trading platform, Europe's largest derivatives market (called Eurex), a huge technology group, and it has its own clearing and settlement organization. It is also in the process of buying 100% of a Pan-European settlement system called Clearstream. More than half of Deutsche Börse's revenues are forecast to come from its IT systems division in 2002.

Successful securities exchanges also offer back-office software packages for brokers that are tightly integrated with the exchange's trading engine. This helps members of the exchange grow their businesses while simultaneously locking the members into using that exchange.

The Future Shape of B2B Exchanges

These examples show that an exchange with longevity must offer a whole suite of community services, not just a trading floor.

In the B2B world, for example, the re-launched MSA MetalSite and NewView are both continuing to provide a public e-marketplace for metals, but it is now just one service in a community of services — just part of their move to create full service B2B exchanges.

Secret # 6:
Make the Right Strategic Partnerships

The universality and ease of use of the Internet means that you don't have to bring people into one physical trading floor to create liquidity any more. However, it is only possible for a new B2B exchange to challenge an entrenched industrial age market if the new entrant can build liquidity at much lower cost. Increasingly, cheap computing power and telecommunications are the weapons that allow Internet-based trading networks to challenge traditional trading mechanisms.

But the successful exchange must be able to build that liquidity quickly and expand to meet the demand in "Internet time." By far the easiest way of achieving this, as proven by the successful B2C applications, is to work with strategic partners from the very beginning.

Potential partners

The potential partners for a B2B exchange include deep pocket investors, buyers in the chosen market space, sellers, existing broker intermediaries, new infomediaries, content providers, IT vendors and trading systems software developers.

As we have seen, some exchanges must adopt a hybrid model (see Chapter 7) which often involves partnering with a leading firm of voice brokers in your chosen vertical. Examples of exchanges that we have seen do this include CreditTrade and ChemConnect.

Customize the market

As part of the laser-like focus and specialization that is required to dominate a particular vertical, a successful B2B exchange must tailor its applications to the specific needs of its chosen market space.

The best way to achieve this is to work closely with the potentially big users of the exchange and literally "get inside their heads."

Vertical knowledge

B2B exchanges are being developed primarily by experienced vertical industry professionals who have seen that, with Internet technologies now being adopted by business, there is an enormous opportunity for them to start up a B2B exchange. These professionals typically have deep knowledge of their particular industry and strong relationships with the main buyers and sellers in that vertical space. This vertical knowledge is critical in order to build credibility for the exchange within that vertical quickly and in order to ensure that the exchange is tailored to suit that particular market.

Where a B2B exchange does not have the necessary level of vertical knowledge on day one, it must move quickly to secure such expertise. The vertical knowledge of an exchange and the early sign up of key industry players are major barriers to entry for potential competitors and ensure that the laws of increasing return apply to that B2B exchange.

Outsource the technology

In our first book, we strongly advised the builders of B2B exchanges to outsource the technology development. It is critical for a successful B2B exchange to focus on its core competency — the specific industry expertise that will enable it to create the best business solution possible for that market space — and let the outside technology experts build the systems.

Indeed, one of the great opportunities spawned by the growth of B2B exchanges lies in the provision of technology, marketing, connectivity, content, and consulting services to these new exchange companies. Leading providers are Commerce One, Ariba, i2 Technologies, Nexprise, and eBreviate.

That advice still holds true today. With a multitude of proven systems around, it makes no sense for a B2B exchange to try and reinvent the wheel.

New age thinking

In the industrial age, a common approach to project development by companies has been to start by engaging a large firm of outside consultants. The methodology behind this approach is largely based on the belief that it is wrong to take key senior executives away from their existing jobs in order to develop a new project. And that an outside firm of consultants can approach all interested parties (including potential competitors) and come up with an independent view.

This approach is not ideally suited to the development of B2B exchanges because they need to:

- emerge and launch in "Internet time";
- have entrepreneurial leadership and be very flexible;
- be designed as neutral third-party applications rather than units within an existing industry player; and
- have very sound vertical knowledge and hands-on industry expertise.

Infomediaries

One of the most obvious areas for an emerging B2B exchange to seek strategic partners is in the development of community services. Since the core competency of an exchange is the centralized trading facility, it is unlikely that the exchange will initially have either the resources or the experience to develop many of the potential add-on services that a full community requires.

Sources of reliable historical market data are key potential partners. The value of a trading facility is greatly enhanced by the availability of market data, such as historical prices, volumes, and analytical research services. While this content will develop on the exchange itself as it grows, it may be necessary in the early stages to buy-in the data from the existing traditional market space.

Secret # 7:
Operate as a Virtual Corporation

In the knowledge-led economy the winners are flexible corporate structures which can "morph" their business plans and innovate in real-time.

The B2B space is still evolving rapidly and only those companies which are light on their feet and truly innovative will be able to survive.

B2B Exchange companies must be able to move quickly, to innovate, and to scale up fast.

The National Transport Exchange (www.nte.com) is an example of the innovative new business models that can be developed. NTE's goal is to improve how companies buy, sell, and manage transportation services. Shippers and carriers identify their available shipment or capacity needs, respectively, and their business requirements on the NTE Public Exchange. The NTE Public Exchange automatically matches compatible shippers with carriers. Thanks to this new level of automation, there are no phone calls and no paper chase. To ease financial settlement, NTE collects from the shipper and provides timely payment to the carrier. NTE carries no inventory itself, it simply brings excess load capacity together with buyers, on-line — it has become a true infomediary.

Since B2B exchanges are still a relatively new species of B2B application, the founders of these companies have the opportunity to start with a clean sheet and adopt the best practices of Internet start-ups. Invariably this means that B2B exchanges should be "virtual corporations."

Anatomy of a virtual corporation

There are eight key guidelines for virtual corporations which I highlighted in 1999 and which still apply today, as follows:

- concentrate on core competencies;
- outsource the rest;
- remain flexible at all times;
- keep staffing levels low;
- plan to operate on a 24 x 7 basis;
- choose professional advisors who specialize in Internet start ups;
- build partnership with key corporate leaders; and
- develop strong funding support.

Outsource, outsource, outsource

In order to be able to concentrate on the core competency of quickly building a customized trading facility, it is critical that the exchange's staff are not distracted by the need to add other services to the exchange. Outsource everything else, including:

- the technology build;
- the addition of content and community services; and
- the provision of logistics and document processing.

Think private, act public

Smart Internet entrepreneurs establish their businesses as limited liability, private companies, but act as if they are publicly-listed companies from day one.

The Future Shape of B2B Exchanges

Acting like a publicly-listed company means that you should prepare to go public from day one. On the other hand, as many B2B dot-coms learned the hard way, you should not rush to go public until you are really ready (see Chapter 2 for a discussion of the dangers of a premature IPO).

Customer care

Exchanges have multiple types of customer and they all demand a very high level of attention. Successful exchanges must focus on marketing to potential customers since new trading members are essential in the early stages in order to build liquidity on the exchange.

In addition to the usual marketing efforts to secure new members, an exchange must have a thorough customer care and user support program. This must include regular training sessions, a 24-hour, seven-day-a-week help desk, and trading desk facilitators to encourage new listings and trades.

Jurisdiction shopping

As an Internet-based application, B2B exchanges must be prepared to position themselves as global players from day one. Where revenues are likely to be generated from all over the world, it makes sense to start off by incorporating a holding company in an offshore jurisdiction — like Bermuda (see Chapter 12).

Chapter **14**

The Anatomy of a 3G B2B Exchange

"It is way too soon to write off B2B exchanges, in fact, they are making a concerted comeback."

In the future, corporate buyers and sellers will be connected to each other, and to all the third-party services that they need in order to do business together, through one or more B2B exchange (both private and public) that provide instantaneous information to all the decision makers in those enterprises.

B2B exchanges that achieve that level of integration are third-generation (3G) exchanges. A 3G B2B exchange includes all of the functionality listed in Figure 14A over the page.

By way of a summary of my analysis of B2B exchanges, I will briefly describe each area of functionality.

Information Portal

The basic function of a marketplace is to provide a place where buyers, suppliers, distributors, and sellers can find and exchange information. B2B exchanges do this in a virtual on-line market (a website), rather than a physical location. The basic functionality of all B2B exchanges thus includes industry news, industry specific information, the moderation of on-line discussions, and the provision of research and industry forecasts.

Figure 14A: 3G B2B Exchanges

	B2B exchanges		
Functionality	1st Generation	2nd Generation	3rd Generation
1. Information portal — news, forms, etc.	√	√	√
2. On-line e-Catalogs	√	√	√
3. Automated RFPs/RFQs	X	√	√
4. Auctions	X	√	√
5. Build and operate private networks for e-procurement by users	X	√	√
6. Fully-integrated clearing and settlement functionality	X	X	√
7. Supply chain management functionality	X	X	√
8. Continuous trading	X	X	√
9. Babel fish communication hub	X	X	√
10. Web-based value-added services	X	X	√
11. Derivatives trading	X	X	√

Source: Author

On-line e-Catalog

B2B exchanges build and manage catalogs. Catalog aggregation provides a one-stop shopping venue for procurement by companies. The exchange's e-catalog streamlines purchasing by aggregating the product catalogs of many suppliers in one place (a website) and in one format.

Instead of phoning and faxing multiple potential suppliers, the exchange's website enables a procurement manager to obtain all of the product and pricing information he/she needs in one centralized place. However, to provide real value, the e-catalog must support electronic searches. In order to support electronic searches, the stock keeping units in the catalog need to be rich with data, fully accessible to the buyer and standardized in format. One major benefit that B2B exchanges bring in this area, therefore, is a common standard for the e-catalog that helps to eliminate the all-too-common inconsistencies in trading partner and product identifiers.

RFP/RFQs

The next level is automated "request for proposal" and "request for quotation" (RFP/RFQ) mechanisms that enable buyers to get proposals or quotes from multiple suppliers. The exchange's systems help users generate purchase orders or RFQs, process invoices, respond to RFQs, and process orders.

To get the full benefit of these applications, users need integration tools to connect the exchange's systems with their internal forecasting and planning systems, inventory management, CRM, ERP, logistics and other applications which they use for supply chain management and customer service (see Chapters 9 and 10).

Auctions

The on-line auction format is one application that has proved to be highly effective for B2B exchanges, as it enhances efficiency while maximizing the return for the buyer or the seller. In addition, an auction market concentrates or pools the liquidity (that is, all the buy and sell orders) into one specific point in time when the auction closes.

The ability of multiple buyers and sellers to collectively set prices for a wide range of goods and services creates a dynamic pricing model and represents a radical departure from the older, fixed-price model of the industrial age.

The Future Shape of B2B Exchanges

Until the Internet came along, businesses were forced to pay fixed prices for standardized goods because one-on-one negotiation was inefficient for centralized, mass producers. Now, Internet-based auctions provide the opportunity for a more efficient, more satisfying relationship between buyers and sellers. In an auction, buyers bid no more than they are willing to pay (and have no excuses for overpaying); and sellers who ask too high a price (by posting a high minimum bid) must soon lower their price, or choose not to sell. Buyers have increased selection, more convenience, and the opportunity to pay less. Sellers have a larger market and the opportunity to charge more.

See Chapter 4 for a more detailed discussion of the way on-line auctions work in B2B exchanges.

Building Private Networks

Building private exchanges leverages off the sunk costs of the public exchange's infrastructure build out and is an important revenue source for emerging B2B exchanges. B2B exchanges can charge software license fees, customization fees, and transaction-based fees, for use of the exchange's core technology in the private network.

Building private exchanges allows B2B exchanges to:

- extend their customer base;
- increase revenue;
- make great connections with potential users of the public marketplace; and
- establish integration standards within an industry.

Private networks built by B2B exchanges use the core functionality of the exchange (eg, the reverse auction application) but with an on-line interface that reflects the customer's specific requests and branding.

Private exchanges therefore allow companies to become familiar with on-line trading so that they will be more prepared to trade in the exchange's more dynamic on-line public e-marketplace. As private exchanges become more common over the next few years, the momentum will build to bring business onto the public e-marketplaces — the pendulum will swing back towards the public part of the exchange.

Fully Integrated Clearing and Settlement Functionality

A 3G B2B exchange resembles a three-layered cake — representing the three layers along the value chain in a transaction: trading, clearing, and settlement.

The trading layer covers all the steps in preparing to make a transaction up to the point of execution. The clearing layer is concerned with the process of determining accountability for exchange of cash and the goods or services between the parties, by confirming the trade. The settlement layer involves the final conclusion of the transaction by delivery of the goods and services and finality of payment.

First- and second-generation B2B exchanges relied on bilateral clearing. In these cases the two parties to the trade had to trust each other to make good on the trade. The B2B exchange's website acted only as the dating agency, which brought the parties together and offered no warranties or guarantees.

Efficient clearing and settlement solutions promote confidence in the marketplace and reduce transaction costs — thereby helping to generate liquidity.

3G B2B exchanges, therefore, own and provide a centralized, multilateral clearing and settlement service that manages the settlement risk issues on behalf of the market.

Supply Chain Management Functionality

B2B exchanges, both private and public, have the capability to tie together the manufacturer with its suppliers (Tier 1) and its suppliers' suppliers (Tiers 2 and 3). This can lead to a collaborative process that generates greater efficiencies in the design of products and significant reductions in the time and cost of manufacturing.

In this way, the B2B exchange becomes a collaborative trading community and the benefits of the exchange extend well beyond the function of bringing buyers and sellers together and result in major process improvements as well.

For example, B2B exchanges can deliver collaborative planning, forecasting and replenishment (CPFR) applications.

The Future Shape of B2B Exchanges

Supply chain management requires deep integration between a company's purchasing process and the information residing in that company's inventory and logistics systems, and with information on the supplier's back-end systems. Connecting major ERP systems to other applications, such as supply chain management and logistics systems, is one of the most complicated tasks facing e-business today.

3G B2B exchanges facilitate this process by setting the standards for whole industries, by building private networks that link individual companies with their suppliers (based on those common standards) and by providing public marketplaces where buyers can identify potential new suppliers.

In summary, the exchange's procurement solutions (as described above) manage the product catalogs, aggregate purchases, and generate a purchase order at the end of the process. The auction engine enhances the procurement process when there are competing suppliers. The exchange's applications automate the RFP/RFQ process, or facilitate an auction (or reverse auction), collect bids, and identify a winning bidder. The supply chain management functions tie the exchange's users together in a collaborative network and the CPFR solutions enable trading partners to share, compare, and alert each other to changes in forecasts or key supply chain metrics.

Continuous Trading

Once a B2B exchange has deep integration with users it can develop a centralized market for standardized (or commodity-like) products (eg, ChemConnect's Commodity Exchange). Competitive bidding between multiple buyers and sellers, with automated matching of orders, creates an extremely efficient price-setting mechanism on-line.

However, continuous trading is only realistic for commodities in which there is regular, high demand. High volume trading by anonymous buyers and sellers can occur during the restricted trading hours of a securities market because the products are pure commodities. In the B2B world, continuous trading is only possible for indirect supplies (such as MRO supplies), pure commodity items, and derivative contracts.

Babel Fish Communication Hubs

The complexity involved in implementing all of the new Internet standards, such as XML, SOAP, WSDL, XSLT, and UDDI, has created an enormous opportunity for 3G B2B exchanges to act as the communication hubs — the "Babel fish" — that translate and map information between all the different parties.

If an exchange's users are suppliers to more than one industry, it may need to support more than one XML standard. If the exchange's users include the largest players in the industry, it may need to support a mandated XML standard for exchanging business documents. It will be important for the exchange to have local repositories of appropriate schemas and document type definitions, XML mapping tools, transformation tools, and a vehicle for ensuring guaranteed delivery of XML documents.

In this way, the B2B exchange acts as a Babel fish, translating all the different XML standards and helping to set a common industry standard.

Business interoperability holds the promise of improved revenues, lower costs, higher quality and faster services for every company. Connecting individual businesses electronically is the challenge. B2B exchanges will connect a company to its suppliers, customers, web services providers, trading partners, and other B2B exchanges — on a "connect once only" basis.

Interoperability with Other B2B exchanges

In January 2001, Transora, one of the industry consortia plays in the consumer packaged goods market, agreed to co-operate with GlobalNetXchange (GNX) to establish what they called a "megahub." Transora and GNX stated that the aim of the megahub would be to make it possible for companies to collaborate with multiple trading partners via a single exchange connection.

The megahub would provide exchanges with low cost EDI and XML transport and translation services over the Internet. The megahub would support exchange-to-exchange interoperability, which facilitates cross-value chain applications such as joint promotions management, CPFR, and other services between member companies.

"Interoperability between exchanges is the only way to make the promise of the Internet a reality for businesses," said Judy Sprieser, Transora's chief executive officer, at that time. "The megahub allows members of one exchange to avail themselves of the services of another exchange without the expense of building a connection to the other exchange. In this way, participants can collaborate with trading partners across the value chain via multiple exchanges."

The Future Shape of B2B Exchanges

The idea of a megahub is being explored further by Transora, which recently announced a reselling agreement with CPGMarket.com. CPGMarket is backed by SAP and is very focused on automating the "back-end" processes for European consumer packaged goods companies.

When I asked Kevin English at Covisint what the prospects are for large exchanges like Covisint to merge with, or create interoperability with, other large B2B exchanges in the future, he told me "Technically, the possibility exists. For relationships to be developed, however, a clear and compelling business case must exist."

The links and interoperability provided by a megahub are illustrated in Figure 14B. In particular, B2B exchanges can share the program-to-program communication and document translation capabilities that derive from the exchange's communication layer (see Chapter 10).

In another example of this growing trend, Elemica, an enabler of inter-company commerce for buyers and sellers of chemicals and related products, and RubberNetwork, an industry consortia exchange for the tire and rubber industry, has recently announced an agreement to create a hub-to-hub connection. They claim that this connection will facilitate more efficient commerce between the tire companies participating in RubberNetwork and their chemical suppliers in the Elemica trading network. Through the RubberNetwork-Elemica hub-to-hub connection, members of RubberNetwork will be able to place orders through that hub intended for one or more of their chemical suppliers in the Elemica trading network. Elemica will route the orders to the correct supplier, based on pre-existing contractual arrangements between supplier and customer. There is clearly a compelling business case for a linkage between these two related industries. Some industry players are suggesting that Elemica will shortly merge with ChemConnect.

The Global Trading Web Association (GTWA) is the largest independent network of B2B exchanges in the world. Focused on accelerating the movement of interoperable global trade, the organization is committed to setting policies for service levels and security, and developing or adopting the technical standards needed for B2B e-business transaction and exchange-based trading. Originally a customer forum for the Commerce One platform, GTWA has amended its bylaws and become an open association of public and private B2B exchanges, which might use any commercial or proprietary platform. Collaborative forums such as the GTWA will facilitate the development of more megahub

Figure 14B: 3G B2B Exchange Interoperability

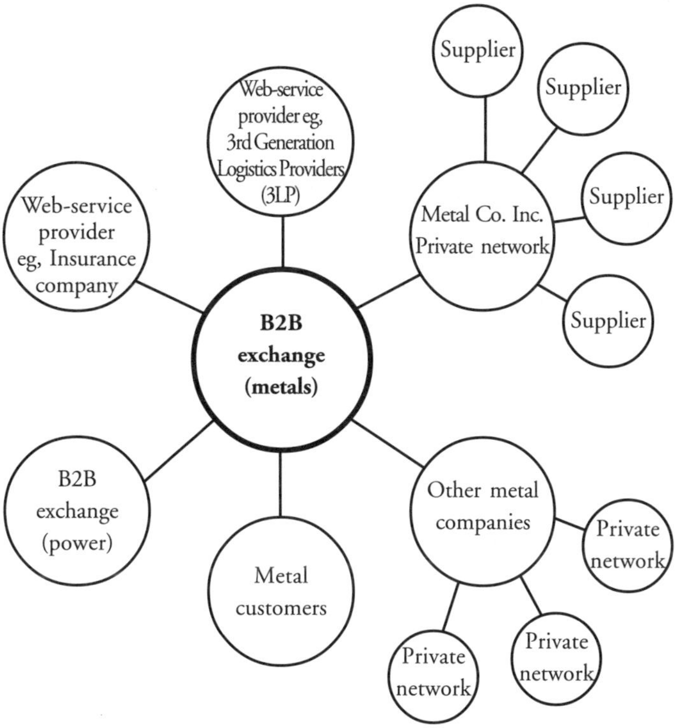

Source: Author

relationships.

However, a realistic assessment of this trend is that it will take several years to come about, since the major B2B exchanges are still focused on dominating their chosen marketspaces — and interoperability will only become a possibility after they have achieved that.

Web-based Value-added Services

Each user of a 3G-B2B exchange obtains access to all the web services it needs through just one connection to a B2B exchange. By linking all these web services together, a 3G-B2B exchange creates additional value for its users.

Applications created by stringing web services together, are known as "federated applications." Through the use of WSDL, the B2B exchange knows the specific type of XML document to send to each web services provider and the web service provider knows what type of XML document to send back to the B2B exchange. This software architecture is known as "loosely coupled" because it allows for dynamic application integration depending on what combination of services is required by each user.

A successful 3G B2B exchange is a hub through which federated e-business applications and web services can be connected in a loosely coupled environment.

Derivatives Trading

First and second generation B2B exchanges have mainly provided trading mechanisms for products that are required to be delivered immediately, or as soon as practicable after the trade is made — the so called "spot market."

It is a natural progression for spot markets to evolve into transactions with future delivery dates. These can take the form of forward contracts or other derivatives such as swaps or futures. 3G B2B exchanges are well positioned to host such derivatives trading and to be the issuer of certain types of derivative contracts.

3G B2B exchanges introduce derivatives to enable the existing buyers and sellers to directly integrate their daily business activity with risk management instruments in one centralized location. Having multiple competing buyers and sellers leads to inevitable market volatility. Because market volatility can involve adverse price moves it substantially increases risk. 3G B2B exchanges provide derivatives to enable users to manage these risks, hedge their exposures and speculate on future prices. This allows the exchange to expand its universe of participants to include players previously "unknown" to the original community of buyers and sellers of the physical products traded in the cash market. The presence of new trading players and new trading products increases transaction volume and builds liquidity on the exchange.

Market Domination

A 3G B2B exchange provides a wide range of services, all complementing each other and attracting users to join the exchange and eventually to use the core trading service — ultimately leading to sustainable liquidity.

Putting those services in order of priority creates a stairway that leads to total market space domination, as illustrated in Figure 14C, over the page.

Many B2B exchanges are still on the first few steps up the stairway. Others, such as ChemConnect, have already reached the top stair. Irrespective, the trend is clear. Many B2B exchanges are building true value for their owners, their users and the industries in which they operate, and they remain one of the killer applications that are driving the use of the Internet by businesses worldwide.

I conclude as I started, by claiming that it is way too soon to write off B2B exchanges as a failure and that, quite the reverse, they are making a concerted comeback.

Figure 14C: Climbing the Stairway to Market Domination

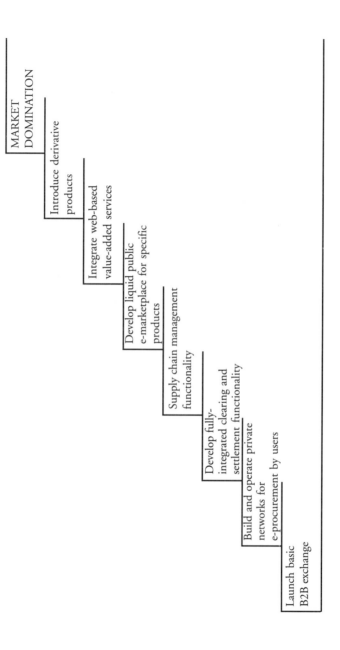

Launch basic
B2B exchange

Build and operate private
networks for
e-procurement by users

Develop fully-
integrated clearing and
settlement functionality

Supply chain management
functionality

Develop liquid public
e-marketplace for specific
products

Integrate web-based
value-added services

Introduce derivative
products

MARKET
DOMINATION

Source: Author

The Future Shape of B2B Exchanges

Appendix:

Directory of Some Successful B2B Exchanges

Name	Industry Focus	Brief Description	Contact Info	Website
Aeroxchange	Aviation/ Aerospace	Aeroxchange is an e-business solutions provider and e-marketplace for the global aviation industry. Aeroxchange was founded by 13 airlines and has been joined by 19 other airlines and hundreds of suppliers, all dedicated to maximizing efficiency across the complex aviation supply chain. Founders include Air Canada, Air New Zealand, All Nippon Airways, America West Airlines, Austrian Airlines Group, Cathay Pacific Airways, FedEx, Japan Airlines, KLM Royal Dutch Airlines, Lufthansa German Airlines, Northwest Airlines, Scandinavian Airlines, Singapore Airlines, and FedEx Express.	Tel: US 1 866 237 6243 or International 1 972 556 8545	www.aeroxchange.com
Agribuys	Food, Fruits, Fish, Cattle, etc	Agribuys is a leading supply chain integrator for the global food industry. Agribuys offers Internet-based solutions for demand planning, transactions, logistics, receiving, and payment.	Agribuys 2150 Hawthorne Blvd. Suite 400, Torrance, CA 90503 USA e-mail michael.o@agribuys.com Tel: 1 310 944 9655 Fax: 1 310 944 9665	www.agribuys.com
Airparts.com	Aviation/ Aerospace	Since 1995, airparts.com has served the Internet aviation community. With over 35 million aircraft parts, they have compiled a large aircraft parts inventory database from leading manufacturers and suppliers worldwide. Members can quickly source the availability of the parts they need.	Airparts.com Centennial Airport P.O. Box 3085 Englewood, CO 80155-3085 USA Tel: 1 970 204 1949 Fax: 1 970 207 0980	www.airparts.com

Name	Industry Focus	Brief Description	Contact Info	Website
Balticexchange	Shipping	Balticexchange.com provides an on-line exchange for ships and cargoes, real time freight derivatives trading, and quality freight market data.	The Baltic Exchange St.Mary Axe London, EC3 A 8BH UK Tel: 4420 7623 5501 Fax: 4420 7369 1622/23	www.balticexchange.com
BayanTrade	Trading Hubs	One of Asia's leading B2B trading hubs. BayanTrade is a joint venture among the Philippines' top 6 conglomerates.	customercare@bayantrade.com Tel: 63 421 2055	www.bayantrade.com
BrokerTec	Financial Services	BrokerTec Global is a fully electronic inter-dealer broker of fixed income securities that was formed by a consortium of some of the world's leading financial services companies. The shareholders include ABN AMRO, Greenwich Capital Markets, J.P. Morgan Chase & Co., Merrill Lynch, and Morgan Stanley.	BrokerTec Global, LLC. One Evertrust Plaza Jersey City, NJ 07302 USA Tel: 1 201 209 7832 Europe: 44 207 959 6700	www.brokertec.com
CATEX	Insurance	Catex is a global insurance and reinsurance technology provider operating and maintaining the world's largest on-line marketplace in the industry.	Catastrophe Risk Exchange, Inc. 475 Wall Street Princeton, NJ 08540 USA frank_fortunate@catex.com Tel: 1 609 683 0888	www.catex.com

Name	Industry Focus	Brief Description	Contact Info	Website
ChemConnect (merged with Envera and CheMatch)	Chemicals and Plastics	ChemConnect has established itself as the world's leading on-line chemical and plastics e-marketplace. The company is committed to significantly improving transaction processes for buyers and sellers in multiple industries around the globe. Some of its investors include Abbott Laboratories, Air Liquide, Albemarle Corporation, BASF AG, Bayer, and Borden Chemical Inc.	ChemConnect, Inc. 2900 North Loop West Suite 1120 Houston, TX 77092 USA solutions@chemconnect.com Tel: 1 713 681 6600	www.chemconnect.com
Converge	Electronics	Converge is a leading B2B global trading exchange for electronic components, computer products, and networking equipment. Converge provides a high degree of market liquidity by aggregating supply and demand from thousands of component, original equipment, and contract manufacturers, as well as distributors and resellers.	Converge Inc. 4 Technology Drive Peabody, MA 01960 USA info@converge.com Tel: 1 978 538 8000 Europe: 31 20 582 6161 Asia: 65 799 8038	www.converge.com
Cordiem	Aviation/ Aerospace	Cordiem provides the $500 billion aviation industry with an end-to-end e-business solution comprising supply chain management, e-procurement, and engineering services. Its founding members included American Airlines, Air France, Delta Air lines, United Parcel Service, and Honeywell International.	Cordiem, LLC. 1200 South Hayes Street Suite 900 Arlington, VA 22202 USA contactus@cordiem.com Tel: 1 703 412 8800	www.cordiem.com

Name	Industry Focus	Brief Description	Contact Info	Website
Covisint	Automotive	Covisint is the technology company whose B2B products and services connect and enable the global automotive industry to reduce costs, increase efficiency, enhance quality, and improve time to market. Covisint was founded by DaimlerChrysler, Ford, General Motors, Nissan, Renault, Commerce One, and Oracle. Since its inception, PSA Peugeot Citroën has also joined the initiative. Covisint has headquarters in Amsterdam, Tokyo, and Southfield, Michigan and offices in Frankfurt, Paris, and Brazil.	Covisint, LLC. 25800 Northwestern Highway Southfield, MI 48075 USA Tel: 1 248 827 6000	www.covisint.com
CPGMarket	Retail, Consumer Packaged Goods	CPGmarket.com is the leading e-marketplace for the European consumer packaged goods industry. Created by Nestlé, Danone, Henkel, and SAPmarkets.	CPGmarket.com S.A. 84, Av Louis Casaï 1216 Cointrin Geneva Switzerland Customercare@cpgmarket.com Tel: 41 22 710 04 76	www.cpgmarket.com
CreditTrade	Financial Services	CreditTrade pioneered the introduction of electronic trading platforms in the credit markets and is at the forefront of hybrid voice and electronic broking system developments.	CreditTrade Limited 180 Fleetwood Street London, EC4A 2HG, UK susan.harris@credittrade.com Tel: 44 207 400 5050	www.credittrade.com

Name	Industry Focus	Brief Description	Contact Info	Website
Currenex	Financial Services	Currenex provides the leading on-line global currency exchange open to all institutional buyers and sellers of foreign exchange (FX) products and services worldwide. Currenex is backed by venture investors including; Amerindo, Barclays Capital, TH Lee Putnam ventures, and The Royal Dutch Shell Group of Companies.	Currenex, Inc. 411 Theodore Fremd Ave Rye, New York 10580 USA info@currenex.com Tel: 1 914 921 8200	www.currenex.com
Daewootrade	Trading Hub	One of Asia's leading B2B trading hubs. Founded by Daewoo Corporation.	Daewoo International Corporation 541, 5-Ga, Namdaemunno Chung-gu, Seoul South Korea Master@daewootrade.com Tel: 82 2 2114	www.daewootrade.com
E2open	Electronics	E2open is the leading global collaboration network for the electronics industry. E2open enables effective collaboration among OEMs, contract manufacturers, distributors and suppliers, and supports the entire product lifecycle, including design, manufacturing, procurement, and asset recovery for computing, networking, and consumer electronics products. E2open was formed by industry leaders including; Acer, Hitachi, IBM, LG Electronics, Lucent Technologies, Matsushita Electric (Panasonic), Nortel Networks, Seagate Technology, Solectron and Toshiba, as well as the prominent investors Crosspoint Venture Partners, and Morgan Stanley.	E2open, LLC. 1075 Old Country Road Belmont, CA 94002 USA information@e2open.com Tel: 1 650 769 3700	www.e2open.com

Name	Industry Focus	Brief Description	Contact Info	Website
Eficentrum	Trading Hub	Eficentrum is a leading B2B trading hub in Latin America.	Eficentrum Av. Insurgentes Sur. No. 3500 Col. Pena Pobre C.P. 14060 Mexico, D.F. contactanos@eficentrum.com Tel: 52 5242 9300	www.eficentrum.com
Elemica	Chemicals	Elemica is a leading network for the global chemical industry, developed by 22 of the leading chemical companies in the world for the benefit of the entire industry.	Elemica, Inc. 1200 Liberty Ridge Suite120 Wayne, PA 19087 USA info@elemica.com Tel: 1 610 786 1200	www.elemica.com
eMerge Interactive	Food, Fruits, Fish, Cattle, etc.	eMerge Interactive is a technology company providing individual-animal tracking, food safety, and supply procurement services to the US beef production industry.	Emerge Interactive Inc. 120nd Terrace Sebastian, FL 32958 USA info@emergeinteractive.com Tel: 1 877 578 2333	www. emergeinteractive.com

Name	Industry Focus	Brief Description	Contact Info	Website
eReinsure	Insurance	The eReinsure platform is a web-hosted software application for placing reinsurance. By centralizing information, reinsurance buyers, sellers, and brokers have the ability to collaborate in arranging risk financing solutions, reducing redundant effort, and ensuring greater speed and accuracy in reinsurance negotiation.	eReinsure.com, Inc. 424 East 500 South Suite 104 Salt Lake City, UT 84111 USA rburke@ereinsure.com Tel: 1 801 521 0600	www.ereinsure.com
eSpeed	Financial Services	eSpeed is a subsidiary of Cantor Fitzgerald. It is a leading developer of B2B e-marketplace solutions and related trading technology solutions, and operates multiple buyer/multiple seller real-time e-marketplaces, including leading electronic energy e-marketplace, TradeSpark.	eSpeed, Inc. 135 East 57th Street New York, NY 10022 USA espeedinquiries@espeed.com Tel: 1 212 938 5000	www.espeed.com
e-STEEL (now part of NewView)	Metals – Minerals and Mining	NewView Technologies (formerly e-STEEL Corporation) is a leading provider of inter-enterprise software solutions that enable buyers and sellers of direct materials in various industries to manage supply network transactions, information, and partner relationships across the boundaries of enterprises. NewView's e-marketplace for steel – e-STEEL Exchange – was launched in 1999 and is one of the leading global marketplaces for steel. The exchange enables buyers and sellers of prime and non-prime products to negotiate, transact, and conclude business with increased efficiency, fewer errors, and reduced cost.	NewView Technologies Inc. 1250 Broadway New York, NY 10001 USA pr@newview.com Tel: 1 212 527 9997	www.newview.com

Name	Industry Focus	Brief Description	Contact Info	Website
Exostar	Aviation/ Aerospace	Exostar is a B2B exchange that is revolutionizing commerce in the aerospace and defense industries. Exostar founding partners – BAE SYSTEMS, Boeing, Lockheed Martin, Raytheon, and Rolls-Royce – have provided the support and vision to create this new industry standard.	Exostar, LLC. 13530 Dulles Technology Drive Suite 200 Herndon VA 20171 USA Tel: 1 703 561 0500	www.exostar.com
FreeMarkets	Trading Hub	FreeMarkets is the leading global provider of sourcing software and service solutions. By combining the power of on-line auctions with in-depth sourcing expertise, FreeMarkets enables the procurement of highly-customized products through reverse auctions.	FreeMarkets, Inc. 210 Sixth Avenue Pittsburgh, PA 15222 USA Tel: 1 412 434 0500	www.freemarkets.com
FXall	Financial Services	FXall is an electronic trading platform offering customers foreign currency trade execution, access to research, and straight through processing. With an increasing number of leading global banks providing liquidity, FXall is designed to aid corporate treasurers, money managers, hedge funds, central banks, and other institutional clients. FXall has offices in New York, London, Tokyo, and Hong Kong.	FX Alliance, LLC. Tel: 1 646 268 9900 Europe: 44 207 173 9600	www.fxall.com

Name	Industry Focus	Brief Description	Contact Info	Website
FX Connect	Financial Services	FX Connect provides real-time, fully interactive foreign exchange trade execution with multiple counter-parties, 24 hours a day. By maximizing front-end efficiency, FX Connect delivers faster, simpler trades than is possible through manual and semi-automated methods. FX Connect is delivered via Global Link, State Street's robust e-finance worldwide network.	State Street Corporation 225 Franklin Street Boston, MA 02110 USA Tel: 1 617 786 3000	www.fxconnect.com
GlobalNetXchange	Retail Consumer Packaged Goods	GlobalNetXchange helps retailers and suppliers improve efficiencies and reduce costs throughout the supply chain by providing web-based products and services tailored to the needs of the retail industry.	GlobalNetXchange, LLC. 333 Bush Street 18th Floor San Francisco, CA, 94104 USA Tel: 1 415 339 0990	www.gnx.com
Goodex	Trading Hub	Goodex is the largest European service- and technology-provider for on-line reverse auctions, RFQs, and sourcing consultancy. With 13 locations in nine European countries, Asia, and USA, and with more than 50 employees, Goodex serves medium- and large-sized customers in a variety of industries. Goodex was founded in 1999 by a group of sourcing experts from General Electric and Bayer AG.	Goodex Aktiengesellschaft Albert-Einstein-Ring 21 D-22761 Hamburg Germany Tel: 49 40 8908160	www.goodex.com

Name	Industry Focus	Brief Description	Contact Info	Website
HoustonStreet	Energy – Oil, Gas, Electricity	HoustonStreet is one of the largest e-marketplaces for physical crude oil and refined products.	HoustonStreet, Inc. 51 Downey Highway Suite 7, Eliot, ME 03903 USA Tel: 1 603 433 6890	www.houstonstreet.com
inreon	Insurance	The e-marketplace, inreon, offers market participants a new platform for reinsurance capacity and establishes new standards for liquidity, transparency, speed, and flexibility. Founding partners include Munich Re, Swiss Re, Internet Capital Group, and Accenture.	inreon, Limited 9 St. Clare Street, 5th Floor London, EC3N 1 LQ UK contact@inreon.com Tel: 44 207 264 2680 US: 1 201 761 0505	www.inreon.com
IntercontinentalExchange (ICE)	Energy – Oil, Gas, Electricity	ICE is an e-marketplace for the trading of over-the-counter energy, metal, and other commodity-based products. ICE was founded by a group of leading US and European financial institutions and some of the world's largest diversified energy and natural resource firms. ICE is the owner of the International Petroleum Exchange of London (IPE), Europe's leading energy futures and options exchange. Based in Atlanta with offices in New York, Houston, Chicago, London, and Singapore.	Intercontinental Exchange 2100 RiverEdge Pkwy Suite 500 Atlanta, GA 30328 USA atlanta@intcx.com Tel: 1 770 933 9522	www.intercontinentalexchange.com

Name	Industry Focus	Brief Description	Contact Info	Website
INTTRA	Shipping	INTTRA is one of the leading providers of B2B ocean freight services. Shareholders include Hapag-Lloyd, CMA CGM, Maersk Sealand, and Columbus Line.	Inttra Inc. One Upper Pond Road Morris Corporate Center Building E Parsippany, NJ 07054 USA Tel: 1 973 263 1889	www.inttra.com
LevelSeas	Shipping	LevelSeas is a common electronic platform for the bulk shipping industry with 34 shareholders including BP, Shell, Cargill, Glencore, Rio Tinto, and BHP Billiton.	Levelseas Ltd. 4th Floor, Fleet Place House 2 Fleet Place London EC4M 7RT UK Tel: 44 0 207 665 3200	www.levelseas.com
MarketAxess	Financial Services	MarketAxess is an Internet-based multi-dealer trading platform that provides rapid price discovery, efficient trade execution, and processing in a wide range of credit products. The initial group of participating dealers consisted of JP Morgan, Bear Stearns, and Deutsche Bank Securities and now includes UBS Warburg, Morgan Stanley, Merrill Lynch, Lehman Brothers, Dresdner Kleinwort Wasserstein, Credit Suisse First Boston, BNP Paribas, Bank of America Securities, and ABN Amro	MarketAxess 140 Broadway, 42nd Floor, New York, NY 10005 USA Tel: 1 877 638 0037	www.marketaxess.com

Name	Industry Focus	Brief Description	Contact Info	Website
MSA MetalSite and MSA ScrapSite	Metals – Minerals and Mining	MetalSite is one of the leading e-marketplaces for buying and selling metals.	Metals Supply Alliances, LLC. 6565 Penn Avenue Pittsburgh, PA 15206 USA Tel: 1 877 544 4452	www.metalsite.com
NTE	Freight	NTE's real-time procurement services and information management tools provide indispensable supply chain value and control for shippers and carriers.	NTE 1400 Opus Place, Suite 650 Downers Grove, IL 60515 USA Tel: 1 630 724 8600	www.nte.com
Omnexus	Chemicals and Plastics	Omnexus is designed and built by the global plastics industry to be the single source for everything a plastics professional needs to succeed in daily business. Founded in 2000 by BASF, Bayer, Dow, DuPont, and Ticona, Omnexus currently offers plastics products and related services from more than 20 global suppliers.	Omnexus 225 Peachtree Street, N.W. Suite 900 Atlanta, GA 30303 USA Customer.service@omnexus.com Tel: 1 877 527 6127 Europe: 41 1 782 8811	www.omnexus.com

Name	Industry Focus	Brief Description	Contact Info	Website
Pantellos	Energy – Oil, Gas, Electricity	Pantellos is one of the leading supply chain services companies for the utility and energy services industries. Buyer partners include Advance Energy, Alliant Energy, Cinergy Service, Inc., and supply partners include A&M Industrial and A.P. Services, Inc.	Pantellos Group Limited Partnership Waterway Plaze One 10003 Woodloch Forest Drive Suite 900 The Woodlands, TX 77380 USA information@pantellos.com Tel: 1 281 863 6300	www.pantellos.com
PaperSpace	Paper	PaperSpace is delivering the next generation of IT and electronic trading solutions to the pulp and paper industry. Acquired technology from paperexchange.com in 2001 and now operates the Paper Exchange.	PaperSpace GmbH Oskar-Messter-Str. 25 D-85737 Ismaning (Munich), Germany customerservice@paperspace.com Tel: 49 89 96282 700	www.paperspace.com

Name	Industry Focus	Brief Description	Contact Info	Website
PartsBase	Aviation/ Aerospace	PartsBase is streamlining the business processes of the aviation industry, using the Internet. Their e-marketplace utilizes a database of approximately 2,500 suppliers, containing over 23 million line items of inventory. Their e-marketplace constitutes one of the largest independent databases of inventory and information in the aviation industry. Current members include Boeing, Honeywell, Federal Express, Airborne Express, United Airlines, Frontier Airlines, BF Goodrich Aerospace, Saab, Southwest Airlines, and Northrup Grumman.	Partsbase.com 905 Clint Moore Road Boca Raton, FL 33431 USA help@partsbase.com Tel: 1 561 953 0700	www.partsbase.com
The Patent and License Exchange	Intellectual Property	The Patent & License Exchange (pl-x) provides financially oriented intellectual property (IP) tools and service to help the IP community manage, value, market, and monetize their intangible assets. PL-X also operates a global IP exchange.	The Patent & License Exchange, Inc. 245 South Los Robles Avenue 5th Floor Pasadena, CA 91101 USA info@pl-x.com Tel: 1 888 465 0690	www.pl-x.com

Name	Industry Focus	Brief Description	Contact Info	Website
PEFA	Food, Fruits, Fish, Cattle, etc.	PEFA.com operates a B2B e-marketplace which runs Europe-wide fresh fish auctions on-line, and an e-catalog-based fish market for worldwide sales of farmed, processed, and frozen fish products.	PEFA.com Vismijnstratt 23 B-83 80 Zeebrugge Belgium info@pefa.com Tel: 32 50 54 7648	www.pefa.com
ProcuraDigital	Trading Hub	ProcuraDigital is a leading trading hub and e-sourcing services partner for large companies operating in Latin America. ProcuraDigital offers reverse on-line auctions and strategic sourcing services for direct and indirect goods. ProcuraDigital has offices in Venezuela, Brazil, Mexico and Chile, as well as the USA.	ProcuraDigital 5200 Blue Lagoon Drive ste. 100 Miami, FL 33126 USA info@procuradigital.com Tel: 1 305 267 6168	www.procuradigital.com
Quadrem	Metals – Minerals and Mining	Quadrem is an e-marketplace for the global mining, minerals, and metals industries. Trading Partners include buyers Alcan Ltd., Alcoa Inc., Anglo American, and suppliers include Abraflex Ltd., Ace Drilling Ltd., and 3M. Quadrem has offices in Asia, Australia, Europe and Latin America, as well as the USA.	Quadrem International Inc. Willow Bend Centre 1, Suite 140 2740 North Dallas Parkway Plano, TX 75093 USA quadremsolve@quadrem.com Tel: 1 972 5437900	www.quadrem.com

Name	Industry Focus	Brief Description	Contact Info	Website
ri3k	Insurance	ri3k is a logistics hub for buyers and sellers of reinsurance.	ri3k Ltd. 1st Floor 10 Ely Place London EC1N 6RY UK info@ri3k.com Tel: 44 0207 400 3500	www.ri3k.com
Riskclick	Insurance	Riskclick's modular web services software is used to create virtual communities that work together across borders and time-zones with complete security and real time access to relevant information and documents for any assignment or transaction. Shareholders include Bank of America, Securitas Capital, and Amadeus Capital Partners.	Riskclick Inc. 215 Park Ave. South Suite 715 New York, NY 10003 USA info@riskclick.com Tel: 1 646 452 8181	www.riskclick.com

Name	Industry Focus	Brief Description	Contact Info	Website
SatyamPlastics	Plastics	SatyamPlastics.com is an e-marketplace for plastics companies around the world.	Sify Plasticscommerce Limited 303 Enterprise Centre Nehru Road Ville Parle (E) Mumbai 400099 India mumbai@satyamplastics.com Tel: 91 22 617 7661	www.satyamplastics.com
ShipyardXchange	Shipping	ShipyardXchange is an e-procurement portal designed by and for the shipbuilding industry. Partners include JSN, Tanksystem, and KVAERNER.	ShipyardXchange AS P.O.Box 126 N-1325 Lysaker Norway mail@syx.com Tel: 47 67 20 67 00	www.syx.com
TraderFirst	Electronics	Traderfirst.com is one of the leading B2B exchanges and ASPs for electronic parts and the semiconductor industry in Asia.	TraderFirst.com Flat A, 12/F, Blk. A 22 Hoi Shing Road Tsuen Wan, N.T. Hong Kong info@traderfirst.com Tel: 852 3422 3038	www.traderfirst.com

Name	Industry Focus	Brief Description	Contact Info	Website
Trade-Ranger	Energy – Oil, Gas, Electricity	Trade-Ranger is an e-marketplace for on-line procurement in the energy and petrochemical industries. Trade-Ranger's founding members are Conoco, The Dow Chemical Company, ENI, Equilon Enterprises, Mitsubishi Corporation, Motiva Enterprises, Phillips Petroleum Company, Repsol YPF, Royal Dutch/Shell, Statoil, TotalFinaElf, Unocal, Occidental Petroleum and BP.	Trade-Ranger Inc. 1330 Post Oak Blvd Suite 2000 Houston, TX 77056 USA contactus@traderanger.com Tel: 1 888 222 1551 or 1 713 332 6750	www.traderanger.com
TradeWeb	Financial Services	TradeWeb is one of the world's leading on-line trading networks for fixed-income securities. Shareholders include Lehman Brothers, Deutsche Bank, ABN-AMRO, UBS Warburg, Salomon Smith Barney, and Merrill Lynch.	TradeWeb LLC. c/o SEMA One Evertrust Plaza Jersey City, NJ, 07302 USA contactus@tradeweb.com Tel: 1 800 541 2268 Europe: 44 207 776 3200	www.tradeweb.com

Name	Industry Focus	Brief Description	Contact Info	Website
Transora	Retail, Consumer Packaged Goods	One of the leading global e-marketplaces for the consumer packaged goods industry, Transora offers an integrated array of collaborative solutions to eliminate inefficiencies throughout the supply chain to deliver breakthrough value. Transora's global operations include regional offices in the Netherlands, Brazil, and Mexico City.	Transora 10 South Riverside Plaza Suite 2000 Chicago, IL 60606 USA questions@transora.com Tel: 1 312 463 4467	www.transora.com
WorldWide Retail Exchange	Retail, Consumer Packaged Goods	The WorldWide Retail Exchange is the leading B2B exchange for retailers and suppliers in the food, general merchandise, textile/home, and drugstore sectors	WorldWide Retail Exchange, LLC 625 North Washington Street Alexandria, VA 22314 USA Tel: 1 703 234 5100	www. worldwideretailexchange. org

Index

C

K

L

M

N

O

P

Q

Quadrem *6, 17, 76*
QuoVadis *234, 235, 243*

R

Ramberg, Christina *221*
Renault *5, 75, 77, 78*
RetailLink *81, 82, 95, 96*
RetailersMarketXchange *6, 8, 18*
RFP *258, 267, 270*
RFQ *22, 48, 79, 155, 156, 157, 158, 159, 160, 163, 258, 267, 270*
RI3K *17, 23, 33, 58*
Riskclick *17, 23, 33*
Rolls-Royce *75, 86, 87*

S

SatyamPlastics *17, 23,*
Sculley, Arthur *3, 9, 21,*
SAP *75, 151, 152, 154, 156, 162, 170, 174, 272,*
Science Applications International Corporation (SAIC)
Schröder, Henrik *84, 85*
ScrapSit *15, 17*
Securities and Exchange Commission (SEC) *206*
Securities Industry Automation Corporation (SIAC) *259*
self-regulatory organization (SRO) *255*
ShipyardXchange *17, 23, 155, 156, 157, 158, 161, 163, 170*
SOAP *148, 157, 159, 161, 162, 164, 174, 270*
Strojka, Tim *84*
Straight through processing (STP) *25, 27, 42, 107, 108, 113, 127, 138, 183, 184, 185, 186, 211*
StreamServe *36, 155, 156, 157, 158, 161, 162, 173, 174*
SWIFT *150, 192, 194*

T

U

V

W

Bibliography

Journals, newspapers, and magazines I took information from include: *Business 2.0, Forbes, Industry Standard, The New York Times, The Economist,* and *The Wall Street Journal.*

On-line information sources on B2B exchanges include: *atmarkets.org, communityb2b.com, eaijournal.com, ecommercetimes.com, emarketect.com, Line56.com,* and *news.com.*

Books

Adams, Douglas. *The Hitchhiker's Guide to the Galaxy,* Harmony Books, 1979

Bhambri, Arvind. *B2B in the Food Industry: What is the Best Marketplace Model?,* www.agribuys.com, 2002

Butler, Steve. *E-commerce Trade and B2B Exchanges Report,* eMarketer, March 2002

Copacino, William C. and Dik, Roger W. *Supply Chain Management: Why B2B eMarkets are here to stay,* Outlook Journal, Accenture, 2002

Daikoku, Gale. *Debunking the Myth: E-marketplaces are not dead!,* GartnerG2 Report, October 2001

Daikoku, Gale and Klemx, Nick. *Evaluating Consortium: E-marketplaces across Industries,* GartnerG2 Report, February 2002

Davenport, Thomas H., Cantrell, Susan and Brooks, Jeffrey D. *Dealing with the unknown: Can B2B e-markets build trust?,* Accenture, November 2001

Davidson, Stephen. *Securing Trust,* www.quovadis.bm June 2002

Evans, Philip and Wurster, Thomas S. *Blown to Bits,* Harvard Business School Press, 2000

Hurwitz Report. *Securing Web Services Integration,* Hurwitz Group, Inc., available from www.vordel.com, November 2001

Johnson, Philip McBride. *Derivatives: a manager's guide to the world's most powerful financial instruments,* McGraw-Hill, 1999

Kollock, Peter. *The World Wakes Up to Online Exchanges,* @Markets, 2001

Krell, Eric. *E-Marketplaces Evolve* Business, Finance, May 2002

Lee, Ruben. *The Future of Securities Exchanges,* paper presented at the Brookings/ Wharton Conference, January-February 2002

Moore, Geoffrey. *Crossing the Chasm: Marketing and Selling Technology Products to Mainstream Customers,* HarperCollins, 1991

Moore, Geoffrey. *Approaching the Chasm,* The Industry Standard, May 2000

Moser, James. *What is Multilateral Clearing and Who Cares?,* Chicago Fed Letter No. 87, November 1994

OnExchange, Inc., *Why Derivatives? An Introduction for eMarketplaces,* www.onexchange.com, 2000)

Offshore News Online, www.offshoreon.com, 2000-2002

Ramberg, Christina. *Internet Marketplaces: The Law of Auctions and Exchanges Online,* Oxford University Press, 2002

Sculley, Arthur and Woods, W William A. *B2B Exchanges: The Killer Application in the Business-to-business Internet Revolution,* ISI Publications, December 1999

Shu, Lauren Jones. *Global B2B Internet Commerce Forecast: Growth Pauses, but Expansion is on the Horizon,* GartnerG2, August 2001

Tasker, Rod. *Project Eleanor — A Global Payments Initiation System,* Identrus LLC., 2002

The Depository Trust & Clearing Corporation. *Straight-Through Processing: A New Model for Settlement,* www.dtcc.com, January 2002

The World Bank. *World Development Report1998/99: Knowledge for Development,* Oxford University Press, 1999

US Treasury. *Corporate Inversion Transactions: Tax Policy Implications,* Office Of Tax Policy Department Of The US Treasury, May 2002

Various authors. *eCommerce in the Fixed-Income Markets: The 2001 Review Of Electronic Transaction Systems,* The Bond Market Association, December 2001

Various authors. *Evolving E-markets: Building High Value B2B Exchanges with Staying Power,* ISI Publications, 2000

Various authors. *High-Level Conceptual Model for B2B Integration Version: 1.0,* Business Internet Consortium, October 2001

Various authors. *US Productivity Growth 1995-2000,* The McKinsey Global Institute, October 2001

Wyld, Dr. David C. *We the People Speak on E-Government: Interviews with Leading B2G Players,* ISI Publications, 2002